OUR DECLARATION:
A READING OF THE
DECLARATION OF INDEPENDENCE

in Defense of Equality

Also by

DANIELLE ALLEN

———

World of Prometheus: The Politics of
Punishing in Democratic Athens

Talking to Strangers: Anxieties of Citizenship
Since *Brown v. Board of Education*

Why Plato Wrote

Education, Justice, and Democracy
(*co-edited with Rob Reich*)

From Voice to Influence:
Understanding Citizenship in the Digital Age
(*co-edited with Jennifer Light*)

OUR DECLARATION

A Reading of the
DECLARATION *of* INDEPENDENCE

in Defense of Equality

DANIELLE ALLEN

LIVERIGHT PUBLISHING CORPORATION

A Division of

W. W. NORTON & COMPANY

NEW YORK | LONDON

For information about permission to reproduce selections from this book,
write to Permissions, Liveright Publishing Corporation,
a division of W. W. Norton & Company, Inc.,
500 Fifth Avenue, New York, NY 10110

For information about special discounts for bulk purchases, please contact
W. W. Norton Special Sales at specialsales@wwnorton.com or 800-233-4830

Manufacturing by Courier Westford
Book design by Barbara Bachman
Production manager: Julia Druskin

ISBN 978-0-87140-690-3

Liveright Publishing Corporation
500 Fifth Avenue, New York, N.Y. 10110
www.wwnorton.com

W. W. Norton & Company Ltd.
Castle House, 75/76 Wells Street, London W1T 3QT

1 2 3 4 5 6 7 8 9 0

For Stefan, Isaac, Nora, and William

And for their peers, the parents of their peers,
and their own children.

"*Although we seem trapped in an age of anger and despair, the alternatives remain the same as in all other ages. We can scuttle—or we can sail the seas.* Navigare necesse est. *One must chart his course and sail.*"

—ALLISON DAVIS, *first tenured African American professor at the University of Chicago, in a graduation address there in 1970*

CONTENTS

PART VII   MATTERS OF FACT

CHRONOLOGY

1774

JULY

Thomas Jefferson writes *A Summary View of the Rights of British America*, his first published account of the grievances of the colonies against King George III.

SEP. 5–OCT. 26

First Continental Congress convenes in Philadelphia; it addresses a petition for redress of grievances to King George III.

1775

APRIL 19

Battles of Lexington and Concord.

MAY 10

Second Continental Congress convenes in Philadelphia.

JUNE 13

John Wentworth, the royal governor of New Hampshire, besieged in his own home, flees to British protection.

JUNE 20

Thomas Jefferson arrives in Philadelphia to join the Second Continental Congress.

JULY 6

Congress approves the "Declaration of the Causes and Necessity of Taking Up Arms," written by John Dickinson and Thomas Jefferson.

JULY 8

Congress approves a petition to the king for reconciliation, known as the Olive Branch Petition.

LATE SUMMER	By now a growing number of politicians in the American colonies view independence from Great Britain as inevitable.
AUGUST 23	The king issues a proclamation declaring all the colonies to be in "open and avowed" rebellion; during the same period, he refuses to receive the Olive Branch Petition.
MID-OCTOBER	The Virginia coast is harassed by the British navy under the direction of Virginia's royal governor, Lord Dunmore; a British naval captain, Henry Mowatt, destroys Falmouth (now Portland), Maine.
OCTOBER 26	King George addresses Parliament and declares the colonists out of his protection, indicating that he would seek foreign alliances to suppress them. Continental Congress appoints a committee of five men, including John Adams (Massachusetts) and Richard Henry Lee (Virginia), to address the question of how New Hampshire should handle its administrative and political needs in the wake of Wentworth's de facto resignation.
NOVEMBER 1	Continental Congress receives the news of the destruction of Falmouth two weeks earlier.
NOVEMBER 3	The Committee on New Hampshire recommends that New Hampshire set up a provisional government.
NOVEMBER 7	Lord Dunmore, Virginia's royal governor, declares martial law in the colony and offers freedom to any slave or indentured servant who joins the British military.
NOVEMBER 9	Congress receives the news that the king refused to receive the colonists' Olive Branch Petition.
NOVEMBER 14	Richard Henry Lee calls on Adams to discuss how to set up new governments.

1776

JANUARY 5	New Hampshire ratifies a new constitution.
JANUARY 10	Thomas Paine anonymously publishes *Common Sense*.
FEBRUARY	Lee has a poster printed based on Adams's advice for setting up governments.
MARCH	Adams writes and publishes his *Thoughts on Government*, a formal statement of his view on how the colonies might set up new governments.
APRIL	Lee begins circulating his poster and Adams's pamphlet.
MAY 10	In Congress, Adams proposes a resolution to endorse any colony's decision to set up new governments.
MAY 14	Jefferson returns to Philadelphia for spring session.
MAY 15	Continental Congress votes on Adams's preamble for the resolution concerning new governments. The Virginia Convention convenes in Williamsburg and votes to set up a new government and to charge its delegates to the Continental Congress with proposing a declaration of independency for all the colonies.
LATE MAY	George Mason drafts the Virginia Declaration of Rights.
JUNE 7	Virginia delegate Lee proposes a resolution for independence in the Continental Congress. Congress debates but defers a vote.
JUNE 11	Congress appoints a committee of five individuals to draft the formal text of a declaration in anticipation of a favorable vote on Lee's resolution in July.

JUNE 28

The Committee of Five presents a draft declaration of independence to the Continental Congress.

JULY 1

Congress continues the debate on Lee's resolution.

JULY 2

All the colonies but one vote in favor of independence. The exception is New York, which abstains. Then Congress turns to editing its formal declaration.

JULY 4

The Continental Congress unanimously approves the edited Declaration as a statement of its position. Congress sends the text to the printer John Dunlap.

JULY 8

Official celebrations occur throughout the colonies.

JULY 9

New York's convention of representatives meets in White Plains and votes for independence, making the decision now fully unanimous.

JULY 15

News of New York's decision reaches Philadelphia.

JULY 19

Congress entitles its document "The unanimous declaration of the thirteen United States of America" and resolves to have the text "fairly engrossed" on parchment. This job is assigned to Timothy Matlack, assistant to Charles Thomson, secretary of Congress.

JULY 17

Thomas Jefferson is assigned to the committee to review and correct Congress's record and decide what should be published.

AUG. 2

Delegates to the Continental Congress begin to sign the parchment Declaration, a process not complete for several months.

1777

JANUARY

With the Declaration now fully signed, Congress resolves that "an authenticated copy of Declaration of Independency, with the names of the members of Congress, subscribing the same, be sent to each of the United States, and that they [the states] be desired [i.e., requested] to have the same put on record." This final job was given to a Baltimore printer named Mary Katherine Goddard, Baltimore's postmaster since 1775.

PROLOGUE

T HE DECLARATION OF INDEPENDENCE MATTERS BECAUSE IT HELPS us see that we cannot have freedom *without* equality. It is out of an egalitarian commitment that a people grows—a people that is capable of protecting us all collectively, and each of us individually, from domination. If the Declaration can stake a claim to freedom, it is only because it is so clear-eyed about the fact that the people's strength resides in its equality.

The Declaration also conveys another lesson of paramount importance. It is this: language is one of the most potent resources each of us has for achieving our own political empowerment. The men who wrote the Declaration of Independence grasped the power of words. This reveals itself in the laborious processes by which they brought the Declaration, and their revolution, into being. It shows itself forcefully, of course, in the text's own eloquence.

When we think about how to achieve political equality, we have to attend to things like voting rights and the right to hold office. We have to foster economic opportunity and understand when excessive material inequality undermines broad democratic political participation. But we also have to cultivate the capacity of citizens to use language effectively enough to influence the choices we make together. The achievement of political equality requires, among other things, the empowerment of human beings as language-using creatures.

Equality and liberty—these are the summits of human empowerment; they are the twinned foundations of democracy.

What fragile foundations they are!

Political philosophers have taught us to think that there is an inherent tension between liberty and equality, that we can pursue egalitarian commitments only at the expense of governmental intrusions that reduce liberty. What's more, in the last half century, our public discourse has focused on burnishing the concept of liberty, not equality. Consequently, we understand the former idea better. We have ideas ready-to-hand about the danger posed to personal freedom by excessive governmental regulation and the value that lies in autonomy and self-creation. What do we know any longer about equality?

Because we have accepted the view that there is a trade-off between equality and liberty, we think we have to choose. Lately, we have come, as a people, to choose liberty. Equality has always been the more frail twin, but it has now become particularly vulnerable. If one tracks presidential rhetoric from the last two decades, one will find that invocations of liberty significantly predominate over praise songs for equality. This is true for candidates and presidents from both parties.

Matters have gone so far, in fact, that we have even failed to notice the disappearance of the ideal of equality from our interpretations of the Declaration. In the 2012 presidential election, the candidates held their final debates in front of a blue backdrop on which the words of the Declaration were reprinted in white. This inspired the presidential challenger to riff on the founders' language. He read out this:

> We hold these truths to be self-evident, that all men are created equal, that they are endowed by their Creator with certain unalienable Rights, that among these are Life, Liberty and the pursuit of Happiness—

Then he dwelled on the ideas of life and liberty to argue for military funding; he focused on the word "Creator" to argue for religious toleration and freedom. And he emphasized the phrase "pursuit of happiness" to advocate caring for the needy, pursuing discovery and innovation, and pruning toward a minimalist government that gets out of the way of individual choices about how to pursue dreams.

What happened to equality? On the subject of equality, no more important sentence has ever been written than the one quoted by the candidate, but he had nothing to say about that ideal. Even more surprisingly, his opponent did not point this out. Nor, for that matter, did anyone else in the frenzy of subsequent media commentary.

I have told this story without naming the candidates because the candidates, the parties, do not matter. Yes, it was the Republican, Mitt Romney, former Massachusetts governor, who glossed the most famous sentence of the Declaration—the very "proposition" about equality around which Lincoln crafted his Gettysburg address—without once invoking the idea of equality. But his Democratic opponent, Barack Obama, our first African American president, never called him on it either.

Political philosophers have generated the view that equality and freedom are necessarily in tension with each other. As a public, we have swallowed this argument whole. We think we are required to choose between freedom and equality. Our choice in recent years has tipped toward freedom. Under the general influence of libertarianism, both parties have abandoned our Declaration; they have scorned our patrimony.

Such a choice is dangerous. If we abandon equality, we lose the single bond that makes us a community, that makes us a people with the capacity to be free collectively and individually in the first place. I for one cannot bear to see the ideal of equality pass away before it has reached its full maturity. I hope I am not alone.

I.

ORIGINS

Dunlap broadside, In Congress, July 4, 1776,
A Declaration by the Representatives of the United States of America
in General Congress Assembled.

THE DECLARATION OF INDEPENDENCE

IN CONGRESS, July 4, 1776.

THE UNANIMOUS DECLARATION OF THE THIRTEEN UNITED STATES OF AMERICA

WHEN IN THE COURSE OF HUMAN EVENTS, IT BECOMES NECESsary for one people to dissolve the political bands which have connected them with another, and to assume among the powers of the earth, the separate and equal station to which the Laws of Nature and of Nature's God entitle them, a decent respect to the opinions of mankind requires that they should declare the causes which impel them to the separation.

We hold these truths to be self-evident, that all men are created equal, that they are endowed by their Creator with certain unalienable Rights, that among these are Life, Liberty and the pursuit of Happiness,—That to secure these rights, Governments are instituted among Men, deriving their just powers from the consent of the governed,—That whenever any Form of Government becomes destructive of these ends, it is the Right of the People to alter or to abolish it, and to institute new Government, laying its foundation on such principles and organizing its powers in such form, as to them shall seem most likely to effect their Safety and Happiness. Prudence, indeed, will dictate that Governments long established should not be changed for light and transient causes; and accordingly all experience hath shewn, that mankind are more disposed to suffer, while evils are sufferable, than to right themselves by abolishing the forms to which they are accustomed. But when a long train of abuses and usurpations, pursuing invariably the same Object evinces a design to reduce them under absolute Despotism, it is their right, it is their duty, to throw off such Government, and to provide new Guards for their future security.—Such has been the patient sufferance of these Colonies; and such is now the necessity which constrains them to alter their former Systems of Government. The history of the present King of Great Britain is a history of repeated injuries and usurpations, all having in direct object the establishment of an absolute Tyranny over these States. To prove this, let Facts be submitted to a candid world.

He has refused his Assent to Laws, the most wholesome and necessary for the public good.

He has forbidden his Governors to pass Laws of immediate and pressing importance, unless suspended in their operation till his Assent should be obtained; and when so suspended, he has utterly neglected to attend to them.

He has refused to pass other Laws for the accommodation of large districts of people, unless those people would relinquish the right of Representation in the Legislature, a right inestimable to them and formidable to tyrants only.

He has called together legislative bodies at places unusual, uncomfortable, and distant from the depository of their public Records, for the sole purpose of fatiguing them into compliance with his measures.

He has dissolved Representative Houses repeatedly, for opposing with manly firmness his invasions on the rights of the people.

He has refused for a long time, after such dissolutions, to cause others to be elected; whereby the Legislative powers, incapable of Annihilation, have returned to the People at large for their exercise; the State remaining in the mean time exposed to all the dangers of invasion from without, and convulsions within.

He has endeavoured to prevent the population of these States; for that purpose obstructing the Laws for Naturalization of Foreigners; refusing to pass others to encourage their migrations hither, and raising the conditions of new Appropriations of Lands.

He has obstructed the Administration of Justice, by refusing his Assent to Laws for establishing Judiciary powers.

He has made Judges dependent on his Will alone, for the tenure of their offices, and the amount and payment of their salaries.

He has erected a multitude of New Offices, and sent hither swarms of Officers to harrass our people, and eat out their substance.

He has kept among us, in times of peace, Standing Armies without the Consent of our legislatures.

He has affected to render the Military independent of and superior to the Civil power.

He has combined with others to subject us to a jurisdiction foreign to our constitution, and unacknowledged by our laws; giving his Assent to their Acts of pretended Legislation:

For Quartering large bodies of armed troops among us:

For protecting them, by a mock Trial, from punishment for any Murders which they should commit on the Inhabitants of these States:

For cutting off our Trade with all parts of the world:

For imposing Taxes on us without our Consent:

For depriving us in many cases, of the benefits of Trial by Jury:

For transporting us beyond Seas to be tried for pretended offences:

For abolishing the free System of English Laws in a neighbouring Province, establishing therein an Arbitrary government, and enlarging its Boundaries so as to render it at once an example and fit instrument for introducing the same absolute rule into these Colonies:

For taking away our Charters, abolishing our most valuable Laws, and altering fundamentally the Forms of our Governments:

For suspending our own Legislatures, and declaring themselves invested with power to legislate for us in all cases whatsoever.

He has abdicated Government here, by declaring us out of his Protection and waging War against us.

He has plundered our seas, ravaged our Coasts, burnt our towns, and destroyed the lives of our people.

He is at this time transporting large Armies of foreign Mercenaries to compleat the works of death, desolation and tyranny, already begun with circumstances of Cruelty & perfidy scarcely paralleled in the most barbarous ages, and totally unworthy the Head of a civilized nation.

He has constrained our fellow Citizens taken Captive on the high Seas to bear Arms against their Country, to become the executioners of their friends and Brethren, or to fall themselves by their Hands.

He has excited domestic insurrections amongst us, and has endeavoured to bring on the inhabitants of our frontiers, the merciless Indian Savages, whose known rule of warfare, is an undistinguished destruction of all ages, sexes and conditions.

In every stage of these Oppressions We have Petitioned for Redress in the most humble terms: Our repeated Petitions have been answered only by repeated injury. A Prince whose character is thus marked by every act which may define a Tyrant, is unfit to be the ruler of a free people.

Nor have We been wanting in attentions to our British brethren. We have warned them from time to time of attempts by their legislature to extend an unwarrantable jurisdiction over us. We have reminded them of the circumstances of our emigration and settlement here. We have appealed to their native justice and magnanimity, and we have conjured them by the ties of our common kindred to disavow these usurpations, which, would inevitably interrupt our connections and correspondence. They too have been deaf to the voice of justice and of consanguinity. We must, therefore, acquiesce in the necessity, which denounces our Separation, and hold them, as we hold the rest of mankind, Enemies in War, in Peace Friends.

We, therefore, the Representatives of the united States of America, in General Congress, Assembled, appealing to the Supreme Judge of the world for the rectitude of our intentions, do, in the Name, and by Authority of the good People of these Colonies, solemnly publish and declare, That these United Colonies are, and of Right ought to be Free and Independent States; that they are Absolved from all Allegiance to the British Crown, and that all political connection between them and the State of Great Britain, is and ought to be totally dissolved; and that as Free and Independent States, they have full Power to levy War, conclude Peace, contract Alliances, establish Commerce, and to do all other Acts and Things which Independent States may of right do. And for the support of this Declaration, with a firm reliance on the protection of divine Providence, we mutually pledge to each other our Lives, our Fortunes and our sacred Honor.

1

NIGHT TEACHING

FOR EXACTLY A DECADE AT THE UNIVERSITY OF CHICAGO, I TAUGHT by day some of the nation's most elite students—many with tousled hair, often rolling from their dorm room beds right into class, one even showing up casually in his boxer shorts. By night I taught adult students who were without jobs or working two jobs or stuck in dead-end part-time jobs, while nearly always also juggling children's school schedules, undependable daycare arrangements, and a snarled city bus service. They should have seemed bone tired when they arrived at class, but they pulsed with energy.

I taught both groups the same books—by Plato, Sophocles, Toni Morrison. We met in the same rooms—sometimes wood-paneled neo-Gothic chambers that heightened for both sets of students the sense of occasion for our conversations; sometimes in the nondescript, fluorescent-lit boxes of mid-twentieth-century collegiate campus architecture. Yet there, too, the conversation itself, by the end of our two hours, would inevitably generate the feeling that something meaningful had transpired.

In afternoons our heated talk kept traffic noise at bay. On winter evenings our small but ever warmer circle of light rolled back the deepening dark. In both circles, we were making worlds: naming life's constitutive events, clarifying our principles, and testing against one another's wits our accounts of what was happening around us.

Yet if you had peeked in on us, what would you have seen? By and large all we were doing was reading texts closely, and discussing them.

We scrutinized single words. When Antigone, in Sophocles's play from fifth-century Athens, decides to stand up to King Creon and bury her brother, the chorus describes her as making laws for herself. She is autonomous, they say, which is simply Greek for "making your own laws." This is the first instance of the word "autonomy" in written literature. What does it mean? Is Antigone's autonomy a good or a bad thing? My day students wanted to know what it meant for Antigone, as a woman, to stand up for herself in the male-dominated world of ancient Greece. My night students wanted to know whether Antigone's courage was something they could learn from to stand up for themselves, for instance, with their bosses.

We engaged such mysteries as what Shakespeare means in Sonnet 94 when he writes,

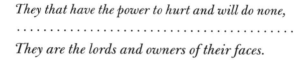

> *They that have the power to hurt and will do none,*
> . . . .
> *They are the lords and owners of their faces.*

How does restraint in the use of one's powers lead to the preservation of one's best self? Neither my day nor my night students felt they had much power, yet my day students had some instinctive sense that, to quote the sonnet again, they might well one day "inherit heaven's graces." My night students were more likely to have seen how power corrupts.

Then there was this mystery: does Toni Morrison want us to believe in the ghosts in *Beloved*? Does she want us to believe there are ghosts in our own worlds? Or are they merely symbols? My night students' lives overran with death—from gunshots and overdoses and chronic disease and battery. They were indeed haunted. My day students, many of them well-heeled and all of them well-insured, were still mostly too young to understand what it means to carry the past around within you.

We listened to music. Again to another Shakespeare sonnet:

> *That time of year thou mayst in me behold*
> *When yellow leaves, or none, or few, do hang*

Upon those boughs which shake against the cold,
Bare ruined choirs, where late the sweet birds sang.

Or Sarah Vaughan singing Rodgers and Hart's "It Never Entered My Mind."* Both groups recognized the musicality in sonnet as well as song, but they brought very different reference points to bear in explaining that musicality. The two groups of students were, I found, experts at different kinds of things.

From my students, I also had much to learn, as teachers often do. They showed me things that I had never seen in texts that I thought I knew so well, as when one of my day students pointed out that the biblical story of the warrior Jephthah's sacrifice of his daughter is used by several of the most important political philosophers of the seventeenth and eighteenth centuries to talk about the founding of nations. Jephthah had sworn to God that, if God gave him victory, he would sacrifice the first thing he saw upon his return home. And his daughter ran out to greet him.

My students also taught me things about learning that I had never known, as when one of my night students, after months of mediocre performances, turned in an essay that was light-years beyond what she had been able to do just a week earlier. From then on her performance remained consistently on that new and suddenly exalted level. To this day, I have no idea what flipped the switch. Now I know that I cannot predict individual learning trajectories and that such inexplicable improvements are among the most fundamental mysteries of human life.

Yet the single most transformative experience I had came from teaching the Declaration of Independence not to my bright-eyed undergraduates but to my life-tested night students. I sometimes taught it as part of the U.S. history unit, sometimes as part of the literature unit, and sometimes as part of the writing unit. Like the huge majority of Americans, few of my day students had ever read its 1,337 words from start to finish. None of my night students had.

I started teaching the text instrumentally. That is, I thought it would be useful. These students with jobs were busy. The Declaration is short. No one would complain about the reading. I could use it to teach history, writing, or political philosophy. And so I began.

* I had hoped to provide you four lines from this song from the 1940 musical *Higher and Higher*, but the permissions charges were exorbitant.

My night students generally entered into the text thinking of it as something that did not belong to them. It represented instead institutions and power, everything that solidified a world that had, as life had turned out, delivered them so much grief, so much to overcome.

As I worked my way through the text with those students, I realized for the first time in my own life that the Declaration makes a coherent philosophical argument. In particular, it makes an argument about political equality. If the pattern of books published on the Declaration is any indication, we have developed the habit of thinking about the Declaration mainly as an event, an episode in the dramatic unfolding of the American Revolution. But it makes a cogent philosophical case for political equality, a case that democratic citizens desperately need to understand.

What exactly is political equality?

The purpose of democracy is to empower individual citizens and give them sufficient control over their lives to protect themselves from domination. In their ideal form, democracies empower each and all such that none can dominate any of the others, nor any one group, another group of citizens.

Political equality is not, however, merely freedom from domination. The best way to avoid being dominated is to help build the world in which one lives—to help, like an architect, determine its pattern and structure. The point of political equality is not merely to secure spaces free from domination but also to engage all members of a community equally in the work of creating and constantly re-creating that community. Political equality is equal political empowerment.

Ideally, if political equality exists, citizens become co-creators of their shared world. Freedom from domination and the opportunity for co-creation maximize the space available for individual and collective flourishing.

The assertion that the Declaration is about such a rich notion of political equality will provoke skepticism. Is it not about freedom? The text, after all, declares *independence*.

The Declaration starts and finishes, however, with equality. In the first sentence, the Continental Congress proclaims that the time has come for the people, which they now constitute, to take a "separate and equal" place among the powers of the earth. The last sentence of the Declaration finds the members of the Continental Congress, as representatives of their newly designated "states," "mutually" pledging to each other their lives, their property, and their sacred honor. They stake their claim to independence—to freedom—on the bedrock of an egalitarian commitment to one another. Only on the basis of a community built with their equality can they achieve their freedom.

And, of course, there is also the all-important second sentence, which begins, "We hold these truths to be self-evident, that all men are created equal."

As my night students metabolized the philosophical argument and rhetorical art of the Declaration, many of them, and I along with them, experienced a personal metamorphosis. They found themselves suddenly as political beings, with a consciousness that had previously eluded them. They built a foundation from which to assess the state of their political world. They gained a vocabulary and rhetorical techniques for arguing about it.

In reading the document with me, my students in fact re-gifted to me a text that should have been mine all along. They gave me again the Declaration's ideals—equality and freedom—and the power of its language. They restored to me *my* patrimony as well as their own, and ours.

2

PATRIMONY

Y ES, I CLAIM THE DECLARATION AS PATRIMONY, AS CAN ANYONE.
Many people—for diverse reasons—will be skeptical of such a
claim, especially when made by a mixed- race (but aren't we all?) African
American woman. Didn't the Declaration defend the liberty and equality
only of white men of property?

That the Declaration is my patrimony I nonetheless insist. Five generations back, not long before the Civil War, a forefather, Sidiphous, came
to the United States from the Caribbean on the promise of work. The
only trouble was, when he got to Florida, he found that the job was a
slave's. Soon thereafter came the Civil War. Four generations of my family's grave markers lie beneath trees trailing Spanish moss on the head-
land of an island just north of Jacksonville. Beside their stones lie those of
two black men from Florida who fought for the Union. Two generations
later the fight continued. In the 1930s my Baptist preacher grandfather
helped found the first NAACP chapter in his north Florida region. And
two decades after that my father left Florida because, as he once told me,
he was tired of constantly looking over his shoulder, always expecting at
any moment to see a posse jump from behind a tree hollering, "Get that
nigger." Is that not wanting to be free?

From the WASP side of my family—my mother's side—I inherited
antiques and china, among other things. My elegant, inquisitive, 1980s
supermom mom idolized her suffragette grandmother, and I always

connected my mother's name—Susan, also my middle name—to my great-grandmother's political hero, Susan B. Anthony, campaigner for women's right to vote. When my great-grandmother found herself in the hospital having a baby on a day scheduled for a suffragettes' march, my great-grandfather, an attorney and social worker, went to the parade in her stead. So goes the family lore. That same suffragette great-grandfather served in a Progressive-era Michigan administration—his distinctive ambition being to reduce juvenile delinquency. During all my growing up, my mother had hanging in her bedroom, as she still does, a framed piece her great-aunt had embroidered that read, "Let me live in the house by the side of the road and be a friend to man."

Equality and freedom. Love of these ideas made my people.

Both sides of my family tied their ideals, these ideas—and their diverse pursuits of freedom, equality, and opportunity—to a love of education. Although I never met my father's mother, a nurse, I've heard from many people that she inspired a love of learning in all around her. The traces of a striking generosity live in the stories her children, my many aunts and uncles, tell about her. She dreamed that my father might go to Harvard. Given where he'd started in life, this was not possible, but he did leave the South for college and earned a doctorate in political science. My mother's side of the family included women college graduates (the University of Minnesota, Wellesley, and the University of Michigan) beginning in the late nineteenth century. My mother, a librarian, followed the reading-obsessed path of her own mother, a high school English teacher.

We were, in short, a family steeped in books. We were also a family of The Book. In my childhood, at an early point, we twice read the Bible through from start to finish. Before we cleared the dinner table of its dirty dishes, still seated each in our nightly seat, in positions that would remain unchanged for nearly eighteen years, my father, mother, brother, and I read a chapter a night, taking our turns verse to verse. It took a couple of years to complete the double cycle.

Slow reading. This too is my patrimony.

Over dinner, my parents often said to my brother and me that when we turned eighteen, we would be on our own. Independence was a real prospect from an early age. Our education, they said, would be our inheritance, and my parents invested everything they had there. We also talked a lot at dinner about freedom and equality. We even talked pretty frequently about the Declaration of Independence. Sometimes we argued over whether the phrase "all men" could refer to everyone or just white men of property. From that discussion flowed other debates, for instance, about the value of the gender-neutral language emerging in the 1980s.

To my embarrassment, however, I never read the Declaration slowly, the way I had been taught to read, until I did so with my night students. It's a cliché to say that we fell in love, but we did. Its words became necessary for us; they became *our* Declaration. Through reading them slowly, we came into our inheritance: an understanding of freedom and equality, and of the value of finding the right words.

3

LOVING DEMOCRACY

I
T'S NOT ENOUGH, THOUGH, TO SAY THAT I INHERITED—AS IF THROUGH
genes—my love of freedom and equality. These things don't pass in
DNA, so figuring out exactly how I came to love democracy demands
some further thought.

To my great surprise, I think I may owe these passions to my grandmother, my mother's mother. She was the so-called black sheep in a family of genteel and gentle people, suspended from kindergarten, as one
story goes, for treating other children badly or, as another tale tells it, in
receipt of failing grades in elementary school for self-control. Very late
in her life she was diagnosed with some form of bipolar disorder, was
medicated, and became kind. I was glad to get to know her then and find
something in her if not to love then at least to feel some affection for. For
when I was small, she was not kind.

After my grandfather died, and my grandmother finally decided, I
think out of necessity, to overlook the fact that her daughter, my mother,
had married a black man, she began to visit us. I was probably around
eight. She insisted on bringing and making us drink Tang because this
is, apparently, what the Space Shuttle astronauts survived on. I recall she
generally smelled pretty rank—and she was full of criticisms, particularly
of me. I drank too much water. I could be expected, for reasons unspeci-
fied, to become an alcoholic. The worst, however, was that I should shave
off all my kinky hair and wear a wig; if I chose not to do that, I should

expect to get nothing from life. No love, no job, nothing. She tended to write letters with key words set out in uppercase: NOTHING.

My mother had an inspired way of dealing with this bullying. She changed the table's seating arrangement to seat my grandmother next to me, instead of across from me. Seated beside me, my grandmother could no longer see me. The thought was that perhaps, if she could not see me, she would not criticize me. This turned out to be true. Invisibility brought at least a lessening of affliction.

It was my younger brother, though, who rescued me finally, after a few years, from my torment. One day, in the wake of another tear storm occasioned by my grandmother's harsh words, he said—and he couldn't himself have been more than eight at the time—"It will only bother you if you let it; you just have to ignore it." In this instance, since my grandmother's words were truly only words and had no other material effects, he was right. I found a way to free myself by ignoring my grandmother; by refusing to take her seriously, I established for myself a platform for agency equal to hers, even if she didn't know it. I could feel for myself how much stronger I was for knowing that my way of seeing the world was equal to hers and that my way, not hers, could be the basis for my life.

I cannot abide seeing someone bullied. Perhaps it is there—in that small but fundamental instinct—that my own driven commitment to egalitarian democracy was born. Even the most intimate relations bring to light how fundamental to human flourishing is equality.

This point, however, simply leads to another question. What seven-league boots can take us from personal to political? How and why does one leap from a concern—which surely we all have—for decency in human relations to a love of democracy? How does one come to understand that these things are connected? And how might this all happen in childhood? Because I did love democracy and, above all, equality before I left youth behind. Working with my night students brought me back to my origins.

My father certainly took up my political education from an early point. The summer I was seven he had me read *Ivanhoe* and—let's go ahead and rehabilitate another repudiated text—*Uncle Tom's Cabin*. But that can't explain my love of democracy. All I remember of *Ivanhoe* is dark forests; all I got out of *Uncle Tom's Cabin* was the notion that good girls die young. From this I drew the lesson that it was best not to be too good.

I think it was a different story of slavery that moved me: the Hebrew Bible tale of Joseph, who was sold by his envious brothers into slavery in Egypt and there achieved a near equality with the Pharaoh. On the basis of his success and having reconciled with his family, he brought them too to Egypt, but then Joseph died. Soon "there was a new king of Egypt that knew not Joseph." Without the accidental protection of a bond between Joseph and the king, the Israelites were enslaved.

> And the Egyptians made the children of Israel to serve with rigour:
> And they made their lives bitter with hard bondage, in mortar, and in brick, and in all manner of service in the field: all their service, wherein they made them serve, was with rigour.

And the Pharaoh commanded that all their sons be killed on birth. I think this is the story that crystallized for me the notion that there is no freedom without political equality. It did not matter how rich, how successful, how powerful Joseph had been. He was still a servant. He could not protect his own. The desire to escape from abusive power was alive in me. Even in my own small circumstances, I had that—a little spit of flame. And somehow I wanted that release for all people. I could free myself from my grandmother by ignoring her, but this was a far remove from what is necessary for escaping tyrannical power. I started banging my head then, I believe, against the question of how people might slip such bonds.

I worked on that question for years—in an undergraduate degree, two master's degrees, and two PhDs as well as books I wrote on punishment, on citizenship, on rhetoric. I pursued it by teaching courses on Hobbes, Locke, and Rousseau, on DuBois and Ralph Ellison, on Aeschylus, Herodotus, Plato, and Aristotle. I sought out the solution through the hell of doing mail-order courses about Homer's Hades and Dante's *Inferno* with my ten-years-imprisoned-only-to-be-murdered-soon-after baby cousin. But I didn't get my answer until I read the Declaration of Independence with a group of adults struggling to survive, for whom nothing was given but who nonetheless believed in the possibility, the necessity, in fact, of their survival.

4

ANIMATING THE DECLARATION

AFTER THE FIRST YEAR OF READING THE DECLARATION WITH my night students, my teaching mission changed. I no longer wanted to use the text merely instrumentally to teach them about other topics. Now I wanted to teach them the Declaration itself for its own sake. I wanted my students to claim the text. They were so much in need of it. I wanted them to understand that democratic power belonged to them, too, that they had its sources inside themselves. I wanted to animate the Declaration, to bring it to life for them, and perhaps even bring them through it into a different kind of life—as citizens, as thinkers, as political deliberators and decision makers. I wanted them to own the Declaration of Independence. I want that for you, too, because the Declaration is also yours.

Our Declaration, then, tries to give that experience of taking possession of the ideal of equality to everyone who cares about democracy, whether in the United States or in the world at large.

Reaching such an audience is a challenge in our contemporary world. Despite globalization, the globe is more than ever a tower of Babel, and even in the United States our culture is also fragmented. We are not all readers, and the reading habits of those of us who are diverge markedly. Bookstores display novels and self-help books to stoke Mother's Day sales; they put out history and politics for Father's Day. History buffs can tell you that George Washington wore clothes made out of North American products for his inauguration; they can tell you he always traveled with seven razors for reasons nobody knows. But other readers don't know who George Washington, the first president of the United States, was. Nonetheless, wherever we may live, freedom and equality are necessary for effecting our safety and happiness.

Although the study of history is riveting and awakens us to contingency, this book treads lightly on the historical side of the tale of the Declaration. While history can serve to help us understand many things much better, it can also function as a barrier to entry. This book is intentionally philosophical; it focuses almost exclusively on the logical argument of the Declaration and the conceptual terrain of its metaphors. We all use philosophical concepts every day, when we contest what is "right," or "good," or "fair," or "just." These concepts—like philosophy itself—belong to everyone everywhere—contested though they are.

My quite conscious decision to foreground the philosophical argument of the Declaration itself is meant to make an encounter with the Declaration easier for readers who have not yet built up a deep historical knowledge base. That does not mean that this book pursues only easy ideas. To the contrary, the philosophy of the Declaration is challenging. But the Declaration presents that philosophy lucidly, and the goal of this book is to do the same.

In other words, I am trying—working against the forces of marketing strategies and our culture—to draw different circles of readers together: the sophisticate and the novice; the frequent and the occasional reader; the history buff and the self-help seeker; the lover of democracy whether at home or abroad. For are we not all democrats? Do we not all need, at some level, to understand what it means to be part of a democratic polity? What concepts, what ideas, do we need to understand the part we play? It is these concepts that I am trying to resuscitate—to renew understanding where the ideas are familiar, to elucidate them for those readers to whom they arrive as new gifts.

In what follows we will begin with a brief account of how the Declaration came into being. The purpose of this account will not be to retell a well-known tale but rather to discover, through that tale of the birth of the Declaration, the art of democratic writing. Democracies are built out of language. To succeed as citizens we need to understand this fundamental political fact. Only once we have clearly in view the importance of specifically democratic art of writing—and of reading, speaking, and listening—will we proceed to our encounter with the Declaration, and unfold, step-by-step, its argument about political equality.

By reading the Declaration slowly, we help ourselves as readers. We help ourselves as writers. We deepen our capacity for moral reflection—for making good judgments about our own actions and those of others. Most importantly, we grow as citizens. In coming to understand political equality, we grasp how to make it real for ourselves and others. We come to feel its necessity. This is the transformative experience I hope to share with you in *Our Declaration*.

II.

WHO WROTE THE DECLARATION OF INDEPENDENCE?

THE WRITER

THE DECLARATION OF INDEPENDENCE IS AN EXEMPLARY PIECE OF democratic writing. That statement is uncontroversial. Yet I do not mean it as most observers do. When most people praise the quality of the Declaration's prose, they mean to credit Thomas Jefferson with unparalleled eloquence. I would never gainsay that he was a superb writer, yet he was not *the* author of the Declaration of Independence. This text was written by a group.

Democracies require a distinctive art of writing, where groups have to weave together the words that they will live by—the words in which they will clothe themselves. By reminding ourselves of how the Declaration came to be, we can make the art of democratic writing—of group writing—visible to ourselves. Group writing is not easy, but, when done well, it heads the ranks of human achievement. It stands even in front of works of individual genius, because it involves a far greater degree of difficulty.

The story of the writing of the Declaration presents a case of the human mind at work on a scale larger than that of a single individual. In this story, we can see human intelligence as a collective force, a powerful instrument for grasping the world, effective because it pools the capacities of multitudes of people. The art of democratic writing entails understanding how to contribute to the collective mind to produce the shared vocabulary that we citizens will use to live together. It's not necessary that everyone agree or play the same part—only that all play their parts well.

By late summer in 1775 a growing number of politicians in the American colonies hugging the Atlantic coast of the North American continent had come to view independence from the motherland, Great Britain, as inevitable. "Independants," these men were called. Now we call them "radicals." Among those "Independants" were the playful but volcanic John Adams of Boston, Massachusetts; a cultured and farsighted strategist from Chantilly, Virginia, named Richard Henry Lee; and Thomas Jefferson, the reclusive intellectual who liked to fire off directions for other men to follow from his mountaintop mansion in Virginia, which he called Monticello.

Adams was stout at forty while, at forty-three, Lee was slender and polished, the fingers of his left hand sundered by a gun accident. Both were, to use a contemporary term, politicos—they believed not only in public oratory but also in backroom strategy sessions, in dramatic performances but also in carefully laid plans. They knew how to make things happen. As Adams put it, writing to his wife, Abigail, about himself, they were both "instrumental of touching some Springs, and turning some small Wheels" to advance great events. By the suffocatingly hot summer of 1775, Adams was setting the northern colonies in motion and Lee the southern.

Autumn found them both in smallpox-plagued Philadelphia as members of the Continental Congress, the decision-making body that the thirteen British colonies in North America—Georgia, South Carolina, North Carolina, Virginia, Maryland, Delaware, Pennsylvania, New Jersey, New York, Connecticut, Rhode Island, Massachusetts, and New Hampshire— had established so that they might steer collectively through the worsening storm of their relationship to the motherland. Fighting between Great Britain and its colonies had begun in earnest at Lexington and Concord in Massachusetts the preceding April. In addition to meeting in Congress from seven in the morning to ten in the evening, six days a week, both men were fast and furiously writing letters to friends and partisans back in Massachusetts and Virginia, their respective "countries" as they called them, helping to advance provincial politics as well as seeking to secure resources for the recently formed Continental army. They were obsessed, for instance, with finding, making, or buying the salt necessary to preserve food for the troops.

The thirty-two-year-old Thomas Jefferson, only lately elected to the

A portrait of Thomas Jefferson from Bailey's Rittenhouse Almanac.

delegation sent by Virginia to the Congress, was also in Philadelphia—or, at least, he was there for parts of the summer and fall. He was there in late June and July, then he went home, and he returned again in early October, staying until the end of December only with reluctance. He had a sick wife at Monticello. He was not a delegate who would ever earn credit for perfect attendance. Nor did he bring with him to Philadelphia much of a preexisting calendar of political activities. When he first arrived, he knew only one other delegate outside of his own Virginia delegation, and in late October we find him with extra time on his hands. On October 31 he wrote to his best friend, "I have set apart nearly one day in every week since I came here to write letters. Notwithstanding this I have never received the scrip of a pen from any mortal breathing." Unlike Adams and Lee, he was not at the center of things.

Not that he had done nothing since his arrival in Philadelphia. To the contrary, on June 26, 1775, a mere six days after he disembarked from his fashionable horse-drawn carriage accompanied by three slaves, Jefferson was assigned a major writing job. Congress had decided to produce a "Declaration of the Causes and Necessity of Taking Up Arms," both to explain why the colonies now had an army and to assert that, despite their June 14 establishment of the Continental army, they sought reconciliation with Britain, not independence. In the days just after Jefferson's arrival, the committee assigned to draft this declaration failed to nail the job. Then, on June 26, Congress turned to Jefferson, who was, when he rolled into town like a princeling, already a famous author.

The preceding summer—July 1774—as Virginia was determining whom it would send to that fall's First Continental Congress, Jefferson had drafted a set of instructions that he hoped might guide the new delegates in their work. It does not appear that anyone asked him to write these instructions; he undertook the job on his own initiative. In his eccentric, slave-built mansion, Monticello, he had, in effect, built his own policy think tank and was firing off directives and white papers to anyone who would listen. When he fell ill and could not make it to Williamsburg for the meeting to elect delegates, he had the instructions delivered to his compatriots by his personal attendant, Jupiter, a slave.

The Virginians did not follow Jefferson's instructions. They considered them too radical—tending too much already toward independence. Instead, they charged their delegates with following the moderate path of reconciliation. But enough people agreed with Jefferson's arguments that his allies sought his permission to publish the document, and it quickly circulated throughout the colonies as *A Summary View of the Rights of British America.* In this document Jefferson argued that, contrary to received opinion, the British Parliament had no authority over the colonies. He also argued—and was one of the first to do so—that George III was personally responsible for the wrongs that the colonies had suffered since 1763, for instance, burdensome taxes on paper and tea, the suspension of colonial legislatures, the introduction of soldiers to control the colonial population, and restrictions on the rights of the colonials to trade and manufacture goods. He wrote that "a series of oppressions, begun at a distinguished period, and pursued unalterably through every change of ministers, too plainly prove a deliberate and systematical plan of reducing us to slavery." He proposed that the colonies ask the king to "redress" their injuries, while also being sure to dispel the king's view that they were "asking favours, and not rights." This text was, in other words, a preview of just the kinds of arguments that would be made in the Declaration of Independence.

When this pamphlet, *A Summary View*, appeared, it was among the most forceful of the "strong independent" treatises yet to have circulated widely, and it made Jefferson famous. Upon his arrival in Philadelphia in

June 1775, he was clearly the man to rescue the committee floundering to draft a "Declaration of the Causes and Necessity of Taking Up Arms." Jefferson was not, however, given the job on his own. The moderate John Dickinson of Pennsylvania, who genuinely wished to pursue the course of reconciliation, was added to the committee. Congress wasn't yet willing to establish a known radical as the sole head of its writing business.

Together Jefferson and Dickinson drafted a text that, like *A Summary View* before it, explained the misdeeds of George III and justified the dramatic action being undertaken by the colonies. From Jefferson's pen came many phrases that anticipate the Declaration, including this: "as it behoves those, who are called to this great decision, to be assured that their cause is approved before supreme reason; so is it of great avail that it's justice be made known to the world." Dickinson changed that to the simpler "we esteem ourselves bound, by obligations of respect to the rest of the world, to make known the justice of our cause." By the time Jefferson drafted the Declaration of Independence, he was ready at last to try something limpid: "a decent respect to the opinions of mankind requires that they should declare the causes which impel them." The 1775 "Declaration of the Causes" was, then, Jefferson's second pass and Congress's first try, at the material that would make its way into the Declaration of Independence. Yet this first Declaration was less radical than Jefferson's *Summary View*; it hewed to the course of reconciliation. Writing as part of a committee— instead of from a solitary mountaintop—Jefferson had to bend. He also had to learn how to restrain his inner dandy so as to simplify his elegance.

Despite his wordiness as a writer, Jefferson was surprisingly not a talker. He spoke infrequently in Congress. When that body met as a whole, he never took the floor to orate at length and is also said to have spoken only sparingly, albeit plainly and directly, in committee meetings. But he listened and took copious notes. After the "Declaration of the Causes," he was given a few more major writing assignments that July. Eventually he would be assigned the job of reviewing and correcting the records of congressional meetings and determining what could be published. The Continental Congress had found a role for him. As one historian has put it, he was Congress's "draftsman." Yet in the autumn of 1775 this role did not put him center stage. In October, when he lamented his empty letter-writing days, he still had time on his hands.

6

THE POLITICOS

I N THE AUTUMN AND EARLY WINTER OF 1775, JOHN ADAMS AND
Richard Henry Lee had no time at all to spare. Their long days continued even past Congress's 10 p.m. adjournment. On the evening of
November 14, for instance, Lee called on Adams, probably between ten
and eleven, at Adams's apartment on Second Street across from the City
Tavern, where delegates often gathered. Adams presumably chose his
abode precisely because it was close to the center of the action. (Jefferson, in contrast, finally settled in lodgings on the outskirts of town.) On
that night, as they talked late into the evening, Adams and Lee wrestled
with the riddle of independence.

What prompted Lee's after-hours visit to Adams? The answer to
that question must be traced back to the preceding June. On June 13,
1775, as colonial militia besieged the king's troops in Boston, John Wentworth, the royal governor of New Hampshire, also found himself under
siege, but in his own home. Born and bred in New Hampshire, heir to a
tight-knit kinship group that controlled the colony, this Harvard College
classmate and friend of John Adams's, was loyal to the king. When Wentworth found himself faced with a crowd of armed men on that June day,
he fled, taking his family to the protection of a British fort. This left New
Hampshire mired in a quandary, for the governor controlled the whole
political and civil administration. He appointed all judges, established
and maintained all courts, and commissioned all officers of the militia.

What were they to do for government? Should they wait for Wentworth to come back? Should they await a new royal government? Or should they try some other solution?

The men of New Hampshire charged their delegates to the Continental Congress with seeking advice from Philadelphia:

> We would have you immediately use your utmost endeavours to obtain the advice and direction of the Congress, with respect to a method for our administring, Justice, and regulating our civil police. We press you not to delay this matter, as, its being done speedily, (yr own knowledge of our circumstances must inform you) will probably prevent the greatest confusion among us.

The delegates from New Hampshire put this query to Congress on October 18. On October 26, Congress appointed a committee of five men, including both Adams and Lee, to answer it.

The committee's work was complicated. Most significantly, Congress itself was now unsure of the exact nature of the colonies' relationship to the crown. Congress was still waiting for a response to its summer "Declaration of the Causes and Necessity of Taking Up Arms," which it had sent off to London in July. It had also included a petition for reconciliation, called the Olive Branch Petition. Because sailing across the Atlantic took anywhere from four to seven weeks, Congress's agents reached London to present the petition to court only in late August. By October 26, when Adams and Lee had been tasked with solving the problem of New Hampshire, no word had yet arrived as to the king's response to the petition. Were the colonies on the cusp of a resolution of their difficulties with the king? As Adams put it, "We are in hourly Expectation of being overwhelmed all at once, with Floods of Intelligence from England, Quebec, St. Johns, Cambridge, and twenty other Places. But at present it is as dead as Midnight."

Yet the blackout of news from London did not suggest an absence of action by the British navy. In late September and October, the British were ravaging colonial sea towns. On November 1, for instance, Congress received a letter from George Washington, commander of the Continental army, detailing the destruction of Falmouth (now Portland), Maine. Two weeks earlier, a British naval captain, Henry Mowatt, had gathered together the people of Falmouth, charged them with rebellion, given them until morning to leave, and then bombarded the town from nine-thirty in the morning till sundown, leaving hundreds of women and children homeless as winter loomed. Similarly, under the direction of Virginia's royal governor, Lord Dunmore, the British navy had been harassing coastal towns in Virginia, especially Norfolk, since October 12, news that also reached Philadelphia only very late in the month.

Without newspapers from London, or intercepted royal orders, the commanders of the American military and Continental Congress could only deduce what the king's orders must have been from the actions of the British navy. In early October, Congress decided that "the last Advices from London" must be "to burn more towns." With the early November news of the Falmouth attack, and Moffat's pronouncement that the people of Falmouth were in rebellion, Congress had to surmise that the king had rejected the petition for reconciliation and was intensifying hostilities. Against this backdrop, on November 3 the committee on affairs in New Hampshire submitted the following recommendation:

> Resolved, That it be recommended to the provincial Convention of New Hampshire, to call a full and free representation of the people, and that the representatives, if they think it necessary, establish such a form of government, as, in their judgment, will best produce the happiness of the people, and most effectually secure peace and good order in the province, during the continuance of the present dispute between G[reat] Britain and the colonies.

For the first time, Congress now recommended that a colony establish a new government for itself. New Hampshire should aspire to form such a government as "will best produce the happiness of the people." Yet Congress described this new government as merely a stopgap measure. It was to last only "during the continuance of the present dispute between G[reat] Britain and the colonies." Nevertheless, it marked a radical break from past practice.

According to John Adams, achieving this policy result—the first actual effort at something beginning to look like the establishment of independent governments—was not easy. His diary notes capture the flavor of the disputations:

> Although this Committee [on New Hampshire] was entirely composed of Members, as well disposed to encourage the Enterprize as could have been found in Congress, yet they could not be brought to agree upon a Report, and to bring it forward in Congress till Fryday November 3. 1775. . . .
>
> By this Time I mortally hated the Words "Province" "Colonies" and Mother Country and strove to get them out of the Report. The last was indeed left out, but the other two were retained even by this Committee who were all as high Americans, as any in the House. . . .

In this same diary entry, Adams now avowed a "desire of revolutionizing all the Governments." Even more significantly, he describes a dissenting committee member as having come at last to share this view as well. Lee was not that dissenter, so we can safely assume that, by this November 3 date, he shared Adams's all-consuming revolutionary passion.

If Lee had not reached such a degree of conviction by November 3, he must have done so by November 13, for by then the news from London had begun to arrive. The king had not merely rejected the colonists' summer petition; he had refused even to look at it. And on August 23 he had issued a proclamation declaring all the colonies to be in "open and avowed" rebellion and to be treated accordingly. In Virginia, Lee's home "country," matters were so precarious that on November 10 Congress had set up a committee to advise on the state of affairs in Virginia, much as it had done the preceding month with the matter of New Hampshire. On November 13 Lee wrote a letter to George Washington, who was far to the north, to share news from both London and Virginia. He was clear on the lesson to be drawn: "All the other letters from London join in confirming it to be the fixt determination of K and Court to leave undone nothing that they can do, to compel implicit obedience in America." There would be no reconciliation, no effort to solve differences through negotiation rather than military compulsion.

Lee did not even yet know what would be for him, when it came, the worst of the news. To open Parliament's fall session on October 26, the king gave a major address, in which he declared the colonists out of his protection and indicated that he would seek foreign alliances to suppress them. An estimated sixty thousand Londoners thronged the streets to watch him ride to his speech in a gold chariot twenty-four feet long and thirteen feet high. In response, Parliament passed an act prohibiting all trade with the colonies and declared "colonial vessels and their cargoes, whether in harbor or at sea, forfeit to the Crown 'as if the same were the ships and effects of open enemies.'" And in Virginia, on November 7, Lord Dunmore declared martial law in the colony, offering freedom to any slave or indentured servant who joined the British military. This proclamation instantaneously radicalized Virginia's slaveholding elite, who had long feared little more than that their slaves might one day rise against them. Bits and pieces of all this news began to filter into Philadelphia only in late November. Yet even without having heard the worst of it, Lee was by November 13, the date of his letter to Washington, determined to thwart the king and Parliament's "infernal plan against the common natural rights of Mankind." He was ready for a serious conversation with Adams and showed up the following evening, November 14, with a question.

The riddle for "Independants" like Adams and Lee was no longer whether the colonies should declare their independence from Britain but how. After all, they had in effect just authorized New Hampshire to do nearly that. But this question of "how" was really two questions. First, how to justify such a step, and thereby persuade others into it, and, second, how exactly to set up political institutions and civil administrations in each colony once the king's institutions had been declared out of existence. Each man developed an answer to one of the "how" questions; together they had a complete solution.

In the king's decision to declare the colonists out of his protection, Lee would find, by the following spring, a clever, logically impeccable answer to the question of how to justify independence. He puts it most forthrightly in a letter to Patrick Henry in April:

> The act of Parliament has to every legal intent and purpose dissolved our government, uncommissioned every magistrate, and placed us in the high road to Anarchy. In Virginia we have certainly no Magistrate lawfully qualified to hang a murderer, or

any other villain offending ever so atrociously against the state. We cannot be Rebels excluded from the King's protection and Magistrates acting under his authority at the same time. This proves the indispensable necessity of our taking up government immediately, for the preservation of Society.

The king's proclamations and Parliament's act had made nonsense of the colonies' civil and political institutions. Their magistracies could no longer function. The result of the king's proclamation, Lee argued, was as good as to cast the colonies into a state of anarchy. Independence had, in short, been forced on them. Lee's work in October on the committee to address New Hampshire's institutional vacuum must have planted the seed of this argument in his mind.

The question about new governments would have followed close behind this thought. If the king was making his own magistracies null and void, with what could they be replaced? The experience on the October committee must also have helped Lee see that Adams was developing an answer to this second question of how exactly to set up political and civil institutions in the wake of the sudden disappearance of the king's magistrates. That November evening Lee paid Adams his visit in the hopes of hearing Adams's answer. He was not disappointed.

That night Adams shared his thoughts about how to set up new governments in circumstances of "sudden emergency." The following morning he sketched his answer a second time in a follow-up letter: "As you was the last Evening polite enough to ask me for this Model, if such a Trifle will be of any service to you, or any gratification of Curiosity, here you have it," he wrote to Lee. Adams's letter begins with the suggestion that his thoughts had been running in the same direction as Lee's; he too thought that the colonies found themselves in a strange situation with a pressing problem, a matter of "sudden emergency," concerning their political institutions. He wrote (and here we can't help hearing the beginning of the Declaration of Independence),

> Dear Sir, The Course of Events, naturally turns the Thoughts of Gentlemen to the Subjects of Legislation and Jurisprudence, and it is a curious Problem what Form of Government, is most readily & easily adopted by a Colony upon a Sudden Emergency.

Adams proceeds to explain how to build new governments. He starts by recommending institutions that balance legislative, executive, and judicial powers:

> A Legislative, an Executive and a judicial Power, comprehend the whole of what is meant and understood by Government. It is by ballancing each one of these Powers against the other two, that the Effort in human Nature towards Tyranny can alone be checked and restrained and any degree of Freedom preserved in the Constitution.

Then he gets down to the details:

> Let a full and free Representation of the People be chosen for an House of Commons.
> Let the House choose by Ballott twelve, Sixteen, Twenty four or Twenty Eight Persons, either Members of the House, or from the People at large as the Elections please, for a Council.
> Let the House and Council by joint Ballott choose a Governor, annually, triennially or Septennially as you will.

In his letter, Adams extends this series of instructions beginning with the word "Let" until it includes eleven items. It is as if he were spelling out a recipe or detailing a stage setting: "Let there be two eggs; let there be a cup of sugar" or "Let there be a sofa stage left; let there be a mirror on the wall stage right." His script is so specific that it concludes with this proposal: "Let the Colony have a Seal and affix it to all Commissions." Adams walks his fellow revolutionaries through the concrete steps that they will need to bring new governments into existence. He even tells them how to make sure their new magistrates are certified as official: there must be a seal to stamp onto letters of appointment.

Adams's purpose in providing such a concrete script is to allay anticipated fears about the difficulty of setting up new governments in conditions of "sudden emergency." He writes, "In this Way a Single Month is Sufficient without the least Convulsion or even Animosity to accomplish a total Revolution in the Government of a Colony." The trick to doing things quickly, Adams indicated, was to rely as much as possible on replicating preexisting institutional forms with which the colonists were already familiar. This meant repurposing British institutions in either a republican or a democratic mold, with the choice to depend on the sentiments of the residents of each colony. The goal for a colony, he says, is "pulling down Tyrannies, at a single Exertion and erecting Such new Fabricks, as it thinks best calculated to promote its Happiness."

In that late-night meeting and in Adams's morning-after letter to Lee, we can see, in truly embryonic form, the emergence of a political strategy. Fully mature, that strategy to bring about independence would look like this: those politicians who sought independence would, first, have to convince the colonies that they now had no governments at all; second, they would have to show them how they might easily, efficiently, and with minimal disturbance have new ones; third, they would need to get one colony—Virginia—to go first to show the others it could be done; and, fourth, they would provoke a cascade of imitators. Then the colonies would have their independence. Lee would make this strategy explicit in April. Virginia, he argued in a letter to Patrick Henry, should "tak[e] up government immediately," "above all to set an example which N. Carolina, Maryland, Pennsylvania, and N. York will most assuredly, in my opinion, follow; and which will effectually remove the baneful influence of Proprietary interests from the councils of America."

Lee and Adams began to put their strategy into motion just after the turn of the year, in February and March of 1776. Each had, for years, been like a gear, or Adams's "springs and wheels," turning the colonies most proximate to his own native colony. Now the two independent gears were engaged and began to turn the whole. In February, Lee prepared a poster, intended for circulation throughout Virginia, that laid out a recipe for setting up a new government; it was much like the script Adams had sketched in November. Conversations about establishing new governments began to spread. New Hampshire had adopted a constitution in January. In March delegates from North Carolina and New Jersey, as well as additional Virginians, asked Adams to write out for them, too, his advice for setting up new governments. After four requests, Adams's writing arm was exhausted; he asked the Virginians to have the essay printed up as a pamphlet.

Adams's pamphlet, called *Thoughts on Government*, was widely read. Here is how the text begins:

MY DEAR SIR,—If I was equal to the task of forming a plan for the government of a colony, I should be flattered with your request, and very happy to comply with it; because, as the divine science of politics is the science of social happiness, and the blessings of society depend entirely on the constitutions of government, which are generally institutions that last for many generations, there can be no employment more agreeable to a benevolent mind than a research after the best.

Much as the Declaration would open its argument in a few months' time, Adams launches his *Thoughts on Government* with a preamble laying out the purpose of government:

We ought to consider what is the end of government, before we determine which is the best form. Upon this point all speculative politicians will agree, that the happiness of society is the end of government, as all divines and moral philosophers will agree that the happiness of the individual is the end of man. From this principle it will follow, that the form of government which communicates ease, comfort, security, or, in one word, happiness, to the greatest number of persons, and in the greatest degree, is the best.

The purpose of government is, he argues, "in one word, happiness." Like Jefferson's *Summary View* and Congress's "Declaration of the Causes," his text, too, provided a preview of coming attractions.

In late April, working from Philadelphia, Lee began to circulate both his own poster and Adams's pamphlet, as he sought to convince his fellow Virginians to use their upcoming colonial convention, scheduled for May 15, both to begin the process of setting up a new government for Virginia and to charge their delegates to the Continental Congress with putting a motion before that body for independence for all the colonies. In the same period Adams drew up an address list for the residences of the delegates to the Congress then in Philadelphia. It is our best remaining evidence of where people lodged that spring. He or his associates must have been busy twisting arms in late-night visits, as we know he sometimes did. (In July, for instance, he wrote, "I have made it my Business ever Since I heard of this Error, to wait upon Gentn. of the Congress

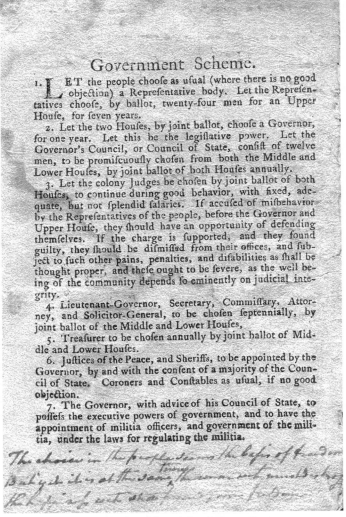

Poster printed for Richard Henry Lee.

at their Lodgings, and else where to let them into the secret and contrive a Way to get out of the Difficulty.") In April both men were working flat out, and after his signature on the bottom of a letter dated April 22, Lee scrawled, "I am so hurried that I scarcely know what I write."

On Wednesday, May 15, 112 members of Virginia's political elite attended a session of their colonial convention in Williamsburg to consider the questions Lee had been pushing hard to put on their agenda: Should Virginia set up a new government? Should its delegates in Phila-

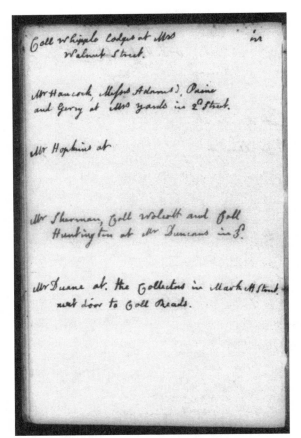

A page from John Adams's diary tentatively dated to April 1775 with notes of where members of the Continental Congress were lodging in Philadelphia.

delphia propose a general declaration of independence? The meeting of the Continental Congress in Philadelphia on the same day would also be momentous. During the middle of May, the City of Brotherly Love, had grown "uncommonly hot," and a week earlier two British battleships had tried to break through colonial defenses on the Delaware River north of Philadelphia. The thundering cannon reverberated in the city. Pressure, both climactic and political, was building. On Friday, May 10, Adams rose in Congress to propose a resolution, supported by Lee, that all the colonies should adopt new governments.

> Resolved, That it be recommended to the respective assemblies and conventions of the United Colonies, where no government sufficient to the exigencies of their affairs have been hitherto established, to adopt such government as shall, in the opinion

of the representatives of the people, best conduce to the happiness and safety of their constituents in particular, and America in general.

As Adams wrote to his wife that weekend, he was someone who liked to "storm and thunder." Congress passed his resolution.

Then Congress tasked Adams to draft a preamble to explain it. This time he, not Jefferson, was to be Congress's draftsman. The Virginian had not yet returned to Philadelphia. He had again been detained at home, this time by a six weeks' battle with migraines following the death of his mother. He would arrive only on May 14, the second of three days of strenuous and draining debate over Adams's preamble. Adams was, however, supported in the drafting of his resolution's preamble by Lee, who had been assigned to the preamble committee. Once again Lee worked in support of Adams's writerly efforts.

Those efforts led to something radical. In his preamble Adams at last put the two men's joint strategy on full, public display. He explained his motion thus:

> Whereas his Brittanic Majesty, in conjunction with the lords and commons of Great Britain, has, by a late act of Parliament, excluded the inhabitants of these United Colonies from the protection of his crown; And whereas, no answer, whatever, to the humble petitions of the colonies for redress of grievances and reconciliation with Great Britain, has been or is likely to be given; but, the whole force of that kingdom, aided by foreign mercenaries, is to be exerted for the destruction of the good people of these colonies; And whereas, it appears absolutely irreconcileable to reason and good Conscience, for people of these colonies now to take the oaths and affirmations necessary for the support of any government under the crown of Great Britain . . . it is [therefore] necessary that the exercise of every kind of authority under the said crown should be totally suppressed, and all the powers of government exerted, under the authority of the people of the colonies, for the preservation of internal peace, virtue, and good order, as well as the defence of their lives, liberties, and properties, against hostile invasions and cruel depredations of their enemies.

Some in Congress passionately wished to resist this direction; the exchange of words was hot. Still, on May 15 the tide of battle turned, and Adams's preamble was adopted. On the same day, in Williamsburg, the Virginians voted unanimously to erect a new government and deliver a resolution for independence to Congress.

Afterward, Adams wrote to a friend in Boston, "This Day the Congress has passed the most important Resolution, that ever was taken in America. . . . This Preamble and Resolution are ordered to be printed, and you will see them immediately in all the News Papers upon the Continent." A delegate on the losing end of the debate considered Adams's proposal and preamble "this piece of mechanism" and "a machine for the fabrication of independence." Adams responded that the resolution was "independence itself." He wrote to his learned, witty, steady wife, Abigail, "I have Reasons to believe that no Colony, which shall assume a Government under the People, will give it up."

In February—when Adams and Lee seem to have begun to set their "independence" strategy in motion—Adams had drafted a to-do list for measures to be pursued in Congress that spring. It included these two items: "Government to be assumed in every Colony" and "Declaration of Independency." With the May 15 vote, he had accomplished the first. In his mind, as he said, that May 15 resolution was already "independence itself." Yet the formal doing of "independency" was still necessary. He and Lee would pull Jefferson into that work.

7

THE COMMITTEE

I N THE WAKE OF ADAMS'S SUCCESSFUL RESOLUTION OF MAY 15, 1776— in which Congress recommended that the colonies establish new governments—an even more frenetic period of activity immediately ensued. One colony after another began preparing constitutional conventions to set up new political and civil administrations for themselves.

Jefferson was drawn to the constitution building, and, as usual, his thoughts turned toward Virginia. The day after the vote on Adams's preamble, two days after he had returned to Philadelphia, Jefferson wrote to a colleague in Virginia proposing that he be recalled home to work on that state's new constitution.

Permission to decamp was, however, not forthcoming, so Jefferson had to content himself by folding his tall frame over the custom-made tabletop writing desk in his lodgings. There he began to draft a proposed constitution for his home "country." Away from the hullabaloo of Congress, Jefferson used his hours out of meetings for that task. By June 13 he would have written not one but three draft constitutions for Virginia. Congress's writer was at work but not, or at least not directly, for Congress. This soon would change.

On June 7 Lee rose in the Philadelphia statehouse, his left hand wrapped, as usual, in a black handkerchief to hide the missing fingers. The May 15 meeting of Virginia's political leadership had, as he had hoped and vigorously worked for, led to instructions to the Virginia delegation to Congress to propose "independency" for the whole of the united colonies. Lee now put forward the motion for independence itself:

> Resolved, That these United Colonies are, and of right ought to be, free and independent States, that they are absolved from all allegiance to the British Crown, and that all political connection between them and the State of Great Britain is, and ought to be, totally dissolved.
>
> That it is expedient forthwith to take the most effectual measures for forming foreign Alliances.
>
> That a plan of confederation be prepared and transmitted to the respective Colonies for their consideration and approbation.

Debate made clear that the resolution would garner only a majority, not the unanimity that all thought independence required. To forestall a majority vote, Congress decided to delay consideration of the Lee resolution until July, by which time several of the delegations would have had time to seek fresh instructions from their home "countries" as to how to vote. That would open the possibility of switches to positive votes from the colonies holding on the longest to the hope of reconciliation. Yet Congress did not wish to lose too much time in the meanwhile. This resolution, like any other major resolution—for instance, Jefferson's "Declaration of the Causes and Necessity of Taking Up Arms" and Adams's resolution to recommend new governments in the colonies—would need a preamble. In order to reduce the impact of the delay, Congress on June 11 appointed a committee of five individuals who would spend the month of June developing the formal text of a declaration, in anticipation of a favorable vote on Lee's resolution in July.

Although Adams's first mention of Jefferson—in his diaries and letters—came only in October 1775, by June of 1776 he had grown not only to admire his pen but to trust him. He wanted him, alongside himself, on the committee to draft the Declaration. Adams worked the hustings and saw to it that Jefferson gained, by one, the most votes for election to the committee. This placed Jefferson at the head of the committee, with Adams coming second. After Adams came the sociable but silent and gout-stricken Philadelphian, Benjamin Franklin; the awkward and upright Puritan from Connecticut, Roger Sherman; and the lawyerly man of affairs from New

York, Robert Livingston. These men knew each other well; Sherman, for instance, had served with Adams and Lee on the committee that considered the New Hampshire question the preceding October. Livingston had written the "Address to the Inhabitants of Great Britain" that accompanied the Olive Branch petition that Congress sent to the King in July 1775.

Congress set up other committees at the same time. Lee was assigned to head a committee to work on the articles of confederation, and both Sherman and Livingston were assigned to it. Adams and Franklin were assigned to the committee charged with preparing a plan of treaties to be proposed to foreign powers. And Adams and Sherman were also assigned to the committee to form a board of war. Livingston and Sherman would be far too busy to contribute much to the writing of the Declaration, and Franklin was both busy and physically afflicted. Adams—capable of sustaining a herculean workload—was ready to join Jefferson in doing the bulk of the work on the draft. Of the two, Adams was far more burdened. Only Jefferson had been left free enough to focus on the Declaration.

The two men tell different stories of how exactly Jefferson ended up being the lead draftsman, yet it's easy to see their stories simply as the idiosyncratic perspectives of two participants in a single conversation. According to Adams, when Jefferson proposed that Adams write the first draft, the men had the following exchange:

ADAMS: I will not [do it]; *You* shall do it.

JEFFERSON: Oh no! Why will you not? You *ought* to do it.

ADAMS: I will not.

JEFFERSON: Why?

ADAMS: Reasons enough.

JEFFERSON: What can be your reasons?

ADAMS: Reason 1st. You are a Virginian and a Virginian ought to appear at the head of this business. Reason 2nd. I am obnoxious, suspected and unpopular; you are very much otherwise. Reason 3rd. You can write ten times better than I can.

JEFFERSON: Well, if you are decided I will do as well as I can.

Jefferson's story about what happened was that when the Committee of Five first met, they discussed the central issues to be handled in the text and then the whole group assigned him the job of drafting the first version. The conversation that Adams recalled could perfectly well have taken place within a committee's back-and-forth or, for that matter, on the way to the meeting. There is no need, as so many commentators have thought, to resolve which of these stories is correct.

Whatever the case, Jefferson produced the first draft. He shared it with Adams and Franklin. They made suggestions and corrections. Jefferson himself had some changes he wanted to make. He made all those changes and then shared a version with the whole Committee of Five. They approved it and on June 28 presented the document to the Continental Congress.

This is not all Jefferson was doing in the three weeks between the initial debate on Lee's resolutions and the submission of the committee draft to Congress. He was, of course, attending Congress six days a week. He was also finishing a third draft for the Virginia constitution, which he dispatched to Williamsburg on June 13. His mind was well steeped in Virginia's affairs. It's no surprise, then, that during the period that Jefferson was working on the Declaration of Independence, he also paid close attention to the bill of rights drafted for Virginia by George Mason. Mason had written,

> SECTION 1. That all men are by nature equally free and independent and have certain inherent rights, of which, when they enter into a state of society, they cannot, by any compact, deprive or divest their posterity; namely, the enjoyment of life and liberty, with the means of acquiring and possessing property, and pursuing and obtaining happiness and safety.
>
> SECTION 2. That all power is vested in, and consequently derived from, the people; that magistrates are their trustees and servants and at all times amenable to them.
>
> SECTION 3. That government is, or ought to be, instituted for the common benefit, protection, and security of the people, nation, or community; of all the various modes and forms of government, that is best which is capable of producing the greatest degree of happiness and safety and is most effectually secured against the danger of maladministration. And that, when any government shall be found inadequate or contrary to these purposes, a majority of the community has an indubitable, inalienable, and

indefeasible right to reform, alter, or abolish it, in such manner as shall be judged most conducive to the public weal.

In the Virginia Declaration of Rights, Mason, using a three-part structure, gave Jefferson a pithy example of how to formulate both the purpose of government and also a right of revolution based on inherent human equality. Here were key ingredients for the preamble that Jefferson sought to draft for the Declaration of Independence. Of course, he had other material as well. There was Adams's recent treatise on government with its axioms on happiness. And as for the colonials' grievances against King George, Jefferson had been compiling such lists since 1774. The ingredients of the Declaration of Independence were ready to hand. As Lee would write to Jefferson later in the summer, from those ingredients Congress's writer in residence had cooked up a remarkably good "Dish for the palates of Freemen."

On July 1 Congress returned to Lee's proposal. On July 2 all the colonies but one voted in favor of independence, some coming to that position only at the very last minute. The exception was New York, which abstained because the instructions that the delegation had from home did not permit it to hinder reconciliation (it would submit a positive vote later in July). Then Congress turned to the question of the text of its formal declaration. On July 4, 1776, the Continental Congress would unanimously approve the edited Declaration as a statement of its position.

John Adams wrote Abigail on the third,

> Yesterday the greatest Question was decided, which ever was debated in America, and a greater perhaps, never was or will be decided among Men. A Resolution was passed without one dissenting Colony "that these united Colonies, are, and of right ought to be free and independent States, and as such, they have, and of Right ought to have full Power to make War, conclude Peace, establish Commerce, and to do all the other Acts and Things, which other States may rightfully do." You will see in a few days a Declaration setting forth the Causes, which have impell'd Us to this mighty Revolution, and the Reasons which will justify it, in the Sight of God and Man. A Plan of Confederation will be taken up in a few days.

Congress had achieved unanimity, even then an almost unheard-of political feat. To do this, however, the delegates themselves had also needed to practice cookery, if not sorcery. Between July 2 and 4, they edited the committee's draft of the Declaration extensively, much to Jefferson's chagrin. Nor, as we shall see, did the writing end even on July 4. The delegates in Congress had wanted to leave their mark, and so did yet another man, Timothy Matlack, one of Congress's clerks, the man who was asked to inscribe the Declaration on parchment.

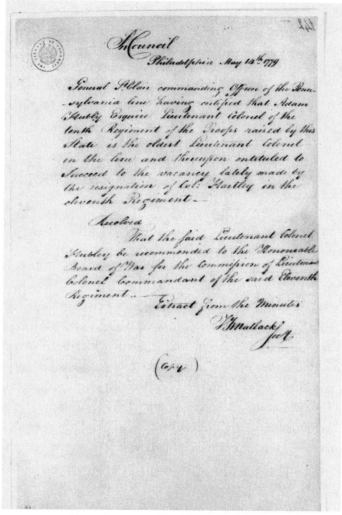

An example of Timothy Matlack's handwriting from a 1779 resolution concerning military promotions copied out and signed by him.

THE EDITORS

AFTER CONGRESS VOTED ON JULY 2 TO DECLARE INDEPEN-dence, it turned to the question of the text of the formal Declaration. Its representatives took up the draft that had been presented by Jefferson's Committee of Five in late June. Congress worked for two days straight emending, correcting, and, especially, cutting the text. If you measure by word count, Congress reduced the Declaration by about 25 percent. Yet most of the argumentative structure initially provided by Jefferson survived. Despite cutting so many words, Congress endorsed that argument and, in so doing, brought the writing job within a hair's breadth of completion.

To see just how group writing works—to understand this democratic art—we need to linger on the writing process. Here is an excerpt of the first draft as worked over by Adams, Franklin, and Jefferson:

> We hold these truths to be ˌself-evident sacred and undeniable; that all men are created equal & independent, that from that equal creation they derive in rights ˌthey are endowed by their creator with inherent & inalienable ˌrights; that, among which ˌthese are the preservation of life, & liberty, and the pursuit of happiness; that to secure these ends ˌrights, governments are instituted among men, deriving their just powers from the Consent of the governed;

Look how messy the work was. People always think that the phrase "we hold these truths to be self-evident" is one of the most important in the Declaration, but it started out as "we hold these truths to be sacred and undeniable." How did it go, the discussion among Adams, Franklin, and Jefferson about whether "sacred and undeniable" or "self-evident" was the better choice? One has to imagine the argument on each side. Did debating these options make Adams "mortally" tired of "sacred and undeniable" as debating the use of "Mother Country" had done the preceding October? These drafts are like snapshots of conversations.

Then, of course, there were the changes that Congress made to the draft that the Committee of Five submitted. Jefferson, whose relationship to slavery was maddeningly complex—an issue to which we will return—wrote high-flown passages about the ills of slavery, charging the British king with having "waged cruel war against human nature itself, violating it's most sacred rights of life & liberty in the persons of a distant people who never offended him, captivating & carrying them to slavery in another hemisphere." Here is the passage in full:

He has waged cruel war against human nature itself, violating it's most sacred rights of life & liberty in the persons of a distant people who never offended him, captivating & carrying them into slavery in another hemisphere, or to incur miserable death in their transportation thither. This piratical warfare, the opprobrium of <u>infidel</u> powers, is the warfare of the <u>Christian</u> king of Great Britain. determined to keep open a market where MEN should be bought & sold, he has prostituted his negative for suppressing every legislative attempt to prohibit or to restrain this execrable commerce_∧ <s>determining to keep open a market where MEN should be bought & sold</s>: and that this assemblage of horrors might want no fact of distinguished die, he is now exciting those very people to rise in arms among us, and to purchase that liberty of which <u>he</u> has deprived them, by murdering the people upon whom he also obtruded them; thus paying off former crimes committed against the <u>liberties</u> of one people, with crimes which he urges them to commit against the <u>lives</u> of another.

Here's what Congress did to that passage:

<s>He has waged cruel war against human nature itself, violating it's most sacred rights of life & liberty in the persons of a distant people who never offended him, captivating & carrying them into slavery in another hemisphere, or to incur miserable death in their transportation thither. This piratical warfare, the opprobrium of infidel powers, is the warfare of the Christian king of Great Britain. determined to keep open a market where MEN should be bought & sold, he has prostituted his negative for suppressing every legislative attempt to prohibit or to restrain this execrable commerce, determining to keep open a market where MEN should be bought & sold: and that this assemblage of horrors might want no fact of distinguished die, he is now exciting those very people to rise in arms among us, and to purchase that liberty of which he has deprived them, by murdering the people upon whom he also obtruded them; thus paying off former crimes committed against the liberties of one people, with crimes which he urges them to commit against the lives of another.</s>

Jefferson also included equally lofty language describing the wrongs done to the colonists by their British brethren. They had permitted the king to send both kinsmen and mercenaries to attack the colonials and, in so doing, had "given the last stab to agonizing affection." The only course was to "endeavor to forget our former love for" the British people. Here's what Jefferson wrote, with some edits by himself, Franklin, and Adams:

at this very time too they are permitting their chief magistrate to send over not only soldiers of our common blood, but Scotch & foreign mercenaries to invade & ˄destroy us [FRANKLIN] ~~deluge us in blood~~. these facts have given the last stab to agonizing affection and manyl spirit bids us to renounce forever these unfeeling brethren. we must endeavor to forget our former love for them, and to hold the rest of mankind, enemies in war, in peace friends. we might have been a free & a great people together; but a communication of grandeur & of freedom it seems is below their dignity. be it so, since they will have it: the road to ~~glory &~~ happiness ˄& to glory is open to us too; we will climb it ˄apart from them ~~in a separately state~~, and acquiesce in the necessity which pro˄denounces our ˄eternal separation ~~everlasting Adieu~~!

And then here is what Congress did to that passage:

˄We must therefore ~~at this very time too they are permitting their chief magistrate to send over not only soldiers of our common blood, but Scotch & foreign mercenaries to invade & ˄destroy us [FRANKLIN] deluge us in blood. these facts have given the last stab to agonizing affection and manyl spirit bids us to renounce forever these unfeeling brethren. we must endeavor to forget our former love for them, and to hold the rest of mankind, enemies in war, in peace friends. we might have been a free & a great people together; but a communication of grandeur & of freedom it seems is below their dignity. be it so, since they will have it: the road to glory & happiness ˄& to glory is open to us too; we will climb~~ ˄must tread ~~it~~ ˄apart from them ~~in a separately state, and~~ acquiesce in the necessity which pro˄denounces our ˄eternal separation ~~everlasting Adieu~~! and hold them as we hold the rest of mankind enemies in war, in peace friends.

Congress had no interest in Jefferson's sentimental and romantic fantasy of the colonists as jilted lovers.

The other major changes in the Declaration relate to God. Jefferson did not originally write most of the text's theological language. Some of that language entered during the work with Franklin and Adams, for instance, the use of the term "Creator" in the second sentence. Then the Continental Congress added several important phrases, particularly in the final paragraph. Jefferson's draft conclusion included no references at all to a divinity. Here was what he proposed as the best way to close the Declaration of Independence:

We therefore the representatives of the United States of America in General Congress assembled do in the name & by authority of the good people of these states, reject and renounce all allegiance & subjection to the kings of Great Britain & all others who may hereafter claim by, through, or under them; we utterly dissolve ~~& break off~~ all political connection which may ~~have~~ heretofore ^have^ subsisted between us & the people or parliament of Great Britain; and finally we do assert and declare these colonies to be free and independent states, and that as free & independent states they ~~shall hereafter~~ have ^full^ power to levy war, conclude peace, contract alliances, establish commerce, & to do all other acts and things which independant states may of right do. And for the support of this declaration we mutually pledge to each other our lives, our fortunes, & our sacred honor.

In contrast to Jefferson, though, the majority in Congress wanted to address itself in its final words not to the world alone but also to the "Supreme Judge of the World" and to "divine Providence." Its insertions are identified below as superscript:

We therefore the representatives of the United States of America in General Congress assembled ^appealing to the supreme judge of the world for the rectitude of our intentions^ do in the name & by authority of the good people of these ~~states, reject and renounce all allegiance & subjection to the kings of Great Britain & all others who may hereafter claim by, through, or under them; we utterly dissolve & break off~~ ^colonies, solemnly publish & declare that these United colonies are & of right ought to be free & independant states; that they are absolved from all allegiance to the British Crown,^ ^and that^ all political connection ~~which may have heretofore~~ ^have^ ~~subsisted~~ between us ^them^ & the ~~people or parliament~~ ^state^ of Great Britain ^is & ought to be totally dissolved^; ~~and finally we do assert and declare these colonies to be free and independent states~~; and that as free & independent states they ~~shall hereafter~~ have ^full^ power to levy war, conclude peace, contract alliances, establish commerce, & to do all other acts and things which independant states may of right do. And for the support of this declaration ^with a firm reliance on the protection of divine providence,^ we mutually pledge to each other our lives, our fortunes, & our sacred honor.

With changes such as these—with God edited in and a condemnation of slavery elided—Congress achieved a text that the men of that day and age could live with, including Jefferson grumpily. Yet even so, the writing was not done.

On July 15 news reached Philadelphia that New York's "convention of representatives" had met in White Plains on the ninth and voted for independence. Now the decision to separate from Britain was indeed unanimous, and on July 19 Congress determined a title for its document. It would be "The unanimous declaration of the thirteen United States of America." Congress also resolved to have the text "fairly engrossed" on parchment; by this it meant elegantly or beautifully, in a large, formal and polished hand. This job was assigned to Timothy Matlack—the forty-year-old cockfighting, brawling excommunicated Quaker—who was clerk for Charles Thomson, secretary of Congress, and a master calligrapher.

All told, Congress placed four different orders for official copies of the Declaration. On July 4 they had the Philadelphia printer John Dunlap produce a poster, which was then reproduced in newspapers throughout the colonies. They pasted this poster or broadside into their original record book for the date of July 4. Then, on the nineteenth, they commissioned Matlack's manuscript. And later, when Congress produced a "corrected journal" of its proceedings—a project that Jefferson helped supervise—the Secretary Thomson gave us a second handwritten but official Declaration. Finally, in January of 1777, Congress placed its fourth order. It resolved that "an authenticated copy of Declaration of Independency, with the names of the members of Congress, subscribing the same, be sent to each of the United States, and that they [the states] be desired [i.e., requested] to have the same put on record." This final job was given to a Baltimore printer named Mary Katherine Goddard, Baltimore's postmaster since 1775, who was described by a contemporary as "an expert and correct compositor of types."

With each of these productions of an "official" text, the writing of the Declaration continued. The two printing houses and the Quaker calligrapher editorialized with upper case and punctuation. Goddard's press, for instance, used all caps to write "Nature's GOD," "CREATOR," and "DIVINE PROVIDENCE." Her workshop treated the argument of the Declaration so as to emphasize its religious grounds. In fact, each of the four official texts changed the use of capital letters and punctuated the Declaration differently, most importantly, adding dashes and periods that were not in the Jeffersonian original. Their changes add texture and meaning to the text, in one case even altering sentence structure.*

To some extent, the differences among the four official texts show the hands of both Adams and Jefferson. The practicing lawyer from Mas-

---

* When Jefferson and his colleagues drafted the text and Dunlap, Matlack, Thomson, and Goddard either printed or transcribed the official versions, rules of punctuation had not yet been fixed. The generation of grammar books that would rigidify rules of punctuation would be published only around the turn of the next century. As Professor Janine Barchas writes, "Before 1800, punctuation . . . was determined by house style, regional idiom, and rhetorical intent" (personal communication, May 27, 2013). This does not, however, mean that we should treat variations in capitalization and punctuation as "accidental" or "invisible." Instead, they are a subtle guide to the interpretive intentions of authors, printers, compositors, and, importantly, copyists. See J. Barchas, *Graphic Design, Print Culture, and the 18th-Century Novel* (Cambridge, 2003), chap. 6.

sachusetts and aristocratic slaveholder from Virginia also differed altogether in their use of uppercase. Adams wrote out a copy of the original draft of the Declaration, and we can hear the thundering orator in it. He capitalizes throughout, giving us, in just the opening sentence, "Course," "Events," "Powers of the Earth," "Nature," "Nature's God," "Respect," and "Mankind." Jefferson, in contrast, capitalized only at the start of sentences. His texts are quiet, just as he was.

Dunlap's and Goddard's broadside versions of the Declaration follow Adams's capitalization; Matlack's version mainly tracks Jefferson. This tells us that on July 4, when Dunlap was at work over his printing press, it was in all probability Adams who was looking over his shoulder. We might have guessed. Jefferson was probably shopping that afternoon. His account books record a purchase on July 4 of seven pairs of ladies gloves and a thermometer. But when it came to Matlack's parchment, if anyone was looking over the clerk's shoulder, it was Jefferson.

Yet for all the influence that Adams and Jefferson had on the final state of the text, the printers and calligrapher were able to add their own voices to the Declaration. We have seen already how Goddard's printing house cast all the words for God in uppercase. Matlack also made his mark, adding color and emphasis, and interpretive layers, as he drew up the formal parchment document.

No mere functionary, or mindless bureaucrat, the Philadelphia native Matlack was himself committed to the cause of independence. When not working in Congress that summer, he could be found at the head of a battalion on New Jersey battlefields or participating in Philadelphia at mass meetings and conventions that were moving toward producing a new constitution for Pennsylvania. On July 17, two days before he was asked to produce the parchment copy, he was elected to Pennsylvania's Constitutional Convention. On July 24 he was elected to Philadelphia's Council of Safety. The rowdy patriot workingman clerk was, in other words, as busy as the congressmen. Squeezing his work on the Declaration in amid duties to city and state, and editorializing on the parchment with capitalization, punctuation, and flourishes, Matlack too helped to write the Declaration. Of all the copies, this one, Matlack's parchment manuscript, was the most important.

On August 2 delegates to the Continental Congress began to sign Matlack's copy, a process not complete for several months. The National

Archives displays this document as the official text, and it served as the basis for an 1823 copperplate reproduction that has become the standard reproduction. The parchment is the basis for the *New York Times*'s annual July 4 reprinting of the Declaration. And it is the basis of the transcription that the National Archives prints on its website. The parchment Declaration is the one that most of us have come to know. As we shall see in chapter 45, Matlack made one of the most important contributions to the text.

9

THE PEOPLE

THE TEXT AS APPROVED AND SIGNED BY CONGRESS WAS, AS WE have already seen, the product of many hands: those of the five men of the committee and the other fifty-one members of the Continental Congress but also the final hand of the clerk, Matlack. Each of the members of Congress contributed opinions about the document that grew out of layers and layers of conversation with one another surrounding the controversy over whether to break from Britain. Perhaps the most astonishing feature of Congress's daily records, the *Journals of Continental Congress*, is how often those pages report the delegation of some matter to a committee of three or five members. In the course of any given year, the busiest members served on dozens of committees. These men were constantly talking to one another.

Yet even those conversations are just the topmost summit on a mountain of talk. When Matlack textured the text with his formal calligraphy, he was at the same time engaged in conversations about how to build a new government with fellow Pennsylvanians; his mind would have been full of their debates. Through his hand—his choices and priorities—their voices are in the text as well. And then there are the words and voices of all those people who participated in conversations with Jefferson, Adams, Lee, and Mason—the conversations that led to Jefferson's *Summary View*, Congress's "Declaration of the Causes," Adams's *Thoughts on Government*, and George Mason's Virginia Declaration of Rights. These streams of talk included women as well as men; there are, for instance, echoes of Abigail Adams's turns of phrases in the documents written by John Adams. Abigail particularly liked to analogize time to the currents of rivers and oceans, and John shared this habit.

Exactly how many layers of conversation did it take to make the Declaration of Independence? Here's a count merely of the "official" discussions that directly fed into the writing of the Declaration.

- Participants in the Virginia Convention had to vote in favor of instructing their delegates to the Continental Congress, Richard Henry Lee in particular, to present a resolution for independence. (1)

- The Continental Congress had to vote in favor of that resolution; it hoped to achieve a unanimous vote. (2)

- This meant that each of the thirteen colonial delegations to the Continental Congress had to vote positively on the resolution. New York's delegates even had to return to New York to secure new instructions from the New York Convention on how they should vote. Not all delegations achieved internal unanimity in their vote for independence. (3–16)

- The Continental Congress had to vote to set up the Committee of Five (17). This means that a majority of the delegations to Congress had to vote to set up the committee, which in turn means that at least seven of the delegations had to agree internally on an affirmative vote. (18–24)

- The Committee of Five had to agree to delegate the first draft to Jefferson. (25)

- In the process of writing, Jefferson had to come to agreement with himself. (26)

- Jefferson, Adams, and Franklin had to come to agreement. (27)

- Then the Committee of Five had to agree that the text was ready for Congress. (28)

- Then Congress, having agreed on independence, had to agree also on the text of the Declaration (29). Here it wanted unanimity, so all thirteen delegations had to reach a positive view of the matter. (30–42)

- Timothy Matlack spoke with members of Congress and undertook the engrossment on parchment. (43)

- Finally, when the time came to sign the Declaration in August, all thirteen colonies had to reaffirm their agreement both individually and collectively. (44–57)

Agreement—whether through consensus or majority vote—had to be achieved in more than fifty separate instances at a minimum.

If we focus on this list of conversations, we cannot avoid seeing that the importance of the Declaration has as much to do with process as with product. This process—the sequence of conversations—had multiple goals. Of course, one was to reach a decision on a draft of the Declaration and whether to sign it. Another was to establish procedures for cooperation—for getting things done by means of talk. In the very process of organizing these conversations about independence and the Declaration, the colonists established patterns of collaboration that would provide for ongoing collective action in the freshly minted and newly united states.

Does the fact that the Declaration of Independence is a sterling example of group art diminish Thomas Jefferson's accomplishment? No. But we do need to redescribe it. The monumental achievement of Thomas Jefferson is, ultimately, to have produced a first draft—and a general argumentative structure—that, through its philosophical integrity and unquestionable brilliance, could survive such intense committee work and bear this much demand for agreement. But the authorship of the document belongs to all those who participated in the conversations leading up to the decision to declare independence and to all those who wrangled over the consensual statement of justification. Lee and Adams stand out, but only as the most engaged gladiators. Matlack entered the fray, too, and countless unnamed others. Ultimately, we have to realize that, when we sit down to read the Declaration, it is *their* argument that we read, not Jefferson's alone. It is the art of democratic writing—process as much as product—that we must learn how to appreciate.

How to do this? Democratic writing—group writing—is not merely difficult; it's exhausting and draining. Recall Adams's state of mind at the end of one set of committee debates: "By this Time I mortally hated the Words 'Province' 'Colonies' and Mother Country and strove to get them out of the Report." Recall, too, the exhaustion expressed by Lee at the end of that April 1776 letter: "I am so hurried that I scarcely know what I write."

Nor is democratic writing a perfect art. Democratic texts have many-headed authors, something like the hydra, that many-headed monster of ancient myth. In the case of the Declaration those multiple tongues continue to speak, often in contradiction of one another, even in twenty-first-century America. The differences between texts written by a group and those written by a single individual are best seen in the language criticizing slavery that was cut out of the Declaration. When groups of people write texts together, some choices are always made on the basis of votes, not truth. There will be compromises. And this makes reading such texts much harder than reading novels or poems or essays written by a solitary artist devoted to philosophical or artistic integrity. To read examples of democratic writing, one has to learn how to discern the traces left by majority vote.

Yet even with these caveats, democratic writing still deserves celebration. There is no other way for a free and equal people to chart its course. Our only chance to achieve collective happiness comes through extensive conversation punctuated here and there with votes, which will themselves over time, in their imperfection, simply demand of us more talk.

Who wrote the Declaration of Independence, then? Too many people to count or name. And how should we read specimens of democratic writing and, in particular, this fine one? If we wish to see just how fine it is, we must read it slowly.

III.

THE ART
OF
DEMOCRATIC
WRITING

The Committee of Five is here represented submitting the draft of the Declaration *to Congress; Jefferson is the tall figure placing a document on the table.*

ON MEMOS

WHEN ONE UNDERTAKES TO READ ANY TEXT—WHETHER FIC-
tion or nonfiction or even a poem—a handful of tried-and-true
questions set one going in the right direction: What *kind* of text have I got
in front of me? Who is the *audience* for this text? And what is the *structure* of the text—that is, how has the author divided the text into parts?
How do those parts help accomplish what the whole has been crafted to
do? Asking these questions about the Declaration will make us better
readers of its democratic art.

I'll start with the first: what kind of text is the Declaration?

Is it a sacred text? Or a treatise? Or perhaps a law? This is a question
we rarely ask.

In fact, the Declaration is just an ordinary memo. As an example, I
have in mind a memo I saw recently from a dean of students office at a
northeastern college. It announced that, going forward, the dining hall
would stay open later on weekdays, and it offered reasons for that change.
The Declaration is the same kind of document: a memo that announces
and, thereby, brings about a change, while also explaining it.

Short for "memorandum," which is Latin for "something that needs
to be remembered," the memo has been a basic tool of human social
organization ever since writing was invented. Although we are used to
thinking of memos these days mainly as interoffice directives, our view
has become restricted. Here's an older and more fundamental meaning:

An informal diplomatic message, *esp.* one summarizing the state of a question, justifying a decision, or recommending a course of action.

In fact, its oldest usage spawned a formula to launch declarations. It went like this: *Memorandum, That it is hereby declared . . .*

As ever speedier modes of duplication and communication have emerged, memos have become only more common and more important. Those who write the best memos set policy for businesses, cultural organizations, and governments. Because of their impact on our memories, writers rule. They wield the instrument by which our world is organized.

The Declaration, too, is a very practical document. It claims to know something about how a particular institution of a particular kind—the kingdom of Great Britain, a free and independent state—should work. It criticizes this institution for failing to work as it should. It announces the separation, on account of this failure, of the colonies from Britain and the coming into being of a new political system. But it also had the job of organizing a group to joint action: revolt from Britain.

What does it take for a group to act in concert? How are decisions made? Who takes responsibility for them? What makes it possible for a group, organization, or institution to collaborate over time? When do they run into trouble? Why? We all know things about how institutions should work. By trying to answer questions like these in relation to our own lives, we build a context for thinking about the Declaration.

Take a family's holiday dinner. Even when people already have many good reasons to want to collaborate, success takes work. In my family as Thanksgiving approaches, there are always the delicate questions: Who will host this year? If two among our extended family have volunteered, how do we decide? We also often have a dilemma with regard to who will take responsibility for the sweet potato pies, or whether we will have both squash and sweet potatoes as part of the meal. Then there is a question of who will get a room in the host's house and who will stay in a local motel. Even in such, relatively speaking, low-pressure situations, families need (1) a lot of communication about who is going to do what; (2) negotiation and agreement about how different family members can contribute in ways that call upon each person's strengths; and (3) some way of resolving disputes. Communication is the beating heart of cooperation.

To recognize that a text, like the Declaration, is a memo is just to see that a piece of writing is helping to organize a group of people. The dullest possible example—like the dining service memo—and a text as remarkable as the Declaration reside at the far points of a single continuum. Both emerge out of the reality that human beings are political creatures, dependent in fundamental ways on our membership in groups and able to use language to organize collective projects. The art of democratic writing exalts the memo.

But memos—or at least, specifically *democratic* ones—aren't just about logistics. What reasons did that dean of students' memo give for the change in dining hall hours? That, given their practice and game schedules, student athletes need more time to get to the dining hall. There's a worldview here: the college valued the efforts of students to excel at more than one kind of activity. In addition to the organizational details, the memo conveyed principles to explain decisions about particular facts. To be democratic, a memo must offer principles.

Take as another example a business memo that caught my attention when, surprisingly, it turned up in the newspaper some years ago—an early warning sign of the coming Great Recession. Charles Prince, CEO of Citigroup, was announcing his resignation in a memo to all employees. He acknowledged that recently downgraded mortgage securities were jeopardizing the business, took responsibility for the business decisions, and announced that he considered resignation the only honorable course. I was particularly struck by the fact that he signed off, informally, with his nickname, Chuck.

Citigroup, a big company, changed profoundly the instant Mr. Prince's memo went out. Like the Declaration, it made something happen. If only those in the boardroom had known that Mr. Prince had resigned, nothing in reality would have changed. The memo also revealed a worldview. Mr. Prince's sign-off suggested that he was everybody's buddy in a company with thousands of employees. How believable is it that the company is as democratic as all that? Still, the memo asserted a specific set of values. References to responsibility and the need to choose the honorable course rounded out those values. Principles applied to facts had led to Mr. Prince's action; such was the clear argumentative structure of the memo.

Describing this sort of business memo in the same breath as the Declaration of Independence is admittedly surprising. For all the clarity of his prose, few of us would be inclined to identify Mr. Prince, like Jefferson, as a prince of prose. And, while the Declaration is a model of human achievement, few would be inclined to say something similar about such business memos. But there remains nonetheless a kernel of truth in the startling comparison. We all work all the time with the basic tools used in the Declaration—principles, facts, and judgments—in order to set a course in life. Bringing in these ordinary memos is a way of highlighting that the basic ingredients for political thought are all around us all the time. The art of democratic writing starts from just those ingredients.

Principles, facts, and judgments: the Declaration takes the ordinary and makes it extraordinary. Mr. Prince's resignation was attended by statements about the future successes sure to accrue to Citigroup—just when the company, and indeed the world, teetered on a precipice. The writers of the Declaration aspired to a sounder judgment.

11

ON MORAL SENSE

DEMOCRATIC MEMOS SEEK TO JUSTIFY PARTICULAR ACTIONS TO broad audiences. Democratic writing—when it is done well—respects the audience's judgment. Who, then, was the Declaration's audience? If the art of democratic writing requires the presentation of reasons to a broad audience, for whom was the Declaration written?

The Declaration makes a strange claim. It says it is for everybody, every single person in the world. What it actually says is:

> *The history of the present King of Great Britain is a history of repeated injuries and usurpations, all having in direct object the establishment of an absolute Tyranny over these States. To prove this, let Facts be submitted to a candid world.*

We are all part of the "world" to which the Declaration submits its facts. With every fresh reading, the Declaration calls out again for judgment. It is not merely those who were alive in 1776 who were members of the candid world; we are too.

The Declaration has expectations of its readers. A reader of the Declaration must be a judge. "Candid" means honest; it also means unstained. As it says here, the Declaration offers a set of facts that are supposed to prove that King George III was tyrannizing the colonies. If we are candid, we will be able to judge these facts fairly.

Do the authors of the Declaration have a strong case? How can we tell? Is it enough to know the facts? Or do we need something else too?

When one child on the playground—call her Hannah—kicks and bites to keep another—let's say Emily—from using the slide, the victim knows that something's wrong. She'll tell her mother, "Mama, Hannah is a meanie." She has, in other words, moral sense, some basic capacity for moral evaluation.

Odds are, her mother will then say something like, "Well, love, when people are bullies it's usually because they're insecure or jealous; she wants to take something from you—the joy of sliding—just because she thinks she can and then she'll feel bigger than you."

This will occasion another question: "What's 'bullies,' mama?" Her mother might say, "Bullies are people who don't care what harm they cause others on their way to getting something they want for themselves."

Perhaps Emily doesn't merely *think* that Hannah is a meanie but even feels downright angry at how Hannah treated her. Not only her mind but her spirit too knows that she's been wronged. She knows the brute fact—someone kept her from the slide. And mind and spirit—helped along by, in this case, her mother—combine to give her moral sense, some general moral ideas—for instance, that people who arbitrarily block the access of others to public goods act wrongly. It probably won't make Emily feel better when her mother says, "Well, dear, at least you have moral sense." But her mother will be right.

The Declaration assumes that its readers are similarly equipped with moral sense. In calling out to its readers as members of the candid world, the Declaration identifies its audience as consisting of the kind of living organisms that can connect facts with principles in order to make judgments. The Declaration also presents us with a particular set of principles and facts and asks us to judge. The Declaration calls out to us, in other words, to act as the political creatures we are. That's what it means to judge the relations among facts, principles, and a community's chosen course of action. It is to be a political creature.

Just as membership in the candid world is not limited in time, it is not restricted in space. Membership is open to citizens of the United States, immigrants, visitors whose home is some place else entirely, and the rest of the world too. When the Declaration asserts that the whole world can and should judge its arguments, when it asks the world to judge it over and over again, the Declaration acts out its belief in human equality. The writers obviously believe that the whole world *can* judge.

For the Declaration we are all equal in having the capacity to judge relations among facts, principles, and courses of action. Indeed, this same capacity is what makes us members of the candid world. We are equal in being political creatures.

I am, however, getting ahead of the story. We have barely even looked at the text yet, but I've already started talking about "human equality" and "the candid world." The question of who the Declaration claims as its audience has already taken us into the substance of its argument.

Our choice of audience—whenever we speak or write—is always freighted with philosophical and political meaning. Do we seek an intimate community of speakers and listeners closed off to others? Or do we seek to open our audience, potentially, to all? As is clear, the authors of the Declaration made the latter choice.

Indeed, the art of democratic writing demands of its practitioners the aspiration to write to any and all, for any and all. It is a philanthropic art: it requires affection for humanity.

12

ON DOING THINGS WITH WORDS

THE DECLARATION, THEN, IS A MEMO THAT RECORDS A DECISION on the part of the colonists to break from Britain. We also know what the Declaration thinks of its audience. It addresses itself, in a philanthropic spirit, to a candid world, inviting judgment. And we know, too, what the Declaration does. This memo organizes a group of citizens and births a nation. A string of words—1,337 of them to be exact—transforms a mass of people from one thing into another, from a set of colonies into a nation of united states. This leads to another important question.

How exactly does the Declaration do what it does? How do the parts of the text allow it to accomplish its work? This is to ask about the structure of the Declaration. The conventional approach to the Declaration's structure is to divide it into blocks of text. For instance, one scholar writes, "[T]he Declaration can be divided into five sections—the introduction, the preamble, the indictment of George III, the denunciation of the British people, and the conclusion." But it's also possible to divide the Declaration into actions.

In the first paragraph, the signers indicate that they will declare the reasons for their actions:

> . . . *a decent respect to the opinions of mankind requires that they should declare the causes which impel them to the separation.*

In the second paragraph they submit facts to witnesses:

> *The history of the present King of Great Britain is a history of*
> *repeated injuries and usurpations, all having in direct object the*
> *establishment of an absolute Tyranny over these States. To prove*
> *this, let Facts be submitted to a candid world.*

Then, after listing the injuries done to the colonies, the Declaration formally declares independence:

> *We, therefore, the Representatives of the united States of America,*
> *in General Congress, Assembled, . . . do . . . solemnly publish and*
> *declare, That these united Colonies are, and of Right ought to be*
> *Free and Independent States,*

Finally, the text concludes with a pledge:

> *And for the support of this Declaration, with a firm reliance on the*
> *protection of Divine Providence, we mutually pledge to each other*
> *our Lives, our Fortunes, and our sacred Honor.*

The Declaration does what it does, then—bravely giving birth to a
new political entity—in four concrete steps: declaring reasons, presenting
facts to witnesses, declaring independence, and making pledges. These
are the parts that, taken together, assembled into a word machine of
sorts—into a "piece of mechanism," to quote John Adams's opponent—
make something happen. To understand how the Declaration does what
it does, we have to understand the interaction among these parts.

Declaring reasons, presenting facts, declaring that a new state of affairs
obtains, and making pledges: these are familiar actions, just like what
brides and grooms do when they marry. Consider. In front of witnesses,
two people pledge themselves to each other, and the judge or religious
official concludes the ceremony by saying, "I now declare you spouses."
As philosophers have shown, what happens at a wedding can teach us a
lot about language. It can also teach us a lot about the Declaration. If we
follow out this metaphor, we will understand better how the actions of
the Declaration fit together.

In a wedding two people walk into a temple, city hall, church, or mosque as individuals. When they say, "I do," and the officiant says, "I declare you spouses," real facts in the world, including legal realities, change. The couple will now be treated differently by everybody who knows them and also by officialdom. For instance, each now owns half of the other's property.

Words can be used not only to tell a story or express emotions or explain ideas but also to "do things," to bring about change in the world. Just as when a couple says, "I do," the words of the Declaration make a new reality. Because these words have been uttered, the text declares, a new confederation of states now exists, and their members have pledged one another their lives, property, and honor. In this the Declaration sounds something like a wedding.

Yet if the Declaration resembles a wedding, it bears an even closer kinship to divorce. The signers, remember, declared,

> *That these united Colonies are, and of Right ought to be Free and Independent States, that they are Absolved from all Allegiance to the British Crown, and that all political connection between them and the State of Great Britain, is and ought to be totally dissolved. . . .*

We can confirm that the Declaration speaks in the dispiriting tones of divorce by comparing it to the high-profile breakup of Charles, Prince of Wales, heir to the British throne, and Princess Diana in 1996. Their divorce decree says this:

> *[I]t was* decreed *that the marriage solemnized on the 29th day of July 1981 at the Cathedral Church of St. Paul in the City and Diocese of London between the petitioner and the respondent be* dissolved unless sufficient cause be shown *to the court within six weeks from the making thereof why the said decree should not be made absolute.*
>
> *And* no cause having been *shown, it is hereby certified that the said decree was on the 28th day of August 1996 made final and absolute and that the* said marriage was thereby dissolved. *(emphasis added)*

Images of wedding rings from An Essay on Marriage; or,
The Lawfulness of Divorce . . . , *published in 1788 in Philadelphia.*

The Declaration not only concludes, of course, with language like this, about "dissolving" relations, but also starts there, precisely with the first sentence: "When in the Course of human events it becomes necessary for one people to dissolve the political bands which have connected them with another, . . . they should declare the causes which impel them to the separation." The arc of the Declaration, then, is this: first the colonists declare themselves divorced from Britain; then, after confirming that divorce, they also declare that they are remarrying, now to one another.

There is something very funny, though, about the divorce and wedding conducted via the Declaration. Why should simply declaring oneself divorced, and then remarried, be enough to make it so? Doesn't a proper divorce, and a proper wedding, too, require a judge or a religious official? And when countless couples get up next June to say, "I do," their pledges will serve to change their lives because that pledge has already been used an equally countless number of times and because every wedding guest knows that this is how those words work.

Other features, too, of the wedding ritual give the words "I do" the power to change reality. In older versions of the ceremony, before the couple exchanged its vows, the minister would read a proclamation asking whether anyone knew of a reason that the young couple should not wed. The proclamation called out, "Speak now or forever hold your peace." Silence was consent. The wedding ritual contains within it the idea that a community's consent is necessary to legitimate a marriage.

In fact, the whole marriage ritual is built out of moments of consent. First, the community consents to let the couple wed, then the couple consents to wed, and finally a minister or judge consents on behalf of the legal system. The parts of the Declaration help build up similar moments of consent for the union it ushers in.

When the signers of the Declaration published their unanimous declaration, traditions did not exist to make their words work automatically. Unlike "I do," their words were not yet a magic formula. They needed to invent rituals to make their words work. This meant defining the moment when each interested party would, as in a wedding, consent. In their case, the interested parties were (1) King George, (2) the citizenry in Britain, (3) their fellow colonists, and (4) the rest of the world.

The signers of the Declaration did not ask King George III to consent to the divorce and remarriage. They insisted that by hiring mercenaries to fight them, he had as a practical matter already divorced them. By fighting back with their own army, the colonies would eventually force King George to acquiesce to a formal divorce.

As to their British brethren, the colonists didn't formally request their consent either, but they did convey regret about the breakup.

In contrast, the signers of the Declaration formally asked all the colonies to consent to the new relationship that they were declaring into existence among themselves. They put most of their effort here, a point to which we will return.

As we have seen, the colonists also presented themselves to a candid world, just as to a crowd of wedding guests. They weren't merely being polite or acting on the idea that it would be nice to know that everybody approved. They had a pragmatic interest in gaining the world's approval. They weren't exclusively philanthropic, after all. They knew King George would try to get other countries to help him subdue his misbehaving colonies. They wanted those countries to refuse to help. That required the colonists to win worldwide consent for their brash divorce and bold remarriage.

Finally, the colonists did, in fact, also seek a judge's approval. When people want to get married, they can go to the courthouse, and, these days, if a people wants to start a new nation, they can go to the United Nations. No such organization, recognized as a superior authority by the colonists, the king of England, and the rest of the world, existed then. Since there was no human judge before whom they might present themselves, the colonists appealed to God, the only judge recognized everywhere, albeit under different names. They appealed "to the Supreme Judge of the world for the rectitude of [their] intentions."

As the colonists knew, the consent of King George and of the candid world would come only after a fight. Similarly, the consent of the "Supreme Judge of the world" would become visible only with a victory in war. As Abraham Lincoln put it during the Civil War, with regard to the warring North and South: "Both read the same Bible and pray to the same God, and each invokes His aid against the other. . . . The prayers of both could not be answered." Victory would be a sign of whose prayers had been approvingly received.

The possible consenters to this divorce and remarriage were no throng of jubilant relatives ready to endorse a union, if only for the party. The parties seeking this divorce and remarriage would have to want their new world badly enough to win it in the fires of war. A will to revolt, like a desire to marry, had to develop before any moment of proposal and consent could succeed.

That is why the signers of the Declaration worked so hard to create rituals through which the colonists, the parties to the new marriage, might come to full consensus or unanimity. All those circles of conversation that led to the writing and adoption of the Declaration provided the necessary ritual.

"Unanimity" is, again, from Latin. *Unus* means "one" or "single," and *anima* means "spirit" or "soul," so "unanimity" means "having a single spirit." The idea of unanimity conveys that people agree with their whole spirits, not just their minds. And spirit conveys the idea of "life force." This comes through in the link between the words *anima* and "animal." A group bound in unanimity, then, has committed its energies fully to a common goal, like a couple saying, "I do."

It took rivers of talk for Jefferson's words to become the "unanimous" Declaration of the colonies. As we saw, those formal and informal conversations had multiple goals. First, the Continental Congress had to reach a decision on a draft of the Declaration and on whether to sign it. Second, the colonists needed to establish procedures for talk-based cooperation. But the third goal of all those conversations is the most important to explaining how the Declaration did what it did. The third, and the fundamental, goal of the conversations that led to the Declaration was to generate the will to revolt.

In a marriage, the discussion about what to pledge is as much a part of the wedding process as the actual exchange of vows. This was equally true for the colonists' efforts to divorce Britain and remarry one another.

The signers of the Declaration used the process of deciding what to pledge to one another as a method for deciding whether to divorce themselves from England and recommit to each other. This doesn't mean the words aren't important, though. A couple can't finally tie the knot until they know what vows they'll use—what principles they'll seek to live by.

The structure of the Declaration reveals, then, four actions that were necessary in order for the Declaration to do its work: declaring reasons or principles, presenting facts, declaring independence, and pledging solidarity. The art of democratic writing routinely joins an analysis of principles and facts to a call to action that will succeed only if supported by solidarity. To claim the Declaration as our own, and to master democratic writing, we first and foremost need to understand that move from principles to facts and then onward to calls for action and, finally, solidarity. The lesson of the Declaration's structure is that solidarity cannot be built without principle.

The text alone did not bring about the colonists' independence. They had long been preparing to claim their autonomy and, in their preparations, their autonomy had begun to exist. With every committee meeting, the windup toy was given another twist. Their work built up stores of potential energy, which the Declaration then released. In one transformative event, with the adoption of the Declaration, potential became actual. This is because with the Declaration the colonists themselves had finally performed their independence, rather than simply preparing for it. Having developed the will to revolt, they revolted.

So how can a memo of 1,337 words—a slender piece of democratic writing—turn a group of thirteen dependent colonies into thirteen independent states? The four actions in the Declaration that give it structure—declaring reasons or principles, presenting facts, declaring a new situation to obtain, and pledging solidarity—achieved this transformation because, taken together, they built a basis for solidarity and used that solidarity to prove to the world that something had changed.

Those 1,337 words were able to change the world because:

1. they recognized that the consent of a community, and the solidarity based on it, can bring new realities into existence;
2. they staked a claim to that consent;
3. they justified that consent;

4. they won that consent;

5. they presented the fact of that consent, and solidarity, before the witnessing world as evidence of a new reality; and

6. they ensured that everyone would remember the fact that had changed the world.

All memos record "something to be remembered." This one, though, brought about the very thing everyone was supposed to remember. Making potential independence actual, it powered a revolution. In Philadelphia on July 8, bonfires were lit, candles glowed in all the windows, and, as Adams recalled, "The Bells rung all Day, and almost all night." In colony after colony, new leaders, "inflexible in their Zeal for Independence," replaced an older cohort opposed to or, at best, lukewarm for independence. Such reluctant revolutionaries were, in Adams's words, "all fallen, like Grass before the Scythe."

13

ON WORDS AND POWER

THE DECLARATION BRINGS TO LIGHT THE INCANDESCENT MAGIC of human politics: the fact that it is possible for people, with ideas, conversations, and decision-making committees—both formal and informal—to weave together an agreement that can define our common life. Paradoxically, it is the combining of ideas with process—such abstract terms—that makes for the wondrous nature—the beauty, even—of the text.

The Declaration is not the only text that achieves this. Something similar might be said about the *Purna Swaraj*, the Indian Declaration of Independence from 1930. There, too, years of talk intersected with political process to achieve an animating statement for a new political order.

Attention to how ideas intersect with process—to decision making— teaches us how to do things with words.

What does consensus look like? A room full of nodding, smiling people? Perhaps that image of a group of jubilant relatives at a wedding? No, as we have seen, consensus is, in short, a mess. Below is the original rough draft, with changes by Jefferson, Adams, and Franklin that had to be made before they could come to consensus about submitting the document to Congress as well as indications of the further changes made by Congress.

This text could be captioned, "Pardon our appearance: consensus in the making."

The "original Rough draught" on which Jefferson marked changes made both by his colleagues in the Committee of Five and by the Continental Congress.

Yet despite the look of a battered term paper from days gone by, the sentences of the Declaration feel sturdy. No doubt this is because each ringing sentence had been hammered out in so many interlocking circles of conversation. Consensus and sturdiness emerge out of construction processes like these. The source of that sturdiness is solidarity.

When Adams told his story about why Jefferson was tapped to write the first draft, he invoked the fact that Jefferson hailed from Virginia. A remarkable proportion of the period's leading figures came from Virginia—not only Jefferson but also George Washington, who would of course lead and win the Revolutionary War and serve as the new nation's first president. James Madison, too, came from Virginia. He would be the fourth president; even more importantly, as the main drafter of the Constitution, Madison midwifed the United States. He, perhaps more than any other of those early wordsmiths, understood the art of democratic writing.

Madison's writerly accomplishments—simultaneously pragmatic and learned—are breathtaking. After the work on the Constitution, Madison, along with two New Yorkers, wrote the *Federalist Papers*, that series of anonymous, yet soon-to-be renowned, newspaper opinion pieces, steeped in history, that swayed public sentiment in favor of the Constitution just as it was coming to a vote in each state. Essay by essay, Madison and his co-authors took apart the arguments against the Constitution with remorseless logic. Then, after the Constitution had been voted in and President Washington elected, Washington, in preparing to give his first inaugural address, asked Madison to read the draft. Madison did so and provided such a forceful critique that Washington—who was self-educated and often deprecated his own writing—prevailed on Madison to ghostwrite him a new speech.

Then, as a congressman, Madison was in the audience when Washington delivered the inaugural address to Congress on April 30, 1789. After the speech, Congress thought the president was due a congressional response, and so the House of Representatives asked its best writer—none other than Madison again—to write it. He was happy to oblige, celebrating in the response the "enlightened maxims" that he had, in fact, sketched out in Washington's speech. After Washington received Congress's response, he thought there should be a response to the response, and once again he asked Madison for help. This rejoinder began, "Your very affectionate address produces emotions which I know not how to express." As my father once quipped, the early history of this country is the story of James Madison talking to himself.

We could stretch this point, and it would still be true: the early history of this country consists of a tight cluster of Virginians—and the occasional New Yorker or man from Massachusetts—talking among themselves. These men knew how to do things with words. That was a crucial source of their power, so much so that we could stretch the point about as far as it will go and say: *this country was born in talk.*

Another point must be made, though, about the figure of Madison. He donated his abilities to the collective conversation—he contributed to Washington's writing, to the work of the Constitutional Convention, to the words of Congress. He did not need the glory of authorship. Nor did Washington disdain help. The art of democratic writing supports the development of collective intelligence and does not seek credit. It does not know intellectual pride.

In the name of the whole: the Declaration is as much about how to solve the central conundrum of democracy—how to make sure public actions can count as the will of the people—as about anything else. It is about how to ensure that public words belong to us all. The fact that these early wordsmiths were men—and, for that matter, white— has never kept me from wanting to learn what they knew about words and power. From them we can learn how to use words to engender the actions, build the institutions, and clarify the principles that belong to a democratic people.

I believe the Declaration succeeded, and succeeds still, because it took on the task of explaining why this quantity of talk, this heap of procedures, these lists of committees, and this much hard-won agreement— such a maddening quantity of group writing—are necessary for justice. The argument of the Declaration justifies the process by which the Declaration came to be. It itself explains why the art of democratic writing is necessary.

Why is all the talk necessary? Because all men are created equal and are endowed by their Creator with certain unalienable Rights, among which are Life, Liberty and the pursuit . . . .

But wait. I am again getting ahead of the story.

We're not ready yet to explain how the argument of the Declaration justifies the existence of the Declaration. To do that we must talk about specific sentences, and, if we're going to do that, we should really start at the beginning. We need to work out just what the Declaration has to say about equality.

IV.

READING
THE COURSE
OF EVENTS

The covers of Anderson's 1773 and 1774 almanacs. Almanacs were, after the Bible, the genre of printed matter with the greatest circulation in the colonies. The 1774 cover echoes a line in Isaac Watts's hymn "O, God, Our Help in Ages Past": "Time, like an ever rolling stream / Bears all its sons away."

WHEN IN THE COURSE OF HUMAN EVENTS...

THE DECLARATION IS NOTHING LESS THAN A VERY SHORT INTRO-
duction to political philosophy. It teaches us to ask: How are things going for us? Are we living well, this group of people to which I somehow belong? These are the fundamental questions of political philosophy.

At the heart of the Declaration are, as I've said, two ideas: equality and freedom. What is this equality that the Declaration is about and where is it? What and where is this freedom?

These days too many of us think that to say two things are "equal" is to say that they are "the same." Consequently, we think the assertion that "all men are created equal," is patently absurd. Everyone knows that Bill Gates is richer, Halle Berry better-looking, and Albert Einstein smarter than virtually all of us. And, of course, Bill and Albert are not as good-looking as Halle, and Halle and Albert are not as rich as Bill, and so on. Everybody is bested by someone at something.

But "equal" and "same" are not synonyms. To be "the same" is to be "identical." But to be "equal" is to have an equivalent degree of some specific quality or attribute. We can be equal in height although we are not the same as people. In what regard, exactly, does the Declaration take us all to be equal to one another?

The matter of freedom is similarly obscure. There is the question of whose freedom? And from what? Or to do what? And with respect to what power? Is it freedom from interference or from domination that we seek? Aren't all of our lives interfered with by law, after all? Yet these interfering laws keep us free from domination by others; they protect us from exposure to arbitrary treatment and so from uncertainty and subordination.

Aren't we also constrained by the necessity of feeding, housing, and clothing ourselves and our families? Yet in meeting these necessities we acquire the capacity to act freely on a broader canvas.

There is, of course, our freedom to vote. But does that freedom translate into any real control? How many of us feel in control of political decisions made at the state and national level? When property taxes go up or decisions are made to reduce investment in education, do we feel that those are *our* decisions? And should we even feel in control of decisions that constrain our friends, neighbors, and passersby? Should they feel in control of decisions that constrain us?

These days too many of us have no idea what to make of the concept of equality; we are also confused about freedom. I routinely hear from students that the ideals of freedom and equality contradict each other. The Declaration argues the opposite case: that equality is the bedrock of freedom.

The Declaration starts its argument about equality in its very first sentence; it follows this salvo with the famous statement that all men are "created equal"; from there it courses onward to amplify the treatment of equality with the complaints against King George; finally, it flows out into its concluding arguments about equality when the signers of the Declaration pledge themselves and their states to one another. To understand the argument, we have to pass slowly through each of its phases: the opening sentence; the important argument about human equality; the remarkable indictment of King George as a tyrant who violates even basic principles of reciprocity; and the concluding pledge of mutuality. This we will do, in reading the Declaration sentence by sentence. In the process, we will master its profound argument about political equality.

There are five facets of the ideal equality for which the Declaration argues. The first facet, as we are about to see, describes the kind of equality that exists when neither of two parties can dominate the other. The second facet concerns the importance to humankind of having equal access to the tool of government, the most important instrument each of us has for securing the future. Something has gone wrong when, as scholars have recently shown, policy outcomes routinely track the stated preferences of the affluent but not those of the middle class or the poor. The third facet concerns the value of egalitarian approaches to the development of collective intelligence. Experts are most valuable when they work hand in hand with a well-educated general population capable of supplying useful social knowledge to deliberations. The fourth facet concerns egalitarian practices of reciprocity. How well do citizens do at thinking of themselves as receiving benefactions from their fellow citizens and owing them benefits in return? And the fifth facet has to do with the equality entailed in sharing ownership of public life and in co-creating our common world. When we worry, for instance, that young people don't vote or are apathetic, we recognize that we've failed to cultivate in them a sense of having an equal ownership stake in what we make together.

Yet important as the argument about equality is, it is not the whole of what we get from the Declaration. There is much more here, too. The argument about equality is set in a stunningly moving meditation on what it takes for people to find their way forward through conditions of uncertainty, under the press of necessity, into a future in which they can flourish. Proceeding sentence by sentence, we will trace the several interwoven threads of this meditation and, along the way, also take ownership of the argument about equality.

15

JUST ANOTHER WORD
FOR RIVER

When in the Course of human events, it becomes necessary for one people to dissolve the political bands which have connected them with another, and to assume among the powers of the earth, the separate and equal station to which the Laws of Nature and of Nature's God entitle them, a decent respect to the opinions of mankind requires that they should declare the causes which impel them to the separation.

That is our beginning, a sentence so long and rich that we can't take it all in with a single glance. We have to begin by focusing on the very beginning, just one clause to start: "When in the course of human events, it becomes necessary for one people . . . ."

Yet even an entire clause is too much to grasp in one go. Let's stop right here: "When in the course of human events, it becomes necessary . . . ."

That beginning seems overdone. Why not just say, "When it becomes necessary . . ."? Why add "in the course of human events"? And what exactly is "the course of human events" anyway?

Since "course" is another word for "river," an image of a waterway lies behind this sentence. Although Jefferson may not have been thinking explicitly about rivers when he wrote the first draft, the language itself, the word "course," has this useful image built into it. We can use this image of a river to work our way into the sentence.

A river has a definite shape. An infinity of droplets combine into a single flow, all moving together in the current's one direction. And all that water is rolling toward some knowable destination. The muddy Mississippi, for instance, may meander, but it descends inevitably into the Gulf of Mexico.

Now the job is to apply those ideas to human events. As a 1773 almanac puts it, "Time, like a Stream that hastens from the Shore, Flies to an Ocean, where 'tis known no more." Imagine an infinity of human events flowing together into a great stream and hastening on.

The Declaration is saying that human events, like the infinity of droplets in a river, cohere. Human events are going somewhere; they have shape and direction; there is meaning to their sequence. We should be able to tell where we are collectively headed. Unlike mindless driftwood, we should be able to see to the river's mouth.

Another important feature of rivers helps us understand what the Declaration says about human events. It takes a huge amount of work to alter a river's path. The city of Chicago, for instance, spent eleven years working to reverse the course of the Chicago River so that sewage would flow away from and not into Lake Michigan. Happily, diverting a river and redirecting a river's course are easier than reversing it, even if such projects take work, too.

The same is true of human events. The course can be altered—with strenuous effort.

The phrase "When in the course of human events, it becomes necessary" implies that the colonists did not just wake up one day and think, "Gee, this looks like a nice day for a revolution." Instead, they had studied the events of the past, including of their own recent experience, and concluded that those events had, like a river, a current. They were flowing in a specific direction: King George was becoming a tyrant.

Because events were flowing in such a direction, the colonists had reached a point where they desired to change course, just like Charles Prince, the CEO of Citigroup, whom I mentioned above. On a much larger scale than Mr. Prince, the colonists would have to dig in to redirect the course of human events.

The seventeenth-century English philosopher John Locke, whose ideas were among those that would influence Madison and the Constitution's framers, argued that government should rest on the will of the people and that people have a right to revolution whenever their government is becoming a tyranny.

The hard part is this: how do you know when a government is turning into a tyranny?

Locke answered that their right to revolution required citizens to see through the fog and haze of events in order to discern a government's true course and destination. He compared the experience to being a passenger in a ship whose course, despite being continually redirected in small ways, consistently heads toward a slave market in Algiers. In his *Second Treatise of Civil Government*, he wrote,

> If all the World shall observe pretences of one kind, and actions of another; arts used to elude the law, and the trust or prerogative [held by the Prince] . . . employed contrary to the end, for which it was given: if . . . a long Train of Actings shew the Councils all tending that way, how can a Man any more hinder himself from being perswaded in his own Mind, which way things are going; or from casting about how to save himself, than he could from believing the Captain of the Ship he was in, was carrying him, and the rest of the Company to [be sold in a slave market in] Algiers, when he found him always steering that Course, though cross winds, leaks in his ship, and want of Men and Provisions did often force him to turn his Course another way for some time, which he steadily returned to again, as soon as the Wind, Weather, and other Circumstances would let him?

Late in his career Locke would work to undermine slavery in the colony of Virginia, and here he uses the fear of being captured and enslaved by Barbary pirates as a metaphor for political anxiety generally.

Citizens need to see through myriad twists and turns of politics in order to tell whether their political leaders are steering toward a slave market in Algiers. This is a very hard thing to do. How are we to tell how things are going for us as a community? How can we see what course we're on?

The twentieth century has provided chilling examples of people's not foreseeing what will befall their community, with the experience of many European Jews before and during World War II being among the most salient. In his memoir *Night*, Elie Wiesel, the Nobel Peace Prize winner and Holocaust survivor, writes about how the inhabitants of the little town of Sighet treated the one man who kept telling them what was coming as a fool. He was a modern-day Cassandra, pouring out the truth but considered mad. What he described seemed to make sense only outside sanity's tree-ringed grove. As a consequence, none of the villagers escaped while escape was still possible.

Then there are the cases where the passengers of the ship can see the dangerous rapids lurking just beyond the horizon but can't get help. Samantha Power's Pulitzer Prize–winning *A Problem from Hell* provides a whole list of examples: Armenia, Cambodia, Iraq, Bosnia, Rwanda, Srebrenica, Kosovo. Power asks why Americans have so much trouble recognizing that a genocide is occurring or is about to occur and believing in the value of a strong response against the perpetrators of genocide.

Her book overflows with stories of how the majority of people failed to see the course being set by political leaders and future perpetrators of genocides. Power describes "an instinctive mistrust of accounts of gratuitous violence," but also the difficulty of settling on a clear understanding of the facts at hand in conditions where nearly every purveyor of information has an agenda. There is, in addition, the difficulty of trying to separate the true consequences of a pattern of actions from whatever claims any actor may make about his actions.

On the other hand, Power records minority reports from people who could, in contrast to everyone else, see what was happening. She writes, for instance, about the Armenian genocide that "U.S. ambassador Henry Morgenthau Sr. examined the facts and saw a cold-blooded campaign of annihilation; [Secretary of State] Robert Lansing processed many of those same facts and saw an unfortunate but understandable effort to quell an internal security threat." Why could Morgenthau see what Lansing could not? Why do we call some people "farsighted"? What skills have they honed that make them better readers of unfolding events than the rest of us? As we trace the argument of the Declaration, we will discover answers to these questions.

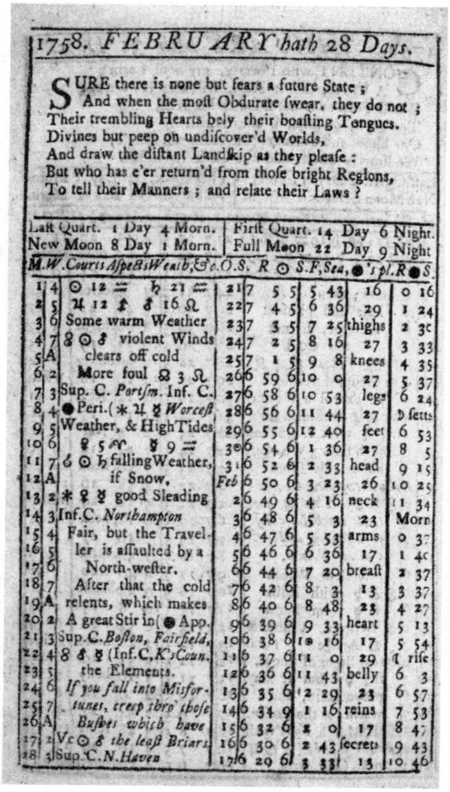

1758. *FEBRUARY hath* 28 *Days.*

SURE there is none but fears a future State ;
And when the moſt Obdurate ſwear, they do not ;
Their trembling Hearts bely their boaſting Tongues.
Divines but peep on undiſcover'd Worlds,
And draw the diſtant Landſkip as they pleaſe :
But who has e'er return'd from thoſe bright Regions,
To tell their Manners ; and relate their Laws ?

Laſt Quart. 1 Day 4 Morn.	Firſt Quart. 14 Day 6 Night.
New Moon 8 Day 1 Morn.	Full Moon 22 Day 9 Night

M.	W.	*Courts Aſpects Weath, &c.*	O.S.	R ☉	S.	F. Sea,	☽'s pl.	R ● S.
1	4	☉ 12 ♒ ♄ 21 ♒	21	7 5	5	5 43	16	0 16
2	5	♃ 12 ♐ ♂ 16 ♌	22	7 4	5	6 36	29	1 24
3	6	Some warm Weather	23	7 3	5	7 25	thighs	2 30
4	7	☍ ☉ ♂ violent Winds	24	7 2	5	8 16	27	3 33
5	A	clears off cold	25	7 1	5	9 8	knees	4 35
6	2	More foul ☊ 3 ♌	26	6 59	6	10 0	27	5 37
7	3	Sup. C. *Portſm.* Inf. C.	27	6 58	6	10 53	legs	6 24
8	4	● Peri.(* ♃ ☿ *Worceſt*	28	6 56	6	11 44	27	☽ ſetts
9	5	Weather, & High Tides	29	6 55	6	12 40	feet	6 53
10	6	♀ 5 ♈ ☿ 9 ♒	30	6 54	6	1 36	27	8 5
11	7	☌ ☉ ♄ falling Weather,	31	6 52	6	2 33	head	9 15
12	A	if Snow,	*Feb*	6 50	6	3 23	26	10 25
13	2	* ♀ ☿ good Sleading	2	6 49	6	4 16	neck	11 34
14	3	Inf. C. *Northampton*	3	6 48	6	5 3	23	Morn
15	4	Fair, but the Travel-	4	6 47	6	5 53	arms	0 37
16	5	ler is aſſaulted by a	5	6 46	6	6 36	17	1 40
17	6	North-weſter.	6	6 44	6	7 20	breaſt	2 37
18	7	After that the cold	7	6 42	6	8 3	13	3 37
19	A	relents, which makes	8	6 40	6	8 48	25	4 27
20	2	A great Stir in (● App.	9	6 39	6	9 33	heart	5 13
21	3	Sup. C. *Boſton, Fairfield,*	10	6 38	6	10 16	17	5 54
22	4	☍ ♂ ☿ (Inf. C, *K's Coun.*	11	6 37	6	11 0	29	☾ riſe
23	5	the Elements.	12	6 36	6	11 43	belly	6 3
24	6	*If you fall into Misfor-*	13	6 35	6	12 29	23	6 57
25	7	*tunes, creep thro' thoſe*	14	6 34	9	1 16	reins	7 53
26	A	*Buſhes which have*	15	6 32	6	2 0	17	8 47
27	2	Vc ☉ ♂ *the leaſt Briars*	16	6 30	6	2 43	ſecrets	9 43
28	3	Sup. C. *N. Haven*	17	6 29	6	3 33	13	10 46

This 1758 almanac captures the emotional texture attached to the desire to see the future.

When the colonists referred to the course of human events, they were taking responsibility for observing the currents within human action that pull us toward destinations, as identifiable—once we arrive, that is—as the Gulf of Mexico. It is our job as citizens to understand those currents—and to debate them and their direction—in the public square, so that we can see, as early as we can, as best we can, and despite the fogs of doubt and misdirection, the destinations that politicians and leaders are steering toward.

The very course of human events depends on it.

ONE PEOPLE

THE OPENING PHRASE OF THE DECLARATION, "WHEN IN THE COURSE of human events," stands as an assertion by the colonists of their farsightedness. It offers us an invitation to adopt their line of sight. From their vantage point, what exactly do they see?

In the opening sentence of the Declaration, the colonists claim, on the basis of having examined the course of human events, that they see the arrival of a moment of necessity. They say, "When in the Course of human events, *it becomes necessary* for one people to dissolve the political bands connecting them with another . . . a decent respect to the opinions of mankind requires that they should declare the[ir] causes." This leads right to a second question about necessity. In what sense is it necessary for the colonists to separate from Britain?

The colonists haven't yet been explicit about why their revolution is a matter of necessity, but the metaphor of a river's course provides a hint. A river is pulled inescapably downward by gravity. Are the colonists saying that some necessary law of nature drives them onward too?

The end of the sentence, where the colonists say that "they should declare the causes which impel them to the separation," provides some confirmation of this idea. "Impel" means that something pretty strong is pushing them. Both "propel," which means "push *forward*," and "expel" which means "push *out*," are related to it. But to be "impelled," if we are to be precise about our Latin etymology, is to be "pushed *toward*" something.

The colonists are not pulled toward the new situation by desire. They are pushed. They imply that they are driven toward their revolution by something like the law of gravity. They go reluctantly.

This does not mean, though, that they have no choice. They have felt and registered the force of the river's current, yes. But then they have made a decision: to swim with that current, rather than against it.

That leaves us with a lingering sense of mystery. What is this strong, gravity-like force pushing them on?

Before we can answer that, we must recognize that this sentence throws yet another problem at us. Before we can identify the mysterious gravity-like force driving events onward, we need to be more precise about who is being impelled and to what. I have said that "the colonists" are being pushed toward a new situation, but this is not what they say. They say that it has become necessary for "one people" to separate from another.

The colonists experience the force of necessity as "one people." They experience it collectively and with some degree of unity. That they identify themselves as "one people" in the very first sentence of the Declaration is surprising. They had long been a very fractious set of quite diverse communities—from all the various parts of England, as well as from Ireland, Scotland, Wales, the Netherlands, and Germany. Some were Puritans with rigorous demands for personal and public morality; others had been convicts, saved from execution by deportation to the colonies. Yet they open the Declaration by claiming the discovery of their peoplehood, as a group separate from, in particular, the British.

What exactly distinguishes one people from another in the first place? Often people take it that differences of language, religion, or race distinguishes peoples, but none of those definitions works here. They don't work, because they don't capture the specific peoples that the colonists have in mind: themselves, on the one hand, and on the other, the British.

The colonists had a lot in common with the people of Great Britain. Most of them spoke the same language. They had the same religion: both groups were mainly Christian, even if there were different flavors of Christianity in each place. They were of the same "race," and the majority shared many cultural traditions with the British, including the common law, school curricula, songs, food, and modes of dress. This means that in the minds of the colonists neither language nor religion, neither culture nor race, established the boundaries of a people.

Was the answer, then, simply geography? The fact of separation by the Atlantic Ocean?

There's much more to it than that. When Jefferson wrote the first draft of the Declaration, "the people" could mean any of three different things. The term could mean a group bound together by language, location, religion, or ethnicity. Or it could be used to describe the poor in contrast to the aristocratic and well-to-do. And in the 1600s and 1700s a third meaning arose through the writings of several eminent philosophers, including Thomas Hobbes, John Locke, and Jean-Jacques Rousseau, who were all, in one way or another, out to destroy the idea that the basis of political rule was a gift from God, passed down king to king, from Adam. The need for political order—the fact of its coming to existence—all three argued, emerges from the need of any multitude of individuals for collective organization. Not a gift from God, political order emerges from the human need to gather together peaceably. A multitude organized politically becomes a people. For these philosophers, a "people" was thus simply a group with shared political institutions. This third meaning seems the best fit for the first sentence of the Declaration. After all, the Declaration is declaring that the residents of the colonies now have a set of political institutions separate and different from those of the mother country.

The thirteen colonies, then, are bound together above all by their political institutions, even if those institutions have only just hatched.

Our Numbers will not avail till the Colonies are united ; for whilſt divided, the Strength of the Inhabitants is broken like the petty Kingdoms in *Africa*.—If we do not join Heart and Hand n the common Cauſe againſt our exulting Foes, but fall to diſputing amongſt ourſelves, it may really happen as the Governour of *Pennſylvania* told his Aſſembly, ' We ſhall have no Priviledge to diſpute about, nor Country to diſpute in.'——

This 1758 almanac written by Nathaniel Ames expresses the unity of peoplehood as joining heart and hand in common cause.

On account of their fledgling institutions, they now see themselves as a people separate from the people in England with whom they share a language, religion, law, cultural traditions, and history. Although the thirteen colonies are still thirteen separate political units and although their new confederation is not yet a single nation, they have become *one people.*

Unified now for the first time, the colonists face their grave moment of necessity together.

What will this people do with it?

17

WE ARE YOUR EQUALS

T HE FIRST THING THE COLONISTS, NOW "ONE PEOPLE," DO WITH their shared moment of necessity is make a preposterous-sounding claim. They say to the kingdom of Great Britain, "We are your equals!"

What they actually say is that it has become necessary for them "to dissolve the political bands which have connected them" with Britain and "to assume among the powers of the earth, the separate and equal station to which the Laws of Nature and of Nature's God entitle them."

The colonists are not only separating from Britain but also claiming to have an "equal station" to their motherland. "Station" is Latin again and comes from the word for "stand." One's station is where one stands with people.

A similar idea is rank. A prince has a lofty station high above a peasant who is in a lowly station. A clergyman has a reasonably high station but not as high as a prince. The prince gets the most respect, the clergyman the next level of respect, and the peasant the least. In an aristocratic society, a person's "station" determines how much respect he gets from others.

Here in the very first sentence of the Declaration the colonists lay claim to a station on the world's stage equal to Britain's. This they do not by pulling Britain down but by pulling themselves up. They want respect.

This must have sounded audacious, if not outrageous. Britain boasted more than three times as many people as the colonies. The British navy presided as master of the Atlantic if not the world. Through both taxation and the capacity to borrow, its government had powerful tools for financing war. The Continental Congress had no power to tax and, consequently, little power to borrow. The British military had numerous experienced officers and well-drilled regiments. The colonial militia were no match in numbers or experience. The British political and legal system dated back to 1066, and the reign of William the Conqueror, a descendant of Viking raiders, who invaded England from Normandy. The colonists, as a single people, had only the decisions of the Continental Congress taken between 1774 and 1776.

Perhaps the colonists' claim to equality might have made more sense in comparison with the continental nations France or Spain?

Such a claim would have sounded equally preposterous. Along with Britain, France and Spain were among the eighteenth century's greatest powers. After China and India, France had the third-largest population in the world, and even Spain, although it had declined from its political apogee at the end of the sixteenth century, had a significantly larger population than the colonies and still held an overseas empire. The newly united colonies would have looked, well, puny when placed alongside those great powers.

Nevertheless, the colonists assert their equality, as a power or confederation of powers, to those other powers.

In what regard could these newly united colonies possibly be the same as the long-lived, vastly wealthy, militarily mighty empires?

Was the physical territory of the colonies perhaps as extensive as that of England, France, and Spain? Only if one pays no attention to the empires possessed by each of those nations. But of course those countries had much more land in the Americas, Africa, and Asia. Even in regard to land, the colonies looked like welterweights.

Perhaps, then, the colonists were asserting their equality because they thought they had the potential to expand to a size equivalent to the European empires?

Territory isn't really what makes the difference here. Imagine that a single person had landed by herself on Mars, claimed it as her country, and declared her new country, "Marsland," equal to the different nations on earth. Would that claim make any sense? Would she be taken seriously?

Certainly not. Or, at least, not at first. Not if she was the only person there. The colonists' claim has something to do with what they as a group of people are doing together, not with the size of their territory, their wealth, or anything else of that kind.

They are the same as the European empires in one way only.

Because the colonies had set up shared political institutions, their citizens have acquired a fledgling capacity to organize their collective lives without help from others and with a clear intention to resist any efforts on the part of others to intervene in their new capacity, as a community, for self-government.

This capacity of the colonies to organize their collective lives was equal to the capacity of Great Britain, France, and Spain to do the same for themselves. The remarkable idea expressed here is that neither wealth nor military power increases the capacity of society to organize itself. That capacity is something a society either has or doesn't have. The capacity of the colonies for collective self-organization was at a bare minimum, but it existed.

Societies have that capacity when they can build functioning political organizations through which collective decisions can be made that have the allegiance, whether explicit or implicit, of the people. Wealth and military power increase the capacity of a society to organize other societies but not to organize itself. The capacity of self-organization lies elsewhere—again, in procedures for decision making and for connecting citizens to one another in a sense of a shared fate.

Simply by virtue of achieving this political capacity, the colonies had made themselves an independent political entity, no less and no more independent than any of the great powers. They were, for this reason, ready to assume, "among the powers of the earth, the separate and equal station" of a self-organizing, sovereign political unit.

The former colonies noted their acquisition of this capacity by changing their names from colonies to states.

At last we can see it. That's the meaning of that change of name. A "colony" identifies a social group whose affairs are organized by someone else. A "state" identifies a social group that organizes its own affairs.

Now that we understand the difference between a colony and a state, we can confidently talk about the newly united "states" that declared their independence and, with this declaration, assumed their separate and equal station among the earth's powers. On the basis of their new capacity for self-government, the new "states" claimed their equality to other states; they claimed a right to be free from domination.

They were equal to all the great powers in the capacity for political organization. And this gives us our first flash of insight into the mystery of what equality means in the Declaration.

It does not mean equal in all respects.
It does not mean equal in wealth.
It does not mean equal in military might.
It does not mean equal in power.
It means equal *as* a power.

Is this change from "in" to "as" overly subtle? I think not. If the newly united states and Britain had been equal "in" power, they would each have had the same amount of something. Each would have the same capacity to influence the world. But to say that they are equal "as" powers is to say that they are equal in something that they are. They share a status. Each is a society that has learned how to use institutions to organize collective life and achieve collective actions. Once a society learns this, it is a power because it has learned how to organize and use power, in particular, the power of words.

In short, the colonists were saying that "our state is equal to your state" insofar as they are both states.

It's surprising to start talking about equality in the Declaration by considering how states are equal to each other, but that is the first way the concept of equality enters our text. In this context, the ideal of equality means being equal as a power and therefore being free from domination. This facet of equality has reverberated through American life. As we will see in the next chapter, some of its echoes are quite surprising.

AN ECHO

INEVITABLY, TRAGEDY ENTERS THE DIALOGUE WHEN WE READ THE Declaration. Shadows, at first faint but nevertheless apparent, fall already on the first sentence.

That first sentence should trigger a nagging feeling of familiarity. If it does, though, we are likely to dismiss the vague tug of memory as coming from how often the opening of the Declaration is quoted. Yet there is more to it than that. An echo of something else is ringing in our ears.

Listen again. The colonists "intend to assume among the powers of the earth, the separate and equal station to which the Laws of Nature and of Nature's God entitle them." Do you hear it?

The phrase "separate and equal" should be vaguely familiar, yet it also feels somehow out of time.

For about sixty-five years, when this country used laws to segregate people by race, the people who wrote those laws insisted that they were providing "separate *but* equal" accommodations. For instance, a Louisiana law of 1890 required all railway companies carrying passengers through Louisiana "to provide equal but separate accommodations for the white and colored races." On June 7, 1892, the legally black, visually white activist Homer Adolph Plessy, planning to challenge the law, bought a first-class ticket for the New Orleans–Covington commuter line and sat in a whites-only carriage. Arrested, he pursued his defense all the way to the Supreme Court, which in 1896 upheld the Louisiana law and entrenched legal segregation, an imposition of inequality whose effects reverberate to this day.

"Separate and equal." "Equal but separate." "Separate but equal." The segregationists picked up the language of the Declaration and gave it a vicious little twist.

The colonists had insisted that their newly united states were to stand as a power "separate and equal" to the other powers of the earth. Because of what it means to be a state—because separation meant freedom from domination—separation in their case necessarily entailed equality. That's why it made sense in the Declaration to say separate "and" equal. In that context, the two concepts were yoked together. The one brought the other with it.

Whereas the colonists sought an external separation, the segregationists—a cross-class alliance of white-power advocates—sought separation internally. They wanted to pretend that different facilities for white and colored races could be "separate but equal."

This kind of separation would not, though, bring equality, and the segregationists knew it. Just the opposite. The goal of segregation was to secure the domination of people of color. Its purpose and its necessary consequence were inequality. To propose, therefore, to link separation and equality in this context was to claim—to pretend—that it might be possible to reverse the social currents established by the separation.

When the colonists said "separate and equal," they claimed that they constituted a free people, separate from the free people of Britain. The segregationists in no way pretended to think that African Americans or, for that matter, Mexican and Chinese Americans (since segregation was used against those groups, too) should be seen as forming independent and free peoples, with their own political institutions. The phrase "separate but equal" was used to do work exactly the opposite of that done by the Declaration: not to raise a people to sovereign status but to keep many people subjected and dependent.

The small change of wording, the segregationists' use of "but," revealed the truth of the matter. Indeed, the word "but" turns a corner; it takes a thought in the opposite direction from where, in the natural course of things, it seems to want to go. It does not yoke together concepts that naturally belong together, like "hand and glove." Instead, it contrasts two concepts that are commonly opposed, as in "young but wise." When the segregationists said, "separate but equal," the "but" revealed that the sort of separation proposed by the segregationists is naturally opposed to equality.

The segregationists piggybacked, so to speak, on the iconic language of the Declaration to pretend that the sort of separation they proposed had a noble lineage. "Separate but equal" became their slogan, which sounded good to people because it sounded lofty, and it sounded lofty because the Declaration opens with "separate and equal." But it was a verbal sleight of hand, and their very language betrayed them. By slipping from "and" to "but," they admitted that the kind of separation they pursued does not and cannot bring equality.

The doctrine "separate but equal" was finally rooted out of U.S. law in the 1954 Supreme Court decision *Brown v. Board of Education*, in which Chief Justice Warren wrote, "We conclude that, in the field of public education, the doctrine of 'separate but equal' has no place. Separate educational facilities are inherently unequal." The language itself was already telling that truth.

An honest phrase meant to liberate and to establish a principle of equality as entailing freedom from domination ("separate *and* equal") was reborn instead as a deceitful phrase ("separate *but* equal") used to subjugate and dominate across generations. This is the stuff of tragedy— an action that results in an outcome opposite to what the actors intended.

In the first sentence of the Declaration, then, one of the smallest words, "and," gives us our first glimpse of the dark clouds that loom, like inclement weather on the horizon, around the Declaration. Slavery, race, the treatment of Native Americans. The Declaration provided tools for liberating some and dominating others.

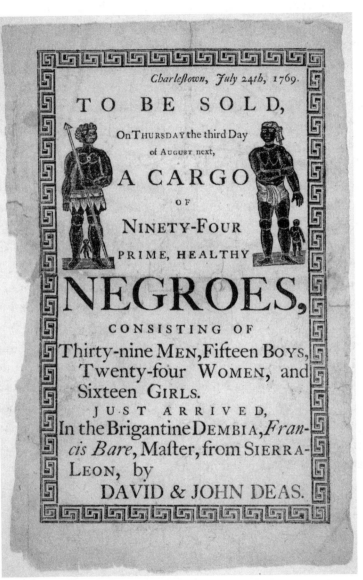

A 1769 poster advertising slaves for sale.

V.

FACING
NECESSITY

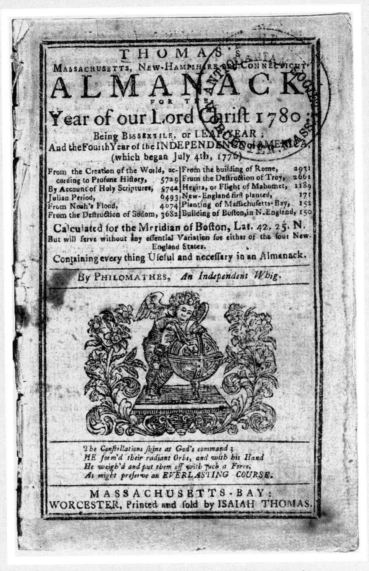

THOMAS's
MASSACHUSETTS, NEW-HAMPSHIRE and CONNECTICUT
ALMANACK,
FOR THE
Year of our Lord Christ 1780:
Being BISSEXTILE, or LEAP YEAR;
And the Fourth Year of the INDEPENDENCE of AMERICA,
(which began July 4th, 1776)

From the Creation of the World, according to Profane History,	5729	From the building of Rome,	2931
By Account of Holy Scriptures,	5742	From the Destruction of Troy,	2661
Julian Period,	6493	Hegira, or Flight of Mahomet,	1189
From Noah's Flood,	4074	New-England first planted,	171
From the Destruction of Sodom,	3682	Planting of Massachusetts-Bay,	152
		Building of Boston, in N. England,	150

Calculated for the Meridian of Boston, Lat. 42, 25. N.
But will serve without any essential Variation for either of the four New-England States.
Containing every thing Useful and necessary in an Almanack.

BY PHILOMATHES, *An Independent Whig.*

*The Constellations shine at God's command;
HE form'd their radiant Orbs, and with his Hand
He weigh'd and put them off with such a Force,
As might preserve an EVERLASTING COURSE.*

MASSACHUSETTS-BAY:
WORCESTER, Printed and sold by ISAIAH THOMAS.

This 1780 almanac cover promises to address everything useful and necessary, including the constellations whose "everlasting course" has been set by God's command.

19

...IT BECOMES NECESSARY...

THE FIRST SENTENCE OF THE DECLARATION HAS TRANSPORTED us across rigorous terrain. Life's currents, like a river's, invariably have a direction, but understanding them is a challenge of surpassing difficulty. In the midst of discerning the course of events—and through the *very* process of discerning the course of events—we make choices about how to define ourselves as individuals and communities. How do groups of individuals come to count as a "people"? They must acquire the capacity to self-organize. This led us to the first facet of the ideal of equality. Equality requires freedom from domination.

Astonishingly, we are still only halfway through that opening sentence. The Declaration demands that we move that slowly, for it is that linguistically and philosophically rich, that rewarding.

Finishing the rest of the first sentence requires us to meditate on the idea of "necessity," one of the central concepts in the Declaration.

20

THE LAWS OF NATURE

AT THIS JUNCTURE, WE MUST RETURN TO THE MYSTERY OF THE gravity-like force impelling the colonists. The first sentence of the Declaration is starting to come into focus, but to uncover the identity of that mystery force we'll have to tackle the sentence's second half. This requires us to start over:

> *When in the Course of human events, it becomes necessary for one people to dissolve the political bands which have connected them with another, and to assume among the powers of the earth, the separate and equal station to which the Laws of Nature and of Nature's God entitle them, a decent respect to the opinions of mankind requires that they should declare the causes which impel them to the separation.*

If this sentence has already taken us across some rough ground, the terrain we need to traverse now gets downright treacherous. The colonists are preparing to assume the separate and equal station "to which the Laws of Nature and of Nature's God entitle them." What exactly does this phrase mean?

The colonists are not claiming to be equal and asking other people to assess their claim. To the contrary. They are "assuming" their new station, or taking it up as already granted to them. They use the word "entitled" to say that their equal status should be taken not "for granted" but "as granted."

"Entitled" is a lovely word that comes from English law. Its first recorded use was in 1381. Since many of the words in English law come from what is called "Law French," a version of French that got imported into English law, the word derives, in fact, from Old French, which means that deep in its roots it, too, is from Latin. For now, however, I'll focus simply on its use in English law.

Here is one early usage from 1530:

By what meanes is he entyteled unto these landes.

These days, a title is, among other things, a formal document used to grant ownership to something. When you buy a house or a car, for instance, the "title" to the house or car is transferred from the previous owner to you. When you hold "title," you have a right to use that house or car to the exclusion of other people. Would-be trespassers must keep out.

When the colonists say that they are "entitled" to their separate and equal station among the powers of the earth, they are not merely saying that they have made themselves equal by getting themselves organized politically. They are also saying that because they have succeeded at organizing themselves politically, they have a right to have everybody else keep out.

Where did they get this right? They couldn't exactly go to a legal office like the Department of Motor Vehicles. Nor could they go to the County Recorder of Deeds.

They make another preposterous claim. They say they got the title from the office of "the Laws of Nature and of Nature's God."

This claim will take some sorting out.

I could take the historian's road and turn to the books that Jefferson and others of the founding generation had been reading. But I've already suggested that one can successfully read the Declaration of Independence by focusing on the structure of its argument. Slow reading, I said, is powerful enough to open up its logic. It's time to put this idea to the test. Can the first sentence of the Declaration itself give us a hand with the challenging idea of the laws of nature?

Here is where the opening image of the river becomes useful. As we've already noticed, the course of a river is governed by gravity, and so we've already spotted one law of nature in this sentence. Now the hard part is to figure out how something like the law of gravity, which governs physical objects, can help us understand what law of nature could possibly give the colonists a title to equal standing on the world's stage.

Consider that opening image of a waterway again. The river was made not of water but of human events. The colonists had the job of understanding the direction and force of its current. They analyzed the particular course of human events by scrutinizing King George's actions. His actions suggested that he was becoming a tyrant. When they discovered that human events were tending against them, they could fight to survive or give in and drown.

An image from Ben Franklin's 1752 Poor Richard *almanac captures the challenges implied by the idea of navigating the course of events.*

In the fight to survive—and, more specifically, to live free from domination—the colonists had little choice but to navigate the currents, or redirect them, in such a way as to establish another direction for themselves.

"They had little choice"—what can that mean?

It means that their drive to survive—and not some kind of abstract historical inevitability—pushed them to chart a new course just as surely as gravity draws a river downwards. This, their drive to survive, is our mystery force.

And they found a way to survive: by forming a union and acquiring the capacity to organize themselves politically.

With this insight, the claim that a natural instinct to survive impelled them to the separation from Britain makes sense. We can understand how such a natural instinct might be compared to the law of gravity.

One of the first political cartoons, this image appeared in
Ben Franklin's Pennsylvania Gazette *in 1754.*

But why did the colonists think they had an actual *right* to be left alone? Does the fact that water flows downhill mean it has a right to do so? Not at all. While no one has ever succeeded, and presumably no one has ever tried, to make a river run up a mountainside, we do periodically dam up rivers and block them from flowing downhill.

Yet it must be admitted that if we ever found a way to dam up all of earth's rivers, we'd soon see the world's environment deteriorate dangerously. Water doesn't exactly have a right to run downhill, but it seems that we ought more or less to respect the fact that it does and accommodate ourselves to it. And respecting certain facts and accommodating ourselves to them is exactly what we do when we respect someone's right to something.

Let's go back to the title to a car. When my neighbor holds title to a sporty little Toyota, which maybe I covet, I nonetheless respect the fact that it is his and accommodate myself to his ownership. When I leave his Toyota alone, I am respecting his right to it.

How exactly do the laws of nature and of nature's God similarly give the newly united states a right to separate and equal station among the powers of the earth? There are two ways to understand this idea.

Sometimes people suggest we should understand the idea as saying the following:

All people naturally want to survive, so when any given group finds a way to survive that does not endanger the survival of anyone else, we should respect their right to organize their survival for themselves. What's more, we should respect these forces of nature not merely because they are great but because they are an expression of God's might.

If you believe in God, it's easy to accept this interpretation of why the laws of nature produce not only facts about the world (like water's running downhill) but also moral obligations. In this case, we are obligated to respect laws of nature because God wrote the laws, and we have an obligation to respect God.

If, however, you don't believe in God, this way of understanding why the laws of nature produce moral obligations doesn't make sense. Nonbelievers, whose numbers have grown greatly in the last two and a quarter centuries, have to take an extra step in order to understand the ideas under discussion here.

The second way of understanding the idea that the laws of nature give the newly united states a right to separate and equal station among the powers of the earth goes like this:

All people naturally want to survive, so when any given group finds a way to survive that does not endanger the survival of anyone else, we should respect their right to organize their survival for themselves. We ought to respect these forces of nature because, if we try to fight them, we will generally do ourselves more harm than good. If we do not respect the right of others to organize their survival for themselves (provided, of course, that they do so without endangering anyone else), we will bring war on ourselves and so jeopardize our own projects of survival.

The Declaration, in other words, gives us two ways of understanding the source of rights. We can see them as coming from nature and/or we can see them as coming from God. It's like belt and suspenders.

Does it matter which interpretation is used to understand the invocation of the idea of "right" or "entitlement"? Or let me put it differently, less delicately. Does it matter whether God is in or out?

AND NATURE'S GOD

INNUMERABLE PEOPLE HAVE TOLD ME THAT THE ART OF DINNER party conversation requires avoidance of politics and religion. Perhaps this is another reason why an invitation to talk about the Declaration makes many people nervous. For this country, the United States, this text is, after all, the so-called ground zero for discussion of how religion and politics intertwine. That God is a presence in the Declaration is indubitably the case. But does that matter? Do the text's arguments about equality and liberty depend on how the text invokes God? Does it matter, to put it bluntly again, whether God is in or out?

The answer has two parts. First, we have to understand why Jefferson, Adams, Franklin, and the Continental Congress put God in. Second, we have to ask what the consequences are for the argument of having God in or out.

How and why, then, did God get into the Declaration?

The only words used by Jefferson for God in the Declaration are "Nature's God," a phrase he uses just once, in the sentence we are now considering. There are other words for God in the Declaration, but they were introduced at later points in the drafting process. The word "Creator," used once, was added during the conversations among Jefferson, Franklin, and Adams, by one of the latter two men. The phrases "Supreme Judge of the World" and "Divine Providence," also each used once, were added during the two days of arguments in the Continental Congress.

In other words, in Jefferson's very spare first-draft picture, nature belongs to God. Presumably this means that nature is given its order by God. Jefferson added God to the first draft, then, to close arguments about why things are the way they are and about whether nature's order is good. Nature is ordered as it is because of nature's God. And, yes, that order is good, because it belongs to God. Jefferson included no mention of Christ and none of salvation, nor did the Continental Congress add any. The God invoked in the Declaration is not a specifically Christian God.*

Although Jefferson used "God" just this once, he put the word "sacred" in the text three times. "Sacred" can have a secular meaning: "worthy of reverent protection and celebration." Or it can mean "made holy by association to a god" and therefore "entitled to veneration and respect." Which meaning is more to the fore in the Declaration?

In his original rough draft, Jefferson wrote, "We hold these truths sacred and undeniable—that all Men are created equal and independent; that from that equal Creation they derive Rights inherent and inalienable, among which are the Preservation of life, and liberty, and the pursuit of happiness; that to Secure these Ends, governments are instituted among men, deriving their just powers from the consent of the governed; that whenever any form of government shall become destructive of these ends, it is the right of the people to alter or to abolish it, and to institute new government, laying its foundation on such principles, and organizing its powers in such form, as to them shall seem most likely to effect their safety and happiness." His sentence is very ambiguous: its use of "sacred" could be either secular or religious.

Then Jefferson's colleagues on the Committee of Five—including, of course, the devout Adams, who often invoked the deity—edited this sentence to say that all men have been endowed by "their Creator" with certain inalienable rights. In introducing a "Creator," a being responsible for originating human life, they tipped the sentence toward a definition of "sacred" that associates it with God. This had an impact, in turn, on the idea of truth being used in the sentence. To say that truths are "sacred and undeniable," in a sentence that also invokes a Creator, would have been a way of saying that those truths are fundamental and foundational,

* Nor is it necessarily a deist god. Jefferson drafted the Declaration carefully so that neither the deist nor the Christian conception of God is presupposed.

even past questioning: truth comes from on high, from God. This is a very authoritarian approach to truth. But, in those early days of drafting the Declaration, as the word "sacred" acquired a religious hue, the phrase "We hold these truths sacred and undeniable" gave way, as we have seen, to this one: "We hold these truths to be self-evident." This was a profound change.

To say that truths are self-evident is an epistemological claim, or a claim about how we know the things we know. How do we know that these truths are true? Because they are self-evident. Well, what does "self-evident" mean exactly? It does not mean that the instant you hear a proposition, you recognize it as true. It means rather that if you look into the proposition, if you entertain it and reflect upon it, you will inevitably come to affirm it. All the evidence you need to judge the proposition for yourself is in the proposition itself. That's why a proposition can be called self-evident. And to call these truths self-evident is to invite everyone into the process of judging them. This is a very democratic approach to truth.

Jefferson also used "sacred" in another place, where it was again edited out. He used the word in the long paragraph about slavery that was cut by Congress. There he wrote, "[The King] has [through the slave trade] waged cruel war against human nature itself, violating it's most sacred rights of life & liberty." Here, as in the opening of the Declaration, it is nature—in this case, human nature—that is sacred, and our fundamental rights too.

Finally, at the end of the document, in the last paragraph, Jefferson wrote that the colonists pledged to each other their lives, fortunes, and sacred honor. Then the debates in the Continental Congress led to the inclusion of the phrases "Supreme Judge of the World" and "Divine Providence" in the final paragraph. Those edits again made an ambiguous Jeffersonian phrase—"sacred honor"—ring with religious overtones. If the colonists considered their honor sacred, it was, they tell us, because they held on to it with care and dedication, as a form of property for which they had responsibility before God.

For Jefferson, then, it was not enough that his readers should understand nature's order and power and the necessities that flow from nature. He also wanted his readers to see nature as sacred, as something meriting reverence and protection. The signers in general agreed, although more emphatically. To see nature as sacred through association with divinity is both to have an answer to the mystery of where its order comes from and to see its laws as inviolable. By resting the principles in this document on God, the signers aspired to bring their readers to share the strongest possible moral commitment to those principles. These are the only theological points that we can confirm were written into the document.

Can people, without believing in a god, achieve for themselves maximally strong commitments to the right of other people to survive and to govern themselves so long as they do not endanger the survival of others? Can they achieve a maximal commitment to the equality of all in these rights?

If so, then the idea of nature's God in the Declaration is not necessary to the work of the text for those readers. If not, then it is.

Or, let me put this another way. You do not have to be a Christian to accept the argument of the Declaration. That much is clear. But do you have to be a theist? That is, do you have to believe in God? The answer is again no.

You do not need to be a theist to accept the argument of the Declaration. You do, however, require an alternative ground for a maximally strong commitment to the right of other people to survive and to govern themselves. One needs a reason to commit to other people's survival and freedom so strong as to command one's reverence. One way or another, one must hold sacred the flourishing of others.

22

KINDS OF NECESSITY

I T IS REMARKABLE THAT WE ARE NOT YET THROUGH THE FIRST SEN-
tence of the Declaration, so intricate, so profound is its exploration of
the kinds of necessity and types of obligation that structure human life.

By way of metaphor, we previously encountered the law of gravity
and thought about what it means to feel nature's force, to be impelled by
nature. Carried along by the course of human events, learning to swim in
and sometimes against its currents—like Lee and Adams in Philadelphia
in that smallpox-plagued autumn of 1775 grappling with the problem of
ungoverned New Hampshire—the colonists experienced something like
gravity's power.

Second, we surveyed the law of nature's God and thought about
whether we should respect the power of nature because it represents
God's law or because it is in our interest to do so.

In both of these cases, the colonists say that they have discovered their
moral obligations by trying to deal with forces imposed from the outside:
by nature, law, and God.

One final type of obligation, one last kind of necessity, also demands
reflection. Here again, but for the last time, is the first sentence in its
entirety:

> *When in the Course of human events, it becomes necessary for*
> *one people to dissolve the political bands which have connected*

*them with another, and to assume among the powers of the earth,
the separate and equal station to which the Laws of Nature and of
Nature's God entitle them, a decent respect to the opinions of mankind requires that they should declare the causes which impel them
to the separation.*

At the end of the sentence, the colonists say that "a decent respect to the
opinions of mankind requires" that they should declare the causes that
impel them to the separation. This time the necessity is internal; it arises
from inside the colonists.

A very short version of this sentence would be: When people start a
revolution, a decent respect for the opinions of mankind compels them to
declare the causes which impel them to that action.

Because they have and should have a decent respect for the opinions of mankind—an internal motivation—they must publicly declare
the causes of their divorce from Britain. This calls to mind the language
of the 1996 decree ending the marriage of Prince Charles and Princess
Diana. The decree said this:

> It was decreed that the marriage . . . be dissolved unless suffi-
> cient cause be shown to the court within six weeks . . . .
> And no cause having been shown, it is hereby certified . . . that
> the said marriage was thereby dissolved.

Just like the Declaration, two centuries later Charles and Diana's divorce
decree refers to causes. Legal language is that durable. Whereas in the
royal divorce people were asked to declare any causes that might block
the divorce, the colonists find themselves required instead to declare
causes that justify it.

Motivated not by outside forces but in their own spirits by respect for
the opinions of the entire population of the globe, the colonists will give
the world something to judge: their reasons.

The fact that the colonists have respect for the opinions of mankind
means that they believe that mankind by and large judges fairly. To think
that all people everywhere always judge fairly would be extravagant.
A decent respect is a modest but fair level of respect. A decent respect

entails no more than expecting most people to judge fairly most of the time. Abraham Lincoln is said to have said, "You can fool all the people some of the time, and some of the people all the time, but you cannot fool all the people all the time." This is another way of expressing a non-extravagant but decent respect for the opinions of mankind.

In describing themselves as motivated by a decent respect for the opinions of mankind, the colonists add another detail to the picture of nature sketched in the Declaration's first sentence. Here's the picture so far:

Nature governs people not only insofar as they are physical objects—like water, rocks, and fire. Nature also governs people as social creatures. The events of social life can generate sudden turnings, particularly when affairs have taken such a shape that the survival instinct activates. States form in order for groups of people to work together to achieve a life in which they can flourish. Successful self-government is a success for nature, because it expands the flourishing of one set of natural creatures, human beings. Because all human beings desire to survive and flourish, they all struggle to interpret the events of their social worlds in order to ascertain whether things are going well or ill for them and their communities and to ascertain whether they need to change course.

Now comes the finishing detail:

Because all human beings seek to survive and flourish and therefore judge the course of events affecting their own lives, they can also judge whether things are going well or ill for other people. Our capacity to judge how things are going includes the ability to discern whether someone is causing others harm or depriving them of liberty. In other words, all people have a sense of fairness that makes it possible for them to be reasonable judges of the causes of others. This is not to say that we all always act as reasonable judges but only that everyone has, at some basic level, the potential to be a reasonable judge. We have, Jefferson would say, moral sense. By nature, in the Declaration's argument, all people have an intuitive sense of fairness.

But why did the signers think that they needed to present their case to all of mankind and not merely to the people of England?

As we have seen, for the new United States of America to be a legitimate nation, the world as a whole would have to recognize it as such. Willy-nilly—whether they wanted to participate or not—the rest of the world had been called as witnesses to a divorce and remarriage. The world's opinion of that divorce and remarriage would determine, finally, whether it stuck.

The colonists decided to deal with the world by presuming it to be populated with fair judges and by making their case to those fair judges. They could presume this because they believed that nature had given all human beings an innate sense of fairness, which, though it perhaps lay dormant sometimes, could nonetheless be activated by spelling out the terms on which fair judgments are made. It could be activated with explanations of principle.

The next sentence of the Declaration undertakes just that kind of activation.

And now at last we've reached the close of the Declaration's opening sentence.

VI.

MATTERS OF PRINCIPLE

LOGICK:

John McMillan

OR, THE

RIGHT USE OF REASON

IN THE

ENQUIRY AFTER TRUTH.

WITH

A VARIETY OF RULES TO GUARD AGAINST ER-
ROR, IN THE AFFAIRS OF RELIGION AND
HUMAN LIFE, AS WELL AS IN THE SCIENCES.

BY *ISAAC WATTS*, D. D.

THE SIXTEENTH EDITION.

PHILADELPHIA:

PRINTED FOR THOMAS DOBSON, AT THE STONE HOUSE, IN
SECOND STREET, BETWEEN MARKET AND CHESNUT STREET.

M DCC LXXXIX.

1789

*One of the most popular logic handbooks
of the eighteenth century taught people how to reason
soundly about their principles.*

23

WE HOLD THESE TRUTHS...

THE FIRST FEW SENTENCES OF THE DECLARATION ARE OFTEN referred to as the preamble. What matters more about them is that they lay out the principles that guide the colonists' judgments about the course of events. In laying out these principles, the colonists—in this remarkable piece of democratic writing—also say a lot about what it means to make judgments in the first place. Insofar as the Declaration offers a meditation on human experience, it particularly scrutinizes what it feels like to try to make consequential judgments about one's future. We judge by connecting principles to facts and on that basis determine a course of action, even in conditions of great uncertainty. To navigate our lives, each of us must set the present in relation to a dimly visible future by relating principles and facts. Doing this is hard—intellectually, psychologically, emotionally. In its compressed expressions of principle, the Declaration conveys just how hard this work is.

Human equality is grounded, fundamentally, in the capacity for judgment, which we all employ in navigating our lives. The second sentence of the Declaration connects equality to judgment, and makes an argument for government as the most important instrument available to us for acting on our judgments about the relation of present to future. To secure our futures we all need an equal opportunity to use the instrument of government. This is the second facet of the ideal of equality presented in the Declaration.

24

SOUND BITES

THE SECOND SENTENCE OF THE DECLARATION IS THE ONE WE ALL know almost by heart:

> *We hold these truths to be self-evident, that all men are cre-*
> *ated equal, that they are endowed by their Creator with certain*
> *unalienable Rights, that among these are Life, Liberty and the*
> *pursuit of Happiness,—That to secure these rights, Governments*
> *are instituted among Men, deriving their just powers from the*
> *consent of the governed,—That whenever any Form of Govern-*
> *ment becomes destructive of these ends, it is the Right of the Peo-*
> *ple to alter or to abolish it, and to institute new Government,*
> *laying its foundation on such principles and organizing its pow-*
> *ers in such form, as to them shall seem most likely to effect their*
> *Safety and Happiness.*

When I finally slowed down to read this sentence in full, I was struck by
how very long it is. Most of us stopped memorizing at the word "equal."
A few intrepid souls perhaps ventured further and memorized all the way
to "pursuit of Happiness." But this is a single sentence, and it stretches all
the way to "their Safety and Happiness."

Is it a problem that most of us know only a handful of ringing phrases?

Many of us think we should be concerned when our political conversations rely mostly on sound bites. Is this one more example of the degradation of discourse?

Not necessarily.

We citizens of democracies hope that our leaders will think for themselves and do the work of having an authentic idea about how to understand and respond to new circumstances, but we don't simply take them at their word that their ideas are the right ones. Instead, we vet their ideas by forcing leaders to compete for votes under intense and strained conditions.

These days we no longer listen to debates that last for days. Instead, we require our politicians to compress whole worldviews into tight summary statements. In their tightest form those summary statements become what the ancient Greek philosopher Aristotle called maxims and we call sound bites.

How does a sound bite work? Imagine a glass of water sitting in the middle of a table. Imagine that the water level in the glass is at the midway point. This is the proverbial glass half full or half empty. How should it be described?

What matters in this example is the following: when someone looks at that glass of water, she can't describe it with words before she makes a decision about how she wants to see it. Whatever decision she makes will be based on how she approaches the world generally. "Optimist" and "pessimist" are something like code words for whatever orientation leads her to describe the glass as half full or half empty.

If she is an optimist, she thinks that things generally work out for the best and that the world will open up if she just applies a little pressure. If she is a pessimist, she thinks the opposite.

Or perhaps our speaker wishes to avoid the conventional framework of a choice between optimism and pessimism. She may, instead, tell us roughly how many ounces of water are in the glass. That move, too, reveals something of the speaker's approach to the world. She refuses conventional choices.

It's not just half-full glasses of water that a speaker will describe one way or another; everything she describes, every situation she recounts, every explanation she gives for her action will reveal her worldview to some degree. Even dissemblers, who positively wish to deceive, are often given away by the fact that their words say more than they can reasonably control. As long as their audiences are listening carefully, that is.

Therapists know this. In fact, anyone who has been to a therapist has probably started to realize that therapists always, so to speak, read between the lines. Even from a sound bite, a listener can work out the speaker's worldview by listening carefully or reading slowly.

The same is true of the Declaration. In the first sentence, the signers described how they saw their world—it was a moment when a divorce was necessary—and they told us how they were going to act. From this alone, we can figure out their worldview.

Why did the signers adopt words like "course of events" and "necessary" and "impel"? I turned over every clue that might help us understand how they saw the world.

And what happened at the end of the sentence? The signers said they would declare the "causes" for their action. After they employ their worldview to describe that world and lay out their course of action, they will do us the favor of telling us what their worldview is. The opening is an example of prolepsis—a rhetorical device in which a speaker assumes that something is the case, before the argument has been made. It is a form of anticipation.

For the rest of the Declaration the signers proceed to tell us what their worldview is. They make explicit the general ideas that govern how they see things, ideas that in the first sentence are just implicit.

Here some more Latin is useful. The words "implicit" and "explicit" come from *plicare*, which means "to fold," as when you fold your clothes.

So think of a sound bite as a suitcase. Writers pack into their sound bites some core principles as well as some instructions to their readers on how to apply those principles to real-world examples. But they're doing the packing in a single carry-on bag. The good news about packing everything up tightly is that readers can pick up sound bites and walk around for days with them, mulling them over. Because the idea is wrapped in something small, it's easily carried around. Sound bites travel. That's why they're valuable.

If a speaker or writer has packed a sound bite well, it will unpack well. By this I mean that from just a few words uttered by a speaker, a careful listener will be able to unfold the full principle implicit in that sound bite as well as its supporting arguments. A careful listener will be able to convert implicit into explicit meanings.

If this communicative transaction is going to work, writers and speakers have to be good at packing, and readers and listeners have to be good at unpacking. Writers and speakers need skills of careful, authentic writing; readers and listeners need the skills of slow reading and close listening, skills very much endangered in contemporary culture. With such skills, citizens can understand and choose among political positions even when those are too often conveyed in sound bites.

A FEW MAXIMS.

DREAD more the blunderer's friendship than the calumniator's enmity.

AVOID him who discovers with rapidity the bad, and is slow to see the good.

THE study of man, is the doctrine of unisons and discords between ourselves and others.

HE knows not how to speak, who cannot be silent.

HE who will sacrifice nothing, and enjoy all is a fool.

THE ambitious sacrifices all to what he terms honor, as the miser all to money.

HE that has no friend and no enemy, is one of the vulgar ; and without talents, powers, or energy.

HUMILITY and love constitute the essence of true religion.

HE has not a little of the devil in him, who prays and bites.

A list of maxims from the
Gentleman's Pocket Almanac *for 1797.*

We needn't fear sound bites if we can master them.

So let's go back again to the sound bite with which we began: "We hold these truths to be self-evident, that all men are created equal."

The value of learning to read slowly and listen closely is not merely that we will understand the Declaration better but also that we will understand every politician better. Slow reading is the best way to learn how to do this. The brevity of sound bites is a problem only when listeners don't know how to convert something short and sweet (or, for that matter, short but sour) into the long implicit thought it contains.

The signers of the Declaration had confidence in their readers.

25

STICKS AND STONES

I N THE LAST CHAPTER I DIGRESSED. I CONFESS, I BIVOUACKED ON
sound bites. Who can blame me for hesitating before plunging into a
sentence as difficult as this?

> We hold these truths to be self-evident, that all men are cre-
> ated equal, that they are endowed by their Creator with certain
> unalienable Rights, that among these are Life, Liberty and the
> pursuit of Happiness,—That to secure these rights, Governments
> are instituted among Men, deriving their just powers from the
> consent of the governed,—That whenever any Form of Govern-
> ment becomes destructive of these ends, it is the Right of the People
> to alter or to abolish it, and to institute new Government, laying
> its foundation on such principles and organizing its powers in
> such form, as to them shall seem most likely to effect their Safety
> and Happiness.

But now I will turn right to the heart of the matter. The matter of principles. How many self-evident truths are listed here?

There seem to be five—one for each clause starting with "that"—
making the following list:

LIST OF TRUTHS

1. That all men are created equal;
2. That they are endowed by the creator with certain inalienable rights;
3. That those rights include life, liberty, and the pursuit of happiness;
4. That governments have been instituted among men, based on the consent of the governed to secure those rights; and
5. That when governments fail to secure these rights, the people have the right to change their government and set up a new one that will do a better job of securing their safety and happiness.

If this is correct, we could say that these five truths add up to a right to revolution since the fifth, concluding truth expresses the right to change our government if it's not protecting our rights to life, liberty, and the pursuit of happiness.

But I'm not sure these really are five separate truths.

When we focus on the repeated use of "that," we are paying close attention to the syntax of the sentence, but we need to attend to punctuation, too. The punctuation reveals something different. And here we really find our many-headed hydra, the democratic author, at work. In every draft that Jefferson copied out and in the draft that Adams copied out, each of the five truths is separated out equally from the others with the same punctuation mark; in most manuscripts, the semicolon is used; in one, it is the colon. But in each of these manuscripts, the punctuation indicates a list of five items of equal status. Then when Congress had official texts made up—first the Dunlap broadside and then Matlack's parchment—the craftsmen added dashes for emphasis. The Dunlap broadside first added a dash after "pursuit of happiness"; then the engrossed parchment turned one dash into two, adding a second one after "consent of the governed."

With these dashes, the democratic author emphasized that Jefferson's list of five truths can also be divided into a list of three truths; they brought out his reliance on the three-part structure of George Mason's argument in the Virginia Declaration of Rights (see p. 68). As in Mason's text, the first three "that's" are all part of a single truth about *human beings*. Then comes a dash, and we start with a second truth about *government*. Then comes another dash, and we get a third and final truth about the *right to revolution.*

If we pay attention to the official punctuation as well as to the syntax, we get a list of truths that looks like this:

REVISED LIST OF TRUTHS

1. all people are equal in being endowed by their creator with the rights of life, liberty, and the pursuit of happiness, among others;
2. humans build governments to secure these rights and political legitimacy rests on the consent of the governed;
3. when governments fail to protect these rights, people have a right to revolt.

Now, if it's correct to think that this sentence includes three truths, then what we have is not exactly a *list* of truths but something else, something philosophers, speaking technically, call a syllogism, a particular method for structuring a logical argument.

You may, though, have noticed that in addition to changing the number of truths in this list, I've sneaked in another revision. The Declaration says that "all *men* are created equal." In this revised list of truths, I've instead written that "all *people* are equal." We are back at the topic my family used to argue over at the dinner table. For whom was the Declaration written?

Like many, I have often gotten hung up on the argument that the phrase "All men are created equal" referred only to men and in particular to white ones with property, the only kind of people who could participate in the Continental Congress. But when I looked closely at the rough drafts of the Declaration, the full text gave me reason to pause. The high-flown passage about slavery that Congress edited out stopped me in my tracks. Here it is again:

[King George III] has waged cruel war against human nature itself, violating it's most sacred rights of life & liberty in the persons

*of a distant people who never offended him, captivating & carry-
ing them into slavery in another hemisphere, or to incur miserable
death in their transportation thither. This piratical warfare, the
opprobrium of infidel powers, is the warfare of the Christian king
of Great Britain, determined to keep open a market where MEN
should be bought & sold . . . .*

This paragraph shares many words with the first two sentences of the
Declaration—nature, nature's sacred rights of life and liberty. Yet here
these words describe Africans being sold into slavery and the violation
of their natural rights. Then Jefferson talks about markets where "MEN,"
which he capitalizes, are bought and sold. In other words, he is calling the
slaves "men." And when he does this, he can't mean males only, because
those markets were for men, women, and children. So when, in the second sentence, he writes that all men are created equal, he must mean all
people—whatever their color, sex, age, or status.

Here it is important to say some things about who Jefferson was. He
was, of course, a slave owner. He took as a concubine one of his slaves,
Sally Hemings, who was also his dead wife's halfsister. She became his
thirty-three-year partner, and the couple had six children, two of whom
died in childhood. What became of the others? Two simply moved
away from Monticello as adults and began living as white people, while
Jefferson freed the two youngest children in his will. In his will he also
freed three other older men alongside them, but he did not free his many
other slaves.

How could Jefferson write so eloquently about slavery as a violation
of the rights of men, women, and children and not disavow his own
complicity in the peculiar institution? Which was the real Jefferson?
The one who wrote these words or the one who lived within the slave
system in ways that both affirmed and contradicted its order? Or was
he simply a repugnant and hypocritical egoist, as one of my friends
once said to me?

Jefferson's story is another mystery of the Declaration.

And tied to these questions about the real Jefferson is yet another
conundrum—this one about words.

Can it matter to a slave, buckling a shoe, whether this document holds
one truth, two, or more? Little kids are also taught to chant, "Sticks and

stones might break my bones but words can never hurt me." Perhaps if we think about the Declaration from the perspective of people who were slaves in 1776, it leaves us having to think, "Sticks and stones *will* break my bones *and* words can never help me."

So here's the conundrum: what exactly are words worth?

26

SELF-INTEREST?

I FIND IT DIFFICULT TO RECONCILE THE FACT THAT JEFFERSON could write words as powerful as those condemning slavery in the first draft of the Declaration, yet also be a slaveholder.

When we focus on this mystery, it becomes obvious that earlier we passed too easily and quickly over Jefferson's idea that everyone has a basic sense of fairness. How could he square that idea with watching his fellow revolutionaries in the Continental Congress delete the paragraphs about slavery? And what about the fact that they didn't even notice the savagery of their own relation to the "Savages," as the Declaration labels Native Americans? Those facts seem to be evidence against the very idea that people have any intuitive sense of fairness.

Although the Declaration encourages us to see people as generally fair, it also forces us to ask ourselves: What keeps people from being fair judges? Why do they even fail to see some people—for instance, "Savages"—as people? What can explain Jefferson?

Self-interest seems like an obvious answer. Jefferson benefited financially, sexually, and, we can imagine, psychologically from having slaves. Perhaps he just couldn't let go of those benefits?

That is surely part of it. But there must be more to it. Here in the Declaration we see Jefferson trying to base his moral commitments on truths that he works out rationally by studying nature. Abstract reflection is one

By His HONOUR

SPENCER PHIPS, Efq;

Lieutenant-Governour and Commander in Chief, in and over His Majefty's Province of the *Maffachufetts-Bay* in *New-England.*

A PROCLAMATION.

WHEREAS the Tribe of *Penobfcot* Indians have repeatedly in a perfidious Manner acted contrary to their folemn Submiffion unto His Majefty long fince made and frequently renewed ;

I have therefore, at the Defire of the Houfe of Reprefentatives, with the Advice of His Majefty's Council, thought fit to iffue this Proclamation, and to declare the Penobfcot Tribe of Indians to be Enemies, Rebels and Traitors to His Majefty King GEORGE the Second : And I do hereby require His Majefty's Subjects of this Province to embrace all Opportunities of purfuing, captivating, killing and deftroying all and every of the aforefaid Indians.

AND WHEREAS the General Court of this Province have voted that a Bounty or Incouragement be granted and allowed to be paid out of the Publick Treafury, to the marching Forces that fhall have been employed for the Defence of the *Eaftern* and *Weftern* Frontiers, from the *Firft* to the *Twenty-fifth* of this Inftant *November* ;

I have thought fit to publifh the fame ; and I do hereby Promife, That there fhall be paid out of the Province-Treafury to all and any of the faid Forces, over and above their Bounty upon Inliftment, their Wages and Subfiftence, the Premiums or Bounty following, viz.

For every Male *Penobfcot* Indian above the Age of Twelve Years, that fhall be taken within the Time aforefaid and brought to *Bofton, Fifty Pounds.*

For every Scalp of a Male *Penobfcot* Indian above the Age aforefaid, brought in as Evidence of their being killed as aforefaid, *Forty Pounds.*

For every Female *Penobfcot* Indian taken and brought in as aforefaid, and for every Male Indian Prifoner under the Age of Twelve Years, taken and brought in as aforefaid, *Twenty-five Pounds.*

For every Scalp of fuch Female Indian or Male Indian under the Age of Twelve Years, that fhall be killed and brought in as Evidence of their being killed as aforefaid, *Twenty Pounds.*

Given at the Council-Chamber in *Bofton,* this Third Day of *November* 1755, and in the Twenty-ninth Year of the Reign of our Sovereign Lord *GEORGE* the Second, by the Grace of GOD of *Great-Britain, France* and *Ireland,* KING, Defender of the Faith, &c.

By His Honour's Command,
J. Willard, Secr.

S. Phips.

GOD Save the KING.

BOSTON: Printed by *John Draper,* Printer to His Honour the Lieutenant-Governour and Council. 1755.

A 1755 proclamation placing bounties on the heads of Native Americans.

way we can come to believe things, to acquire truths and principles to guide our actions.

The trouble is, it's not the only way we come to believe things.

We also acquire a lot of what we believe through habit. We're born into worlds that seem to us natural at first. Maybe, like my husband, we're born into a Catholic family and never meet anyone who isn't Catholic until we're ten. We'll think the whole world is Catholic and that it's just the way everyone is. We'll think Catholicism is natural. Or any other cultural or religious tradition that is the world into which we are born.

For that matter, maybe we're born into a world, for instance, ancient Athens, where all the men vote and move freely well beyond their homes, while all the women are largely restricted to their households and play no role in politics. Because things have been done one way for a long time, they seem natural. Because we grow up with them, they seem given, even though they might be changed.

Nature, in other words, isn't such an easy thing to grasp.

What happens, then, when what we know from abstract reflection conflicts with what we know from habit, as it did for Jefferson?

The history of the world suggests that habit is the more powerful source of knowledge. People are able to replace old habits with new ones, based on ideas that show them the truth lies elsewhere, only with great difficulty. Quite often they change only when forced to by the people who are worst off under reigning conditions.

Although George III eventually came to consider George Washington "the greatest character of the age," he wasn't about to change how he thought about the colonies without being forced by them to change.

Ultimately, the same thing was true about slavery. During the Civil War, slaves liberated themselves from plantations. In great numbers they escaped and then often offered to serve in the Northern army. Their readiness to fight ultimately forced both North and South to change their policies toward runaway slaves and laid the foundations for freedom.

In the case of native Americans, new ideas about human equality did not gain traction before a genocide had been completed.

When we recognize the power of habit, we are left with an obvious question. Why do we celebrate principles so much, mere words, if habit is so much more powerful?

Principles and the words that convey them are, at least, a starting point. They generate tensions, conflicts, dialectics, out of which over very long time spans, changes do emerge. Without them, where would we be?

Also, we can change our ideas and our principles a lot faster than we can change our habits. There's a lot to learn about human beings from studying what it takes to get our habits to catch up to words and principles that have run on ahead.

So what are words worth?

A starting point.

No less.

No more.

And, no, we're not done with the problem of how Jefferson could be simultaneously the architect of an egalitarian political philosophy and an owner of slaves. This problem will dog us.

Although I will return now to the second sentence, I don't imagine for a moment that I have shaken tragedy's long shadow.

27

SELF-EVIDENCE

THERE'S SOMETHING QUITE STARTLING ABOUT THE PHRASE "WE hold these truths to be self-evident." Perhaps it can be made visible most easily with a comparison.

The Catholic Church, too, is committed to a set of truths. At every mass priest and parishioners together recite a list of their beliefs called the *Credo*. One version, called the Apostle's Creed, starts like this: "I believe in God, the Father almighty, creator of heaven and earth. I believe in Jesus Christ, his only son and Lord." Each section begins with the words "I believe," and that's why this recitation is called the *Credo*. Latin (again), "credo" simply means "I believe."

The Declaration launches its list of truths altogether differently. Jefferson and his colleagues do not say, "I believe," or even "we believe," that all men are created equal. Instead, they say, "We hold these truths to be self-evident," and then they give us a set of either three or five truths, depending on how you count.

What's the difference between "We believe" and "We hold these truths to be self-evident"? In the Catholic *Credo*, when one says, "I believe," the basis for that belief is God's revealed word. In contrast, when Jefferson and his colleagues say, "We hold these truths to be self-evident," they are claiming to know the truths thanks to their own powers of perception and reasoning. These truths are self-evident, and so humans can grasp and hold them without any external or divine assistance.

In order to understand what "We hold these truths to be self-evident" really means, then, it is important to know what "self-evident" means.

Sometimes people take it to mean that we can instantly understand an idea, but that's not really right. It's true that sometimes the idea of self-evidence is used for things that we simply perceive. For instance, when I look out my window I immediately perceive that the world includes things like trees and flowers. If outside my window there are many different kinds of tree—hickory and maple and oak, for instance—when I look at them, I nonetheless rapidly perceive that they are all the same kind of thing. That many different kinds of a particular sort of growing thing are all trees is self-evident. We can call this self-evidence from sense perception.

The immediacy of perception, though, is not the same as instantly understanding an idea. And, in fact, to call a proposition self-evident is not at all to say that you will instantly get it. It means instead that if you look into the proposition, if you entertain it, if you reflect upon it, you will inevitably come to affirm it. All the evidence that you need in order to believe the proposition exists within the proposition itself.

This second kind of self-evidence comes not from perception but from logic and how language works.

For instance, we define a chair as an object with a seat and some structure of legs to hold that seat up; and the artifact serves the purpose of having someone sit on it. Then, if I say that a chair is for sitting on, I am expressing a self-evident truth based only on the definition of a chair. Of course a chair is for sitting on! That is how I've defined the word, after all. That's a pretty trivial example of self-evidence. If that were all there were to the idea of self-evidence, it wouldn't be very interesting.

So here is where matters get more interesting: one can string together more than one kind of self-evident proposition—let's call them "premises"—in order to lead to a new piece of knowledge, a conclusion, which will also count as self-evident, since it has been deduced from a few basic self-evident premises.

Aristotle called this method of stringing together valid premises to yield a self-evident conclusion, a syllogism. Above, I said that "syllogism" is a technical word. Here is a basic example:

FIRST PREMISE: *Bill Gates is a human being.*
SECOND PREMISE: *All human beings are mortal.*
CONCLUSION: *Bill Gates is mortal.*

This is a bit like math. We can use a Venn diagram to show how the syllogism works. Venn diagrams represent sets of things and how they overlap, and the argument of a syllogism can be thought of as expressing facts about sets and their members. Bill Gates is in the set of human beings. And the set of human beings is entirely contained within the set of mortals. It follows that Bill Gates is in the set of mortals. The validity of this syllogism becomes self-evident when those facts are represented as in this Venn diagram:

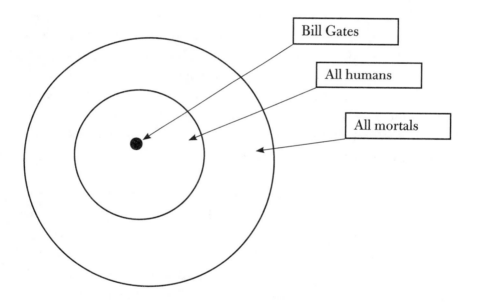

Now, in this syllogism, our two premises are both self-evident truths based on sense perception. We know Bill Gates is a human being by looking at and listening to him. As to the idea that human beings are mortal, we know that human beings die by seeing it happen all around us and never seeing a counterexample. Then we take these two premises, each self-evident through sense perception, and generate a third self-evident proposition, in this case a conclusion, through deduction. From the two premises, we can deduce the certain conclusion that Bill Gates will die.

The Declaration introduces a similar kind of argument when it says, "We hold these truths to be self-evident." At first glance, it looks as if we just have three separate self-evident truths. But if we look closer, we notice that our truths also represent an argument with two premises, which are true from sense perception, and a conclusion that is deduced from them.

Here's how it works.

After the Declaration says, "We hold these truths to be self-evident," the text proceeds to identify three truths: one about human beings, one about government, and one about revolution. The truth about human beings, though, is a three-part truth.

It is self-evidently true:

> *that all men are created equal, that they are endowed by their Creator with certain unalienable Rights, that among these are Life, Liberty and the pursuit of Happiness.*

How do these three claims make a single truth? Human beings are equal in all acquiring the same rights at the moment of their creation. From the moment of their emergence as living beings, human beings seek to survive, to be free from domination, and to be happy. This is something we simply observe about human beings. For that matter, we observe it about other animals, too. For instance, I've never seen a cat that didn't want to survive, to be free, and to be happy.

Then, with the next truth, we come to the difference between human beings and animals. The Declaration says, it is self-evidently true

> *—That to secure these rights, Governments are instituted among Men, deriving their just powers from the consent of the governed.*

This is a truly salient point. The signers are saying that, in contrast to the animal kingdom, the world of human beings is indeed full of kingdoms and other kinds of governments. The so-called animal kingdom is a kingdom only metaphorically. There are no governments among animals. Animals have social hierarchies, and they have their own methods for seeking their survival, freedom, and happiness, but human beings use politics. Human beings display self-conscious thought about social organization, and politics is the activity that flows from that self-consciousness about

An anonymous political cartoon from the
Massachusetts Sentinel, *published in 1788.*

power. Again, this is simply a matter of observation. From the beginning of time to the present day, human beings have formed governments. Human beings have done this just as regularly as birds build nests.

Then the Declaration puts these first two truths together. Since human beings seek their own survival, freedom, and happiness, and since they have a special tool for doing so—namely, the ability to form governments—it makes sense for them to stick with any particular version of that tool, any particular government, only if it's doing the work it's been built to do.

Compare it to a bird with a nest. What's the point of a bird's staying in a nest if it turns out that the nest has been built out of material inimical or poisonous to the bird? What's the use, in other words, of having a government, if it doesn't serve the purposes of protecting life, liberty, and the pursuit of happiness for which governments are set up in the first place?

The Declaration puts it this way: It is self-evidently true

> —*That whenever any Form of Government becomes destructive of these ends, it is the Right of the People to alter or to abolish it, and to institute new Government, laying its foundation on such principles and organizing its powers in such form, as to them shall seem most likely to effect their Safety and Happiness.*

From the facts, first, that people are simply wired, as are all animals, to seek their survival, freedom, and happiness, and, second, that human beings use governments as their central instrument for protecting their life, liberty, and pursuit of happiness, we can deduce that people have a right to change governments that aren't working for them.

This makes an argument that goes like this:

PREMISE 1: All people have rights to life, liberty, and the pursuit of happiness.

PREMISE 2: Properly constituted government is necessary to their securing their rights

CONCLUSION: All people have a right to a properly constituted government.

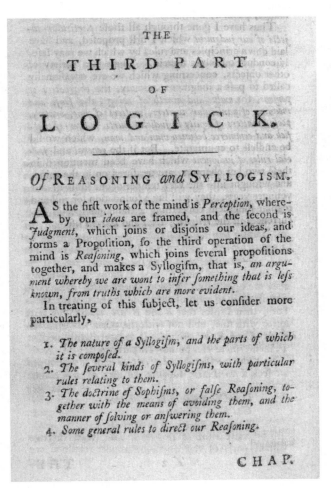

Isaac Watts's eighteenth-century handbook explains how to construct syllogisms to reason from more-evident truths to those less known.

In fact, a philosopher would say that a premise is missing from that argument and that the full formally valid syllogism would look like this:

PREMISE 1: All people have rights to life, liberty, and the pursuit of happiness.

PREMISE 2: Properly constituted government is necessary to their securing these rights.

PREMISE 3: [All people have a right to whatever is necessary to secure what they have a right to].

CONCLUSION: All people have a right to a properly constituted government.

Politicians often craft maxims simply by dropping out pieces of their argument. With the missing premise inserted, the Declaration's truths fit together almost like the pieces of a mathematical equation; we intuitively feel the puzzle pieces snap together. That is how self-evidence should feel.

28

MAGIC TRICKS

SURPRISINGLY, MATHEMATICS CAN TAKE US STILL FURTHER AND help make the structure of the Declaration's argument even easier to see.

For instance, the point about syllogisms is easier to understand if we cheat a little and write out the premises and conclusions of the syllogism as if they were a mathematical equation. For instance,

Bill Gates = a human. A human = a mortal.

Then you cross out the pieces in the middle which are repetition—they sort of cancel each other out—and that leaves you with

Bill Gates = ~~a human. A human~~ = a mortal. → Bill Gates = a mortal.

We are used to doing this sort of operation with numbers, and there is nothing special about it. So why do I think this operation will be helpful with the Declaration's truths?

Looking at some actual numbers makes it easier to figure that out. For instance, one could say the following two things:

$$3 \times 4 = 12$$
$$12 = 2 \times 6$$

And then one could also say that
$$3 \times 4 = 2 \times 6$$

Now, consider the numbers in the third equation, on either side of the equal sign. When one looks at them, one has the definite sense of looking at two different things. What's written out on each side of the equal sign is different. But even though the two sets of numbers look different, they're not different, of course, because they both amount to 12. Math lets us see when things that look different are really the same. That is also what is happening with the Declaration's truths.

Jefferson was conducting a magic trick of sorts. With the list of self-evident truths, he was holding up a couple of things that initially look different, only to whisk away the cloth and reveal that they amount to the same thing because of some shared feature. But what exactly is the shared feature in each of the truths that the Declaration lists?

Let's go back to Bill Gates for a moment. In that example, it looks as if "Bill Gates" and "mortals" are two different things or two different categories, but each has a necessary connection to the category "human being," so "Bill Gates" and "mortals" have a necessary connection to each other also. The terms "Bill Gates" and "mortals" are not, however, equivalent to each other. The equal sign that I stuck between Bill Gates and mortals claims too much; that's the sense in which using an ordinary mathematical equation is cheating. But what matters is to see that "Bill Gates" and the category "mortals" are linked through a third term: "human beings."

The magic in this passage of the Declaration similarly depends on using a single term to connect all of its truths. Here, again, is our stripped-down version of the truths:

All people have rights to life, liberty, and the pursuit of happiness.
Properly constituted government is necessary to their securing their
*   rights.*
All people have a right to a properly constituted government.

The word "rights" appears in all three sentences. That was the concept that brought the first and second sentence in relation to each other to generate the third sentence. If we wanted to make it even easier to see how the Declaration's self-evident truths are connected, we could rewrite them like this:

All people have rights to life, liberty, and the pursuit of happiness.
The rights to life, liberty, and happiness are secured by properly
constituted governments.

And if people have a right to whatever is necessary to secure what they have a right to, then

All people have a right to a properly constituted government.

At first, the fact that all people have rights to life, liberty, and the pursuit of happiness and the fact that all people have a right to a properly constituted government looked as if they were different things. But they essentially amount to a single right, because governments are the instrument human beings use to protect the rights to life, liberty, and the pursuit of happiness. Jefferson has set up these points so that two things that look different, two observable facts about the world, turn out to be fundamentally the same.

What do I mean by saying that two observable facts about the world turn out to be fundamentally the same?

The fact that people seek their survival, freedom, and happiness and the fact that people seek to build functioning governments turn out to be equivalent. If we have a right to do one, we have a right to do the other. Our individual pursuit of happiness leads us to form collectivities through which we pursue the safety and happiness of the whole.

This is the sort of idea in the Declaration that I find stunning in its simplicity and power.

To understand that power, think of the historical context. In an age when some sixty thousand Britons turned out to see their king process to Parliament in a gold chariot twenty-four feet long and thirteen feet high, with three gilt cherubs on top, a sea god above every wheel, and windows large enough for them to get a good view of him, how shocking it must have been to declare that the road to a functioning government did not pass through monarchy. In an age in which the wealth required to pay for such a chariot—and for the wars of the man riding in it—required extraction from an empire that, with its various forms of exploitative labor, reached around the world, how radical it was to think of the happiness even of farmers and laborers as the ground and limit of politics.

With their simple lines, the signers of the Declaration sought to overturn not merely then-existing governments but centuries of received opinion. And they called what they were doing a matter of self-evidence!

Having come to understand the Declaration's propositions, we can now see what the idea of self-evidence is. It is something like the math example. If we can establish that each of two things has a necessary relationship to a third thing, we automatically learn something about the relationship of those first two things to each other. Self-evident ideas emerge from such relationships of necessary connection.

Yet this merely leads us to another question: If the Declaration's three truths all fit together through a relationship to the concept of "rights," where did that concept come from in the first place?

In the Declaration the idea of rights entered when Jefferson, Adams, and Franklin wrote that "all men had been endowed by their Creator with certain inalienable rights." The Declaration's rights come from a "Creator."

I have been skirting the deepest water in this sentence—the question of the role of that Creator.

29

THE CREATOR

W<small>E CAN'T PRETEND TO UNDERSTAND THE SENTENCE THAT</small> begins, "We hold these truths to be self-evident," until we navigate through the daunting presence of the Creator in its middle. This is our toughest task.

In the last two chapters, we saw how the Declaration's truths boil down to this:

> *People have rights to life, liberty, and the pursuit of happiness.*
> *Properly constituted government is necessary to their securing their*
>   *rights.*
> *[People have a right to whatever is necessary to secure what they have a*
>   *right to].*
> *People have a right to a properly constituted government.*

And they do. But remember how when we were counting the Declaration's self-evident truths, it seemed at first that there might be five? Only upon reflection did we realize that there were three.

We were initially led astray because the first self-evident truth has three parts. Here's how it goes. It is self-evidently true

(1a)   *that all men are created equal,*

    (1b)   *that they are endowed by their Creator with certain unalienable Rights,*

    (1c)   *that among these are Life, Liberty and the pursuit of Happiness.*

"That all men are created equal," which is the most important phrase in the Declaration and probably also the most mystifying, is in fact just *part a* of this tripartite truth.

Importantly, this is not, as we've seen, the first time that "equality" appears in the Declaration. In the very first sentence, the colonists describe themselves as founding a country that would take its "separate and equal" place on the world's stage. In that context, equality was a matter not of size, power, or wealth but of status. England, France, Spain, and the newly united states on the Atlantic seaboard had equal status simply in being states, capable of making decisions for themselves and organizing a shared life for their citizens. Respecting their equality meant leaving them free from domination; it meant keeping out so that they could pursue their own flourishing.

The meaning of equality in that first sentence can help us understand the idea here that all people are created equal. The signers don't mean that we all have the same size, power, wealth, or even ability. As in the first sentence, what we share is a *status*.

What exactly is that status? *Parts b* and *c* of that first tripartite truth provide the answer. It is self-evident that all people

    (1b)   *are endowed by their Creator with certain unalienable Rights,*

    (1c)   *that among these are Life, Liberty, and the pursuit of Happiness.*

Our shared status is that of being creatures endowed with the same set of inalienable rights.

To understand this shared status, then, we need to understand two things. We need to know what it means to be "endowed" with something and who or what this Creator is that has endowed us with these rights.

"Endowed" comes—of course—from Latin, from the word *doto*, which describes giving a dowry to a bride about to be married. This, however, just generates another problem. What exactly is a dowry?

In England and then Britain, from medieval times through the Victorian era, when a woman was to be married, her family would give her some money to take with her into the marriage. Dowries were used in many other parts of the world as well and in some places still are. In the British case, this money was hers to keep regardless of what happened to her husband. If something went wrong with the marriage, and the couple divorced, the dowry traveled with the wife back to her former family or to a new husband. The purpose of this dowry was to make sure that there was a permanent basis for the wife's support. Since the wife and her money could not be separated, there is a sense in which the money became a part of her.

What, then, does it mean to say that all people are endowed by their creator with inalienable rights to life, liberty, and the pursuit of happiness? It must mean that these rights are property that we get, like a bride, but in this case from God, not our families. Nobody should take this property away from us, just as no one should rob a bride of her dowry.

Although the word "endow" was first used for providing money to someone, it eventually came to mean "to enrich or furnish with any quality or power of mind or body." If we have been endowed with inalienable rights, with what have we been enriched or furnished? In particular, we have been equipped with the powers of mind, spirit, and body necessary to live, to be free, and to pursue happiness.

Yet this is not all that we have received. In its second truth, the Declaration tells us that government is the tool that humans use to secure life, liberty, and the pursuit of happiness. We have been furnished with our powers of mind, spirit, and body in order that we may live, be free, and pursue happiness *by means of politics.*

The powers of mind, spirit, and body with which we have been created, and which we use in politics, belong to us simply because of who we are. Simply by coming into being as humans we have them. We also have the right to keep these powers permanently: that is, after all, the meaning of an endowment. Consequently, any effort to take these powers away from someone is an effort to rob him of his fundamental human property.

This leads us to the two most challenging questions: How is it that we come into being as humans in the first place? And how is it that we come not merely to have these powers of mind, spirit, and body but also to have a *right* to them? These questions, in turn, lead us straight back to the Creator.

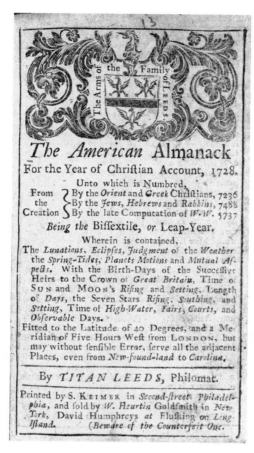

Like many almanacs, this 1728 example dates celebrated events from creation.

In addition to referring to a Creator, the text, as we have seen, invokes "Nature's God." If our Creator is nature's God, then human beings come to be, simply, by being born. It's as easy as that. We just are a part of nature. And the way we are is also a part of nature. And because God is the source of nature, we can take it as granted that nature is good, which means that *our* nature is good too.

Why is it, though, that we possess our powers of mind, body, and spirit, which enable us to live, be free, and pursue happiness by means of politics, as a matter of *right*? To understand this, we have to go back to the idea of the dowry. We must be precise about how dowries worked. What did it take for a bride to have a right to property that would travel with her as her endowment?

Four parties had to participate to make a dowry work as a *right* for the dowryholder. Someone had to give the bride a dowry. This was her family. Then there was the recipient of the dowry, the bride. Third, there were the legal authorities, the representatives of the legal order by which the bride was deemed to have a right to her dowry, who punished anyone who tried to steal the wife's dowry. The bride owned her dowry, in practical terms, as a matter of right, *because* people stood ready to protect her possession of it. Fourth, and finally, there was the person who might have tried to take away the bride's or the wife's property but didn't, because of respecting her right.

When it comes to our inalienable human rights, who plays each of these four roles?

As to the first, we already know that the Creator provides us with our dowry or endowment. As to the second, clearly we are like the wife who holds the endowment. And as to the fourth, the thief might be anybody.

But what about the third role? That of the police officers, say, who make sure that no one robs the bride of her dowry? What order and what authorities enforce our right and thereby make it real as opposed to notional?

Nature's order is the only one that the Declaration identifies the Creator as having a role in, so somehow nature's authorities must be the ones to enforce our rights. The Declaration's explanation of how nature provides this protection comes in its second and third truths:

> *That to secure these rights, Governments are instituted among Men, deriving their just powers from the consent of the governed,*
> *That whenever any Form of Government becomes destructive of these ends, it is the Right of the People to alter or to abolish it, and to institute new Government, laying its foundation on such principles and organizing its powers in such form, as to them shall seem most likely to effect their Safety and Happiness.*

What is the answer to the question how rights are to be protected? Governments are "instituted," says the Declaration, precisely to do that job. They are instituted to "secure" our rights.

Human beings have been furnished with the powers of mind, spirit, and body to live, be free, and pursue happiness. But, as we have seen, we have also been furnished with the powers to do these things *by means of politics*. Because politics comes as naturally to human beings as does living, being free, and pursuing happiness, politics is the tool nature has developed to protect those fundamental human powers. By providing protection to those powers through politics, nature turns those powers into rights. The instrument we use to secure our rights and to effect the safety and happiness, which we pursue individually and collectively, is government. Egalitarian access to the instrument of government is therefore fundamental to the pursuit of happiness. This is the second facet of the ideal of equality in the Declaration.

In other words, nature makes us creatures who are prepared to protect ourselves and gives us the tools we need for that work. We ourselves are the ones who punish people who try to take away our inalienable rights to life, liberty, and the pursuit of happiness. This is true of all of us, equally.

That we ourselves simply are the authorities nature has created to protect as rights our powers to live, be free, and pursue happiness is the crashing, resounding, remarkable conclusion of the Declaration's third truth.

Yet this leads to another quandary. Is the Declaration implying that we're just like any other wild creature? When our young are endangered, we'll fight ferociously to protect them. If our rights are just a matter of our willingness to protect ourselves, how do we differ from animals? It would be pretty disappointing if inalienable rights consisted only of this.

In fact, the Declaration has already shown us the answer to these questions. Its claim about our inalienable rights is indeed more than the simple notion that this is a so-called dog-eat-dog world and that we, too, are dogs.

First, there is the Declaration's observation that human beings' self-protective instincts are channeled into a distinctively human activity: politics. As I have said, human beings display self-consciousness about social organization, and politics is the activity that flows from that wakeful relationship to power. While other animals exhibit forms of social organization, the diversity of social types displayed in the human world flows from that wakefulness. Politics is an activity where people, thanks to their wakefulness, can organize themselves and set up institutions so that they can all collectively protect themselves *without* having to fight with each other. Politics is an activity we come by naturally that should enable us to prevent our degeneration into a post-apocalyptic landscape of unrelenting devastation.

Second, the very fact that nature has given us an instinct for politics—an instinct that allows us to turn away from the path that leads from self-protection to mutual annihilation—is evidence that nature is organized to provide for our flourishing. Our tools of self-protection are good—we have a moral as well as a practical right to them—because they enable nondestructive forms of self-protection.

Although our inalienable rights are rights only because we are reliably our own protectors and enforcers of them, it is our ability to carry out our self-protection in a nondestructive way—an ability given to us by nature's God—that allows us not only to protect our rights but also to enjoy them in peace, just as the bride hopes to enjoy her dowry.

This prospect of peace is our great gift, our dowry, our endowment from our creator, nature's God.

CREATION

ALL PEOPLE ARE CREATED EQUAL. THIS MEANS EQUAL IN BEING endowed with capacities to pursue their individual and collective safety and happiness through politics—through the instrument of government. The second facet of equality presented by the Declaration highlights the importance of equal access to the instrument of government.

This sentence has already yielded a rich reward, but there is still more here. Just like the first sentence of the Declaration, the second one requires us to explore subjects beyond equality. The first sentence raised the difficult topic of God, and this one does too. Does Jefferson's use of the idea that "all men are created equal" perhaps mean that he was a creationist who believed in the Hebrew Bible's description of how God made the world? Or can his invocation of creation fit with evolution?

Questions like this cannot but rise to the surface now, marked as our world is by controversies over evolution and creationism. But those are not the right questions to ask about Jefferson or about the Declaration.

Jefferson drafted the Declaration more than eighty years before Charles Darwin published *On the Origin of Species*. Only then would the theory of evolution be launched once and for all.

In the early Christian church, long before Jefferson wrote, the case for creationism was set against an argument made by the ancient Greek philosopher Aristotle that the earth was eternal—that it had always existed and would always exist. Aristotle thought a divine force provided order

This 1739 almanac by Nathanael Ames mentions Aristotle's theory of the eternal existence of the earth.

SIR *Richard Blackmore* speaks of the Heathen's being bewildred concerning the firſt Original and beginning of the World as follows, *viz*.

THE Pagan *World to* Canaan's *Realms unknown*
Where Knowledge reign'd, and Light Cæleſtial ſhone,
Loſt by Degrees their Parent Adam's *Name,*
Forgot their Stock, and wonder'd whence they came.

But it ſeems to me, that if we were not favour'd with the Inſpired Hiſtory of *Moſes*; we could, not by the bare Dictate of Reaſon be of theOpinion of *Ariſtotle* and ſome other of the Heathen Philoſophers, namely, that the World was *ab Eterno*. The *Chaldeans* who are amongſt the moſt ancient Writers next to *Moſes*, give us an Account concerning the *Beginning of the World*, and 'tis probable the Tradition of ſo memorable a Thing was not wholly loſt to thoſe ancient Ages; and altho' they reckon *Forty three Thouſand* Years from the Beginning of the World to the Time of *Alexander*, yet this Way of Computation is acknowledged by *Diadorus Siculus* and *Plutarch* to be meant of Lunary Years or Months, which being reduced to Solary Years will fall out to be much about the Time aſſign'd by *Moſes* for the Creation.

to the universe, and he called this divine force the unmoved mover. The unmoved mover set the universe in motion not by creating it but by giving everything in nature its goals or ends.

In Jefferson's day the central controversy was simply over whether the Bible was literally true in its entirety. The argument had, however, been spinning along for quite some time. For instance, the Renaissance painter and scientist Leonardo da Vinci thought that the existence of fossils raised questions about the Bible's historical accuracy. But the biggest issue in colonial America was the validity of the Copernican revolution. In 1543 the Polish-born, Italian-trained astronomer Nicolaus Copernicus, published a book written in Latin called *On the Revolutions of the Celestial Spheres*, which laid out an astronomical system based on the recognition that the earth revolves around the sun, not the other way around. Seventeenth-century American almanacs, many published by lecturers and students at Harvard, devote considerable attention to explaining and arguing for Copernicus's views. Even in the late eighteenth century, almanacs were still presenting his theory as scientific novelty.

What did Jefferson himself believe? He did not think the Bible was literally true. He believed in some godhead as the source of nature's order but not in the authority of revelation. On this ground, he should properly be called a "deist," a word that comes from the Latin, *deus*, for god and

In the first Orb above the Sun is Mercury, who performeth his course about the Sun in 88 dayes.
In the next Orb is the glittering Star Venus, who finisheth her Course about the Sun in 225 dayes.
In the middle of all the Planets is the Earth, who performeth her Revolution about the Sun in a year; and is turned round upon her own Axis in the space of 24 hours. The Moon is a secondary Planet, retaining the Earth for her Center, about which she performs her Revolution in 27 dayes, and returns to the Sun in 29. d. 12. h.
Next to the Earth is Mars accomplishing his Revolution in two years.
Next is Jupiter, who hath several little Stars moving about him, as the Moon moveth about the Earth, he runs his Course in 12 years. Saturn the highest of the Planets finisheth his Course in 30 years.
Far above all these is the Orb of the fixed Stars, who make their Revolution in no less then 25920 years. Whose distance by reason that their Parallax is insensible, cannot be by any man determined.

This 1675 almanac presents core ideas of the Copernican revolution.

that was identified in 1563 by a French theologian as a "totally new" term adopted by those who wished to distinguish themselves from atheists. Indeed, Jefferson would be charged with atheism in the years following his arrival at the White House in 1801.

Yet Jefferson also believed that the great religions had discovered moral truths, or principles, that reason itself could find too. On this basis he produced his own version of the Bible—*The Jefferson Bible*, we call it, although he called his book *The Life and Morals of Jesus of Nazareth*. In this book he tried to strip out of the New Testament any suggestion of supernatural intervention in the created order so as to leave only the simple moral truths that Jesus had outlined. By literally cutting up a Bible and gluing the bits into a new book, he extracted from the Bible only the parts that reason could approve. He also intended that this book, as he

JANUARY, Second Winter Month.						
Days.	☉	♄	♃	♂	♀	☿
1	♑ 11 42	♍ 26	♈ 2	♉ 10	♒ 28	♐ 21
7	17 49	26	3	21	♓ 5	24
13	22 41	26	3	26	11	♑ ½
19	29 48	26	4	♒ ½	17	7
25	♒ 5 54	26	5	5	22	15

Of the SUN.

MR. WHISTON says the Sun is 763,000 miles in diameter, and is 230,000 times bigger than the Earth, and is eighty-one millions of statute miles distance from the Earth, each of which miles is 5280 English feet.

Of the EARTH.

THE Earth, according to Mr. Whiston, is 7970 miles in diameter; which will make nigh 24000 miles in circumference. It revolves about its Axis in 23 hours 56 minutes: It moves in the space of one hour 56,000 miles, and is 365 days 6 hours and 9 minutes revolving about the Sun.

Of the Divisibility of MATTER.

THE ingenious Mr. Lewenhoek says, that in the Milt of one Cod-Fish there are more little animals, than there are inhabitants on the face of the earth. Several thousands of them can stand upon a needle's point. And Dr. Keil has shewn, that the smallest visible grain of sand would contain more of the Globules of that fluid (which serves these animals for blood) than ten thousand two hundred and fifty-six of the highest mountains in the world would contain grains of sand.

A Damnd Lye

Of the Fixed STARS.

DR. HOOK and Mr. Flamsteed say, that the distance of the fixed Stars from the Sun is so great, that a bullet shot out of a musket would not reach them in 5000 years.

Another

This 1774 almanac presents several newfangled scientific claims; a reader has annotated the third "A Damnd Lye" and the fourth "Another."

wrote to a friend in 1816, would be "a document in proof that *I* am a *real Christian*, that is to say, a disciple of the doctrines of Jesus" (emphasis in original).

What the elusive Jefferson wrote in the Declaration, what the devout John Adams and Roger Sherman and the openly deist Benjamin Franklin, as well as the diverse members of the Continental Congress, revised and approved, did not commit him or them to a view about the age of the earth. Nor did their words commit them to a judgment about when and how the animals that we now see populating it came into being. As the idea of the Creator is used in the Declaration, it committed the signers only to believing that the natural world, as we know it through observation, originates in a divine source and takes its order, too, from that divine source.

Maybe that divine source brought us creation via the big bang and evolution; maybe in some other way. That doesn't really matter for what Jefferson wrote, or for what the signers affirmed.

And so it doesn't matter either for what the Declaration means. This is a topic we can put aside.

31

BEAUTIFUL OPTIMISM

W E MUST NOW FOCUS AGAIN ON THE SECOND FACET OF EQUAL-
ity that the Declaration has brought into view, on what lies
beneath the idea that all people need access to government, the tool
nature has given us for securing our safety and happiness, individually
and collectively. We have yet more meaning to unpack from the phrase
"All men are created equal."

As we do this, we will come face-to-face with the Declaration's most
beautiful aspect.

"Beauty"—an overused word—is also an odd word to apply to a document that's about politics. Of course, I've already used it several times
for the Declaration. I said that the beauty of the text—a beauty it shares
with important founding texts from other times and places—arises from
how the text combines ideas with process. The text has in it the wizardry
of politics—the fact that it is possible for a multitudinous heap of people to build a shared life by doing things with words. Yet that beauty is
pedestrian compared with what we are about to see.

The Declaration's combination of ideas with process is built on the
foundation of a sublime optimism about human potential. We should
take the time to appreciate that optimism.

In fact, this optimism resides in the same sentences we've just been sift-
ing through. We still haven't understood everything in that all-important
second sentence:

We hold these truths to be self-evident, that all men are created equal, that they are endowed by their Creator with certain unalienable Rights, that among these are Life, Liberty and the pursuit of Happiness,—That to secure these rights, Governments are instituted among Men, deriving their just powers from the consent of the governed,—That whenever any Form of Government becomes destructive of these ends, it is the Right of the People to alter or to abolish it, and to institute new Government, laying its foundation on such principles and organizing its powers in such form, as to them shall seem most likely to effect their Safety and Happiness.

For the moment, let's focus on the last clause: "That whenever any Form of Government becomes destructive of these ends [of securing the rights of life, liberty, and the pursuit of happiness], it is the Right of the People to alter or to abolish it, and to institute new Government, laying its foundation on such principles and organizing its powers in such form, *as to them shall seem most likely to effect their Safety and Happiness*" (emphasis added).

Can I put the central point plainly and directly? Here the Declaration identifies the fundamental feature of human equality. It is this: None can judge better than I whether I am happy; each can judge for herself, just as well as I can for myself, whether she is happy. As judges of our own happiness, we are equals.

The Declaration's assertion that we are all created equal has confounded generations of readers. Given how varying our abilities are, in what way are we all equal? My answer was that we are equal in sharing a *status* as rights-bearing creatures, a status that flows from the fact that we are also equal in being political creatures, a status that requires for its realization that we all have equal access to the tool of government.

Beneath those types of equality lies something even more fundamental, even more profound. Each of us is capable of participating directly in politics because each of us is the best judge of her own happiness.

"When in the *course* of human events it becomes necessary. . . ." I introduced the images of rivers and of a slave ship heading toward Algiers, then a center of slave trading, to explain those very first words of the Declaration. I took that image of the slave ship from the seventeenth-century philosopher John Locke, one among a host of earlier writers whom the founders took seriously. He thought that people have a right to revolution and wanted to explain how we can learn to exercise that right appropriately. In his *Second Treatise of Civil Government*, he argued that the experience of judging the actions of abusive political leaders is like being a passenger on a ship with a secret destination.

The ship's captain might steer this way and that, put in to one or another port to avoid crosswinds or deal with leaks or find a fresh crew or provisions, but despite the to-ing and fro-ing, the passengers will discern the boat's general direction. The passengers will be able to judge where they are headed and whether they need to save themselves.

Locke's image is remarkable. We need to be clear about exactly what his image of the slave ship meandering toward Algiers stands for. It doesn't stand merely for our relation to politicians. Even more importantly, the image stands for the connections among past, present, and future. Our experience of the present is like that wandering journey: full of details, many of which might initially seem random or disconnected. But within all those details there will be a pattern. And because the future does emerge from the present continuously, it must emerge from directions and trajectories that can be discerned, or spotted, within the complex detail of a seemingly shifting itinerary.

This does not mean that there is a grand design in history—just that present and future are continuous with each other. Although it is difficult, we should be able to grasp the future, at least dimly, by scrutinizing the present. The issue isn't exactly whether the future can be foreseen. It is whether we can know, given the discernible patterns in the conduct of certain powerful groups and persons, that some particular outcome will probably occur if we and others do not act so as to prevent that outcome. The reason we can't know the future, even in cases where we are aware of especially clear social and political trends, is that we don't know who, after observing those same trends, might decide to counter them. Yet we can grasp the future: by connecting foresight to action.

This is an astonishing idea: that we can grasp the future. Yet the Declaration makes an even more surprising claim: *everyone* is capable of grasping the future by scrutinizing the present. What's more, not merely are we all capable of this; we, in fact, all *do* this. The Declaration drills down into the heart of human experience: each of us is constantly evaluating patterns in the treatment we receive from others in order to judge whether they are trustworthy. Will they treat us well or badly in the future? Must we counter current trends?

Let me offer a simple, even commonplace, example to clarify this point.

A boy and girl meet at a party. They have a fun conversation. They exchange phone numbers. The girl says to the boy: call me. A day goes by, no phone call. Another day goes by, again no phone call. The girl thinks, maybe he is shy. She calls him. He answers. He is running out the door. He is glad to hear from her, he says, and he also says that he will call her back the next day, when he is less busy. The next day comes. He does not call. Another day comes and still he does not call. Although the boy had said how pleased he was to meet her at the party, and how glad he was to get her call when she phoned, by now she knows that he will not treat her well. Even if he is genuinely interested in her, the pattern in his actions is clear: he does not keep his word; he is not attentive to her. Based on the present, she makes a judgment about how her future interactions with this boy are likely to be, and she moves on. It will not make her happy, she knows, to be existentially waiting.

As a recent movie hero put it, "Past action is the best predictor of future action." Human beings all foretell the future. We are equal in being prognosticators. That is not to say that we are equally good at it; it is to say only that we all do it. We all have the capacity. Some of us exercise it better than others. Most of us err much of the time in our effort to see what is coming; we need to bring humility to the endeavor. Nonetheless, as the Declaration sees us, nearly all of us scrutinize the relationship of present to future well enough to move inch by inch toward happiness.

This is what is so dazzling in the Declaration: its unbounded optimism in the capacity of human beings to see the future in the present well enough—not perfectly, but well enough—to move toward securing happiness. Thanks to this capacity, we are collectively able "to alter or to abolish" our existing government and "to institute new Government, laying its foundation on such principles and organizing its powers in such form, *as to [us] shall seem most likely to effect [our] Safety and Happiness.*"

The colonists did just that. They did the very thing that the Declaration says we can do. They instituted new Government, laying its foundation on such principles and organizing its powers in such form, as to

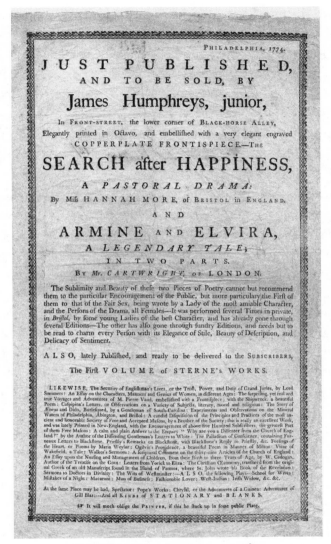

This 1774 poster advertises a new play,
The Search after Happiness, *written by Miss Hannah
More and published in Philadelphia.*

them seemed most likely to effect their safety and happiness. Collectively, using politics, they inched their way toward happiness.

They believed this was possible because they believed in human equality. The fundamental feature of human equality in the argument of the Declaration is, we now realize, this: None can judge better than I whether I am happy; each can judge for himself, just as well as I can for myself, whether he is happy. As judges of our own happiness, we are equals.

This gem of an idea is the prize of our quest. Hold fast to it, and one must also immediately grasp the importance of self-knowledge. One will grasp as immediately the unrelenting work for which each of us, in face of this equality, must take responsibility—achieving self-understanding is like hard, slow tunneling. Hold fast to the idea that we all judge our own happiness best, and one can calculate the value of conversation; only when others tell us about themselves, and about what they see, have we any chance of setting their happiness and ours in relation to one another. Hold fast to this idea, and one has the root of democracy. Only a political system built out of conversation—where multitudes share what they have come to understand with others—has even a scintilla of a chance of making good on the fundamental human truth that none can judge better than I whether I am happy.

The process by which the Declaration came to exist—the structure of committees and meetings in every colony and in the Continental Congress, the need for consensus at so many different levels—brought to life these abstract ideas about human potential. They gave living form to the importance of conversation for setting individual and collective happiness in relation to one another.

Think of the institutions of democratic government, then, as the instrument that democratic citizens use to hold the massive shared, even if acrimonious, conversation in which we figure out how to relate our prospects for happiness to those of others. To secure our futures we all need an equal opportunity to use the instrument of government. What's more, equal access to that instrument is necessary simply to protect our human equality as judges of our own happiness. This is the second facet of the ideal of equality presented in the Declaration.

MATTERS OF FACT

The wicked Statesman, or the Traitor to his Country, at the Hour of DEATH.

This 1774 almanac depicts the traitorous statesman,
dying beneath his list of crimes. The caption reads,
"The wicked statesman, or the traitor to his country,
in the hour of DEATH."

32

PRUDENCE...

T WO FACETS OF THE IDEAL OF EQUALITY PRESENTED IN THE DEC-
laration of Independence have now emerged. Equality designates
freedom from domination. It designates the need for equal access to the
tool of government. Subtle ideas about God, nature, and necessity were
also woven through the argument of the text's first two sentences. Then,
in our final turn with the second sentence, we came face-to-face with the
Declaration's most astonishing, even awe-inspiring, claim: *we are all
equally engaged in the business of prognostication, and as judges of our
own happiness, we are equals.* In that idea we encounter the Declaration's
sublimely philanthropic spirit—its love of humanity—once again.

But there is in the text a counterweight to the Declaration's philan-
thropy, a spirit of prudence. Following quick on the heels of the Declaration's bold optimism, this spirit of prudence raises its head and draws
our attention to just how difficult it is to judge our own happiness and see
the future. Individually—on our own—we often fail, even if no other individual could judge our happiness better than we do ourselves. How then
can we counteract our individual weakness? This brings us to the Declaration's third facet of equality. We need to build a collective intelligence,
and this requires egalitarian approaches to learning and discovery, and to
the analysis of how the present connects to the future.

The methods by which the colonists built their list of grievances
against King George are importantly egalitarian. Their methods for han-

dling the matters of fact will reveal the third facet of equality: everyone has something to contribute to the shared work of cultivating a collective intelligence that maximizes the community's knowledge capacities.

Although the list of grievances, in contrast to the preamble, does not appear to be philosophical, it nonetheless leads us not only to the third but also to the fourth facet of equality. After the colonists spell out all their particular complaints, they sum them up in a general accusation: the king has not responded to their petitions for redress. Justice in human relationships requires the kind of equality expressed by principles of reciprocity. Such principles provide the basis for interaction through which both friends and fellow citizens can achieve equality of agency in their relationships with one another. The king has violated these principles, principles rooted in human equality that anchor freedom. The importance of reciprocity—of fair give-and-take in human relations—links equality to freedom. This is a subtle idea that demands careful thought. Pursuing it will bring to light the fourth facet of the ideal of equality.

Also lurking in the next few sentences, even before the third and fourth facets of the ideal of equality, is a spirit of prudence, a sober counterweight to the spirit of optimism that has infused the Declaration so far.

33

DREARY PESSIMISM

THE DECLARATION SHIMMERS WITH A SUBLIME OPTIMISM. ALL people can judge their own happiness well enough to inch toward better futures. So the text argues.

Yet we can easily imagine an immediate objection. Don't we all know people who over and over again get into bad relationships with others who abuse them?* If people commonly do that, why should we think that we are all such good judges of our own happiness? If it can be so difficult to set a course toward happiness, so hard to escape even from the path of personal abuse, why should anyone ever expect to transform a whole society? Can the Declaration's optimism really be justified?

This is not merely a political question but a human one. What are the facts of human psychology that make it difficult for us to change our circumstances, both our nearest and most intimate relationships and our broader political situation? With questions such as this, the third sentence of the Declaration rises into view.

---

* In chapter 10, I wrote, "What does it take for a group to act in concert? How are decisions made? Who takes responsibility for them? What makes it possible for a group, organization, or institution to collaborate over time? When do they run into trouble? Why? We all know things about how institutions should work. By trying to answer questions like these in relation to our own lives, we build a context for thinking about the Declaration." Here where I use examples from our ordinary intimate lives, "bad relationships," I am doing just what I proposed in that earlier chapter—showing how the important political concepts of the Declaration grow out of what some might even call trivial features of human experience.

Prudence, indeed, will dictate that Governments long established
should not be changed for light and transient causes; and accord-
ingly all experience hath shewn, that mankind are more disposed to
suffer, while evils are sufferable, than to right themselves by abolish-
ing the forms to which they are accustomed.

If the first two sentences of the Declaration lifted us to sublime heights,
the third dashes us on the rocks of pessimism: *mankind are disposed*
to suffer while evils are sufferable. Here the signers acknowledge that
people often *do* live with injustice and oppression for a long time, longer even than the oppressor's mechanisms of control might be able to
explain.

Yet that question—why should we have so much confidence in people's ability to get out of bad situations?—is not the one that Jefferson's
contemporaries would have asked him about his draft. They had a different kind of worry.

Writers often progress from a sentence where they argue for something to one that responds to a potential objection to what they have just
said. In between one sentence and the next, in other words, there is often
an invisible question.

In between the second and the third sentence of the Declaration,
there is just such an invisible question—the very question that Jefferson's
contemporaries would have been most likely to ask. Here, again, is the
third sentence, which answers that imagined question:

Prudence, indeed, will dictate that Governments long established
should not be changed for light and transient causes; and accord-
ingly all experience hath shewn, that mankind are more disposed to
suffer, while evils are sufferable, than to right themselves by abolish-
ing the forms to which they are accustomed.

If that is the answer, then the question must be something like this: "If
people have a right to revolt whenever things aren't going well for them,
why won't they revolt all the time?" Or we can even put it more simply: "Why don't people constantly launch revolutions, even over trivial
wrongs?"

And the Declaration's answer is: "Prudence and habit."

First, there is prudence. People are aware that undoing the whole structure of their lives is a dangerous undertaking, so they are cautious. They hold off until it looks absolutely necessary. They recognize that the seriousness of any revolutionary undertaking requires that the causes be weighty and long-lived. Only such causes can justify radical action. Then there is habit. People do not easily *abolish the forms to which they are accustomed.* People invariably get used to things, even things that are damaging to them.

How exactly does habit inure us to bad situations? Is the idea, here, that fear of the unknown keeps people from embracing change? That is part of it, surely, but habit has other effects too. Take the child of alcoholics who doesn't realize there's a different way of being in the world. She is so used to her parents' toxic environment that she can't even tell it's not normal. Children especially accept a painful reality as normal for lack of experience. Even for adults, though, habit makes it harder to judge the true meaning of a situation.

While there could be a worry that the Declaration's optimism might be unjustified because people stay in damaging situations for too long, this tendency was a source of comfort, not concern, for Jefferson's contemporaries. They will not have to fret, Jefferson reassured them as he drafted the text, that the Declaration's approach to politics will make for a state of perpetual revolution. He provides this assurance: people do not easily rise up; it is not in our ordinary experience.

Yet the text also provides further reassurance for those who are anxious about too frequent revolutions. We have to pay attention to the remark that "mankind are more disposed to suffer" than to alter their situations. Prudence and habit are helped along by nature. It's not enough to recognize that people often grow accustomed even to situations in which they cannot thrive. Just as significantly, we humans have a remarkable capacity for endurance.

Ominous as it sounds, this is not all bad.

Think, for instance, of a prisoner of war. Our capacity to endure is an invaluable part of our nature. Somehow we have a capacity to keep some hope alive, even in destructive conditions that we cannot change, while our other faculties shut down. After some period of mere survival, if we are blessed with escape, we may yet have the chance of recovering and of finding some place, some soil in which in some fashion we can again not merely survive but thrive.

Although people should be captains of their own happiness, many endure for a long time even bad environments that they *could* change. Since one should not lightly undertake to transform one's life, there is something reasonable about this slowness to rise. But there's also something natural. Nature has, it appears, equipped us to endure.

Don't worry, the Declaration rushes to reassure its readers, people aren't too quick to revolt.

But if we are not too quick, are we perhaps too slow?

We have followed the arc of the Declaration from audacious, even sublime, optimism to grinding pessimism. The first two sentences painted us as proactive and self-actualizing, yet the third makes us sound like pack animals—donkeys or dray horses—so cautious and calcified that we willingly carry around heavy loads without making a change.

What has become of the right to revolution?

Do we have it in us to change our world, or don't we?

34

LIFE'S TURNING POINTS

THE DECLARATION HAS A RIDDLE AT ITS CENTER. IT GOES LIKE this:

Question: I am proactive and self-actualizing but also cautious and conservative: what am I?

Answer: A human being.

People can be both cautious and conservative and also proactive and self-actualizing by turning from the one into the other. But why, how, and when does this transformation occur? How do people overcome the pattern of endurance to make a change? When does the time come for revolt?

The next sentence—the fourth—provides the answer:

But when a long train of abuses and usurpations, pursuing invariably the same Object evinces a design to reduce them under absolute Despotism, it is their right, it is their duty, to throw off such Government, and to provide new Guards for their future security.—

The transformation from caution to activism begins with observation. One has to spot the patterns in one's experiences, a "design."

Our efforts to understand the situations in which we find ourselves are akin to watching a skywriter. As the pilot starts making his loops, you can't at first make out what the message says. The words manifest themselves slowly, one letter at a time. Some of the first letters start to break up before the last ones are done. But there comes a point when—all at once—you have that aha moment, you just know what it says: "Dine at Mike's!" for instance.

The word "evince" suggests that the data points themselves, the fragments of our experience, reveal a pattern to an observer. Life's chaos must resolve itself into meaning.

I am, of course, cheating a bit here. In the Declaration's fourth sentence, "design" doesn't simply mean "pattern." It also means "plan" or "intention." When actions "evince a design," they very specifically reveal a pattern that comes *from* someone's intentions.

Because our intentions give our actions patterns, the patterns in our actions can reveal our intentions to a careful observer. In trying to master our social and political fates, what matters is to identify patterns in our environment that have been caused by human beings.

Consider someone who keeps getting passed up for promotions. His boss keeps patting him on the back and telling him he's great, but her actions speak the truth. Whatever she may say, she clearly does not wish to promote him. Finally, he has to face the fact that despite whatever nice things his boss whispers, she is really out to get him or, at least, has no desire to assist him.

The colonists have experienced—or so they claim—a train of events that evince a design "to reduce" the colonists "under absolute despotism" or, we might say, tyranny. Despots tell other people to do whatever they want whenever they want them to do it, and resistance is costly.

What happens when we figure out that our boss or someone else with power over us does not want to aid us or is even out to get us—in the language of the Declaration, to "reduce" us? We might fall into depression or continually try to come up with ways to get our boss to take us seriously. But in the end we are apt simply to quit, even before we line up another job.

The time for revolution has come, argues the Declaration, when one realizes that a string of events all point in the same direction: to the effort of someone else to dominate us. It is as if the skywriter's message, in this case not the bemusing puzzle of a summer's day, has resolved itself into something sinister: I AM HERE TO REDUCE YOU.

Most of us have had moments of recognition—a sudden perception that alters life's course. Scales fall from the eyes. As when a wife empties the laundry and finds, emerged from the pockets of her husband's running shorts, a damp photo of a woman. Then she might report:

Just once, later
in the day, I felt a touch seasick, as if
a deck were tilting under me—

Suddenly a farrago of little memories of things not quite right and moments slightly odd—a pocketful of worry beads long mindlessly fingered—now sorts itself into an obvious strand of meaning: *He has betrayed me.*

People provide different descriptions of moments of painful epiphany. Take these poets' words:

and I am sweating a lot by now

Or

What are these words, these words?
They are plopping like mud.

Or

Over my heart, too, there sweeps a surge of bitterness and I am
smitten as if a sword had stabbed me through and through.
. . . .
I am in torment; my brain is in a whirl.

We all know what it is like physically to discover a painful truth: the flushed cheeks or creeping nausea; the experience of time's sluggishness; the disconnection from what has been. A grief-stricken lover might express his experience this way: "Stop all the clocks, cut off the telephone."

Somehow our bodies react as fast as, or even faster than, our minds to the experience of recognition, to life's turning points. And if we translate the phrase "turning point" into Latin, we get the word *revolution*. A moment of recognition augurs a turning point in life; it presses us physically on toward relief through revolution.

Why, though, do we experience life's turning points physically as well as emotionally and intellectually? Why can dread manifest itself as nausea? It's as if our bodies communicate the need for change. That feeling—nausea out of dread—is our survival instinct, activated. One can't not act on that instinct, not begin to think about what to do.

The fourth sentence of the Declaration captures this movement from discovering the depths of one's trouble to feeling the force of one's survival instinct. Here it is again:

> *But when a long train of abuses and usurpations, pursuing invariably the same Object evinces a design to reduce them under absolute Despotism, it is their right, it is their duty, to throw off such Government, and to provide new Guards for their future security.—*

When one finally sees an enemy for what she is, can one do anything other than try to protect oneself from her?*

It is one's right; it is one's duty.

The hard emphasis of these two clauses back-to-back conveys the immediate force of the survival instinct.

Here the Declaration does not say to whom we have this duty to protect ourselves. Is it a duty to God? To nature? To ourselves? Can it be a duty to anyone other than oneself? Our bodies make us feel this duty, most urgently to ourselves, whenever we feel sick at such a painful or even traumatic realization. Severe unease catalyzes action at last.

When, after a long train of abuses, a string of truth-telling actions, we finally recognize that someone else is our enemy, a yoke of necessity, as the ancient Greeks would say, falls upon us. Then the instinct to survive,

---

* A reader may wonder why an enemy is "she." In everything I write, I alternate between using the female and the male for the third-person generic pronoun so that there is a fifty-fifty distribution. The first time I use the generic pronoun in any piece of writing, I always start with the female to make up for centuries of past practice; it's just chance that when I got to this sentence it was time for "she."

welling up from deep within, demands a change. Not too soon. Just in time. Just before it is too late.

The Declaration follows up this set of thoughts by, in effect, repeating them. Here is the fifth sentence of the Declaration:

> *Such has been the patient sufferance of these Colonies; and such is now the necessity which constrains them to alter their former Systems of Government.*

"The patient sufferance" of putting up with evils suddenly yields to a feeling, often quite intense, that requires action. This is the movement that the Declaration describes. What else is a feeling of necessity, such as the text invokes, other than that ascent out of nausea into clearheaded resolve as one begins to plan for change? The colonists will change—they will alter—their systems of Government.

Alter: change. Like altering a dress so that it fits better. Such a small and quiet word for a revolution.

The Declaration can get away with such a small, quiet word because the real revolution has already happened—as one of life's turning points—when those who once suffered patiently suddenly see that he who is supposed to be a friend is in fact a foe. That experience is wrenching—painful but also forceful and dramatic. One picture clashes with another. A new reality displaces the old one. "It is their right; it is their duty" to throw off the old way of life. These clauses capture the true moment of revolution.

The right to revolution dwells in our survival instinct. It *must* kick in. Not right away, perhaps, but before it is too late. This is how we can reconcile the Declaration's optimism with its pessimism: people are unlikely to overuse revolution; but even when they are accustomed to harsh circumstances, there will come a point when the need arises to survive free from domination, and revolution will become simply necessary. Everyone has that survival instinct.

35

TYRANNY

OW HAS LIFE BROUGHT THE COLONISTS TO A TURNING POINT? The Declaration claims that the actions of Britain's king "evince a design" to reduce the colonists to subjection; the actions of the king have revealed him to be an enemy.

To prove that they do not act lightly, the colonists must give their reasons. How have they come to see the king of Great Britain as an enemy? To explain this, they will submit facts to the world. We have come to the heart of the Declaration:

> *The history of the present King of Great Britain is a history of repeated injuries and usurpations, all having in direct object the establishment of an absolute Tyranny over these States. To prove this, let Facts be submitted to a candid world.*

Indeed, we are all part of that candid world, and the Declaration asks us to be judges. We are to be judges of fact. Those "facts," the Declaration tells us, are supposed to prove "this." But what is that exactly? That King George has perpetrated "injuries and usurpations," a long list of which we are about to see? Yes. But not that alone.

The facts should also prove that King George is a would-be tyrant. He is not becoming a tyrant accidentally. He positively seeks to control all of life's major domains and to eradicate counterbalancing powers that might check him. He pursues a world where his powers unfold directly and completely. He intends to secure domination over the colonies.

Why do King George's intentions matter? Aren't the outcomes of his actions enough? Doesn't it suffice, as the basis of complaint, that he has inflicted "injuries and usurpations," regardless of why he did?

Not quite.

When a person injures others by accident, we can often educate him about his behavior so that he will stop. Knowledge can change the behavior of those who are well intentioned but do wrong out of ignorance. But when a person *intends* to do wrong—*intends*, for instance, to dominate others—the problem is profound. One would have to restructure radically the pattern of incentives facing the tyrant or change the whole structure of that person's internal motivations, not a job for ordinary political conversation. With an accidental tyrant, then, there's still a chance of bringing the tyrant around with words. With a purposeful tyrant, the time for talk is past.

The colonists' claim that they have reached one of life's critical turning points—the time has come for war. They need to prove, of course, that King George's actions add up to a pattern that spells "tyranny." They also need to prove that he has pursued that pattern of activity with self-awareness. Only this can justify their decision to abandon persuasion.

There's also something that the colonists need to prove about themselves. In this sixth sentence of the Declaration we find the text uncharacteristically repeating a word within a single sentence:

The history *of the present King of Great Britain is a* history *of repeated injuries and usurpations.*

"History" meant as "a time line of events" has revealed "history" meant as "a pattern." The repetition is meaningful. King George's behavior is of long duration, long enough to count, emphatically, as history. The colonists need to prove that they are not revolting too soon. Their patience is what the Declaration emphasizes. "History . . . history . . . ," it says. "Time has passed," we hear.

The colonists are not dealing with an accidental tyrant, with whom they might still try persuasion; nor are they imprudent. They have timed things just right. This is because they are good anticipators. While the colonists want to paint King George in the colors of a tyrant, they want to cast themselves as people who can look at the tumbling cascade of current events and *rightly* discern, as through a kaleidoscope, the future emerging from them.

Their list of complaints against King George is not just a description of what he has done but also a prediction about what he is becoming. Their list must prove their capacity to predict. The Declaration therefore seeks to prove four things to us:

1. that King George has sponsored harms to the colonists, in particular usurpations and injuries;
2. that the pattern of these harms spells "tyranny";
3. that King George is not generating this pattern by accident; he is becoming a tyrant on purpose; and
4. that the colonists are good anticipators; they know how to spot the warning signs of tyranny correctly.

How will the Declaration prove these four things? The text now presents the list of facts submitted to the candid world. There are eighteen of them, although one of them—the thirteenth—has itself nine subparts. Here they are:

1. *He has refused his Assent to Laws, the most wholesome and necessary for the public good.*
2. *He has forbidden his Governors to pass Laws of immediate and pressing importance, unless suspended in their operation till his Assent should be obtained; and when so suspended, he has utterly neglected to attend to them.*
3. *He has refused to pass other Laws for the accommodation of large districts of people, unless those people would relinquish the right of Representation in the Legislature, a right inestimable to them and formidable to tyrants only.*
4. *He has called together legislative bodies at places unusual, uncomfortable, and distant from the depository of their public Records, for the sole purpose of fatiguing them into compliance with his measures.*

5.   *He has dissolved Representative Houses repeatedly, for opposing with manly firmness his invasions on the rights of the people.*

6.   *He has refused for a long time, after such dissolutions, to cause others to be elected; whereby the Legislative powers, incapable of Annihilation, have returned to the People at large for their exercise; the State remaining in the mean time exposed to all the dangers of invasion from without, and convulsions within.*

7.   *He has endeavoured to prevent the population of these States; for that purpose obstructing the Laws for Naturalization of Foreigners; refusing to pass others to encourage their migrations hither, and raising the conditions of new Appropriations of Lands.*

8.   *He has obstructed the Administration of Justice by refusing his Assent to Laws for establishing Judiciary powers.*

9.   *He has made Judges dependent on his Will alone for the tenure of their offices, and the amount and payment of their salaries.*

10.   *He has erected a multitude of New Offices, and sent hither swarms of Officers to harass our people, and eat out their substance.*

11.   *He has kept among us, in times of peace, Standing Armies without the Consent of our legislatures.*

12.   *He has affected to render the Military independent of and superior to the Civil power.*

13.   *He has combined with others to subject us to a jurisdiction foreign to our constitution, and unacknowledged by our laws; giving his Assent to their Acts of pretended Legislation:*

13a.   *For Quartering large bodies of armed troops among us:*

13b.   *For protecting them, by a mock Trial, from punishment for any Murders which they should commit on the Inhabitants of these States:*

13c.   *For cutting off our Trade with all parts of the world:*

13d.   *For imposing Taxes on us without our Consent:*

13e.   *For depriving us in many cases, of the benefit of Trial by Jury:*

13f.   *For transporting us beyond Seas to be tried for pretended offences:*

13g.   *For abolishing the free System of English Laws in a neighbouring Province, establishing therein an Arbitrary government, and enlarging its Boundaries so as to render it at once an example and fit instrument for introducing the same absolute rule into these Colonies:*

13h.   *For taking away our Charters, abolishing our most valuable*

Laws, and altering fundamentally the Forms of our
Governments:

13i.   *For suspending our own Legislatures, and declaring themselves*
       invested with power to legislate for us in all cases whatsoever.

14.   *He has abdicated Government here, by declaring us out of his*
       Protection and waging War against us.

15.   *He has plundered our seas, ravaged our Coasts, burnt our towns,*
       and destroyed the lives of our people.

16.   *He is at this time transporting large Armies of foreign Mercenar-*
       ies to compleat the works of death, desolation and tyranny,
       already begun with circumstances of Cruelty & perfidy scarcely
       paralleled in the most barbarous ages, and totally unworthy the
       Head of a civilized nation.

17.   *He has constrained our fellow Citizens taken Captive on the high*
       Seas to bear Arms against their Country, to become the execution-
       ers of their friends and Brethren, or to fall themselves by their
       Hands.

18.   *He has excited domestic insurrections amongst us, and has*
       endeavoured to bring on the inhabitants of our frontiers, the mer-
       ciless Indian Savages, whose known rule of warfare, is an undis-
       tinguished destruction of all ages, sexes and conditions.

These eighteen facts spell "tyranny." Just how they do is the question
we will have to answer next.

FACTS?

I F WE SKIM THE DECLARATION, BRIEFLY ALIGHTING ON A FEW NOW hallowed phrases, we inevitably skip the list of grievances. Yet if there were no grievances, there would be no Declaration.

The Declaration has asked us to judge. What are we to judge if not these complaints? We have to ask: were the colonists right about King George?

Judging these complaints is not easy, however. The abstract principles of the Declaration are understandable without much reference to history—to the lived events of 1776. But these complaints?

At first it seems as if making our way through them is impossible without serious historical knowledge. And the signers did not help us here. As Stephen E. Lucas, a scholar of rhetoric, has pointed out, they left out the names, dates, and places of the specific episodes underlying each grievance. The signers made it hard to see the real histories behind these complaints.

But is that perhaps the point? Could it be that the Declaration's grievances are in fact composed to be nonspecific and general?

To see that this is the case, we have only to compare the grievances to any formal legal complaint. Here is one example: the 1999 indictment of a Pentagon employee, Linda Tripp, on wiretapping charges, which were later dismissed, for taping her phone conversations with Monica Lewinsky, the intern with whom President Clinton had an indelicate liaison:

STATE OF MARYLAND,

HOWARD COUNTY, TO WIT:

The Grand Jurors of the State Of Maryland for the body of Howard County, do on their oath present that

LINDA R. TRIPP,

late of said Howard County, did, on or about 22ⁿᵈ day of December, 1997, at Howard County aforesaid, wilfully and unlawfully intercept a wire communication in violation of Section 10-402(a), *Courts and Judicial Proceedings Article, Annotated Code of Maryland*, to wit: did tape record a telephone conversation between the said LINDA R TRIPP and Monica Lewinsky without the consent of the said Monica Lewinsky, a party to said conversation, contrary to the form of the Act of Assembly in such case made and provided and against the peace, government and dignity of the State.
(Illegal Interception, Section 10-402(a)(1), *Courts and Judicial Proceedings Article, Annotated Code of Maryland*)

SECOND COUNT

And the Jurors aforesaid, upon their oath aforesaid, do further present that the said

LINDA R. TRIPP,

did, between on or about 16ᵗʰ day of January, 1998 and on or about the 17ᵗʰ day of January, 1998, at Howard County aforesaid, through her agent, wilfully and unlawfully disclose the contents of the aforesaid wire communication to employees of *Newsweek* magazine and others, knowing and having reason to know that the information was obtained through the interception of a wire communication in violation of the Maryland Wiretapping and Electronic Surveillance Act, Sections 10-401, *et seq., Courts and Judicial Proceedings Article, Annotated Code of Maryland*, to wit: did authorize and instruct her agent and attorney, James Moody, Esquire, to play the contents of said unlawful tape recording for *Newsweek* magazine reporters and others, which was done by the said James Moody, Esquire at the offices of *Newsweek* magazine in Washington, District of Columbia, on or about the 17ᵗʰ day of January, 1998, contrary to the form of the Act of Assembly in such case made and provided and against the peace, government and dignity of the State.
(Illegal Disclosure of Intercepted Communication, Section 10-402(a)(2), *Courts & Judicial Proceedings Article, Annotated Code of Maryland*)

Stephen Montanarelli
State Prosecutor

The specificity of this indictment with regard to names, dates, places, and actions is intimidating. Adding all this information to each of the Declaration's grievances could have, of course, been done, but it would have taken a lot more words and turned the economical list into a cumbersome compendium. When, in 1776, the lawyer John Lind wrote a response to the Declaration to defend the king, it took him 110 pages to flesh out and then address the Declaration's complaints.

The Declaration asks the whole world to judge its grievances, but surely the signers did not expect everyone to undertake a major research project before making that judgment. Still, if not the facts of the matter, then what is there to judge?

Once again the Declaration forces us to confront general ideas. Even in its list of grievances, the Declaration directs us away from history and toward abstraction.

How, though, can a list of concrete complaints possibly direct our attention toward general ideas? We will have to dig into that list to see what it is really doing. Let's start, at random, with the third complaint:

> 3. He has refused to pass other Laws for the accommodation of large districts of people, unless those people would relinquish the right of Representation in the Legislature, a right inestimable to them and formidable to tyrants only.

If we put aside, for a moment, what we know about the history behind this grievance, we can see that the complaint raises an interesting problem of the relationship between specific experiences and general ideas. Does this complaint mean something specific like, for instance, that the king wouldn't pass laws to let people settle some specific plot of land, or does it mean something general, that, for instance, he generally would not pass laws that would have been helpful to a large number of people?

The latter general idea is what's at stake. King George refused to pass laws being requested by, for example, the residents of the Massachusetts Bay Colony, unless those residents were willing to relinquish the right to elect representatives. Because the Declaration does not name the residents of Massachusetts Bay, we know the text is not directing our attention toward them. Instead, it asks us to reflect in general on the relationship between legislation and public participation.

In exchange for taking care of public business, King George wanted ordinary people to stop participating in politics, the colonists assert. Although the king has allegedly injured a particular group of people—

the people of Massachusetts Bay— they don't matter here. The nature of their injury is what matters. As if we cared not about the murder victim but about the method of the killing: was it a knife or gun?*

So what *is* wrong with insisting that people give up their right to representation in the legislature in exchange for the passage of laws that they in fact desire? Maybe it's the most efficient way to get things done.

Such a deal might get the job done in the present, but then later, when a citizen no longer has someone to speak for her in corridors of power, she is lost. She won't be able to get her future business taken care of because she sacrificed one of her most important weapons: a voice speaking on her behalf when decisions are made. To take away a person's voice is to leave that person vulnerable. The efficiency is not worth the trade.

This complaint, Grievance 3, boils down, then, to this: King George was taking stances that undermined the sovereignty of the people, the ability of ordinary people to have a say in what their government does.

Once we see this, and if we look closely again at our list of complaints, we quickly realize that Grievance 3 is not the only one that provides evidence that King George was undermining rule by the people. In fact, Grievances 4, 5, and 6 also suggest that general idea.

Here they are again:

4. He has called together legislative bodies at places unusual, uncomfortable, and distant from the depository of their public Records, for the sole purpose of fatiguing them into compliance with his measures.

5. He has dissolved Representative Houses repeatedly, for opposing with manly firmness his invasions on the rights of the people.

6. He has refused for a long time, after such dissolutions, to cause others to be elected, whereby the Legislative powers, incapable of Annihilation, have returned to the People at large for their exercise; the State remaining in the mean time exposed to all the dangers of invasion from without, and convulsions within.

---

* Another example might be a case that reaches the Supreme Court, as in the 2003 decision *Lawrence v. Texas,* in which the lawyers and justices were not addressing the specific needs of John Lawrence and Tyron Garner but were dealing with more theoretical questions of what is demanded by the right of privacy.

Each of these complaints broadly describes an erosion of the power of the people. From them we can therefore also learn the opposite: what it takes to make people power real.

Why, for instance, does it matter that King George has made the legislative bodies meet at some distance from the depository of public records?

In that detail dwells an entire story about politics and political order. A depository of public records is where a legislature records its decisions. It puts down in writing what it has agreed on. For instance, that whiskey should be taxed at nine cents per gallon. Or that, perhaps, no one who lives upstream can build a dam that will prevent water from getting to the people who live downstream.

The purpose of keeping a universally accessible record of agreed-upon rules is to give people a way to check those rules when they come under dispute. Having written records makes it much easier to hold people to plans and commitments; this makes it easier to coordinate action. When a community uses a depository of public records to keep itself straight about what it has agreed, it is trying to live by the rule of law.

In complaining that King George frustrates access to the depository of public records, the colonists imply that they want to live by the rule of law but that the king is obstructing their effort.

Professional philosophers have trouble pinning down the precise meaning of "the rule of law." They do agree, though, on some of its features. You need to know what the rules are before you act. The rules can't change without a reasonable effort being made to alert you to the change. Also, your actions need to be judged after the fact by whatever laws were in place and had been made publicly known before you acted. The rule of law protects us from arbitrary punishment.

The important point with regard to Grievance 4 is that we can't have the rule of law without a capacity to make laws publicly known. It's not enough to pass rules and to use them to judge people. If the legislature hasn't ever told anyone what the rules are, the system of rules is by definition unfair. A public depository and other institutions like it are fundamental to setting up a rule-of-law system in the first place.

When we looked at Grievance 3, we saw that it consisted mainly of a complaint that King George was undermining rule by the people. But in the process of looking at a handful of related complaints—Grievances 4,

5, and 6—we learn that they identify another problem as well. The colonists also complain that King George is preventing the healthy establishment of the rule of law.

Noticing this makes visible the general idea behind two more of the facts on our list: Grievances 1 and 2. Here they are again:

> *1. He has refused his Assent to Laws, the most wholesome and necessary for the public good.*
>
> *2. He has forbidden his Governors to pass Laws of immediate and pressing importance, unless suspended in their operation till his Assent should be obtained; and when so suspended, he has utterly neglected to attend to them.*

King George, the colonists are saying, is causing the legal system to break down completely. At stake are not trivial laws but laws that are "the most wholesome and necessary for the public good." The violence done by King George to the rule of law and popular sovereignty is preventing the colonists from pursuing the common good.

We are beginning to see how this list of facts works. It is by no means random, was not drawn up without thought or purpose, but is organized in clusters, each of which relates to a general principle about how politics should work. Here are our first two: We should have the rule of law. The people should have a say in their government.

King George is a tyrant because he violates these principles, and the list of grievances in the Declaration provides a definition of tyranny. This definition, not the facts of the matter, is what we are in a position to judge.

Before we can judge that definition, though, we will have to work out the rest of its details.

LIFE HISTORIES

BEHIND EACH COMPLAINT IN THE DECLARATION LIE SPECIFIC events, which require the work of a historian to access, and general ideas, which any reader can work out. There are also life histories. These, too, any reader can summon up.

What do I mean by life histories?

People were living through the experiences captured by these grievances. Without knowing specifically who was living through each case, we can still imagine something of the shape of the human experience buried beneath each one.

Let's use Grievance 4, about the public depositories, as an example. Here it is again:

> *4. He has called together legislative bodies at places unusual, uncomfortable, and distant from the depository of their public Records, for the sole purpose of fatiguing them into compliance with his measures.*

Imagine a small gray gable house of pinewood, with a pitched roof and an overhanging second story, its simple horizontal lines punched through by three chamber windows underneath a second, small oak gable. The first floor is one large room serving as both parlor and hall; its two windows and low door line up beneath the windows above. A lean-to

The following is a LIST *of* STAGES *that run from* BOSTON, *and also of the* PLACES *from which they start.*

ALBANY Mail Stage goes through Worcester, Brookfield and Northampton to Albany ; sets off from white horse tavern, Newbury street, Boston, every Mon. and Thurf. morning at 6 o'clock, and arrives at Albany every Thurf. and Mon. noon.

days at 4 o'clock afternoon ; leaves Plymouth every Mon. and Fri. 6 o'clock morning, and arrives in Boston at 4 o'clock afternoon same days.

SALEM Mail Stage starts from Major King's tavern every day in the week, (Sundays excepted) at 3 o'clock after-

This 1799 almanac lists journey times between various points and Boston. The mail stage from Salem to Boston takes twenty hours.

housing a leatherworker's shop nestles against the house. Not many timber houses built in Boston at the end of the seventeenth century survived the spate of fires that periodically razed part of the colonial port, but this one has passed into a second generation. It's now sometime circa 1774.

Imagine dusk. The front door opens out into a very small well-kept garden, which in turn opens directly onto a sidewalk, one of the first in the colonies. We can see a whale oil lantern burning in the first-floor window to the left of the door. Inside sitting at a small oval-shaped walnut table are a man, in his late twenties, and his wife.

Imagine, then, their conversation. He's just told her he must leave early in the morning to ride to Salem for a meeting of the general assembly. Perhaps she asks him not to go, expressing worries such as Abigail Adams, finding herself in similar circumstances, conveyed to John: "I am cumbered about and scarcely know which way to turn." Or "I find myself unequal to the difficulties." Perhaps her husband curses Gage's decision to make Salem the seat of government, as John Adams did in his letters to Abigail: "Who knows who suggested this wrong-headed, and iniquitous measure?" Together, feeling themselves under duress, they make plans for how to man their leatherworks in his absence.

On it goes. . . . Behind each of the complaints are stories of specific people chafing under the arbitrary exercise of power.

And maybe being asked to meet at an inconvenient location was no more than an annoyance, but how about Grievance 17?

17. He has constrained our fellow Citizens taken Captive on the high Seas to bear Arms against their Country, to become the executioners of their friends and Brethren, or to fall themselves by their Hands.

Poster of an eighteenth-century ballad in which Black Ey'd Susan laments the disappearance of Sweet William, pressed into service.

For this one, we have to imagine at least two locations. First, a ship on the Atlantic, maybe a whaler, call it the brig *Polley*. It's been out for nearly a year, having sailed from Nantucket to the South American coast. On its way home it crosses paths with a British navy man-of-war, call this the HMS *Harwich*. The *Harwich* fires at the *Polley* and brings her to. Soldiers board and "strictly search" the brig, arresting all the common sailors on the whaler, though not harpoonists and the like, since they are irreplaceable experts who are legally protected from impressment. The common sailor William, whom we are watching, is young, nineteen, but he is already on his fourth whaling expedition. He has a young wife, Susan, in Sherburne, on Nantucket's sandy shores, a town that is desolate in the annual absence of its many mariners. She spends her time visiting other women whose men are gone; underneath the unending rounds of gossip, a general nervousness circulates. The women all know the same facts: in the face of the huge mammals they chase, the whalers are at best frail; the elements are treacherous; there are "sudden and unforeseen accidents of wind"; and then there is the British navy. Other men begin to return home, and William does not come. Nearly home, he has been arrested by the British; he is, after all, a British subject and therefore a fair target, so the British admiralty reasons, for impressment. Now he finds himself impressed to serve in their navy, shackled when the man-of-war puts into port. William's absence stretches and, without word from him, without the earnings from his journey, Susan, distraught, must seek credit from relatives to pay her rent, to buy the beef, flour, and molasses that she needs. Only after months does she at last receive a letter from William telling her his fate.

Why does any particular fact count as evidence that King George was trying to develop a tyranny? In order to figure out what's wrong with each thing that King George is accused of doing, it helps to inhabit each fact, to live inside it. To use our imaginations to experience its details.

This narrative about William's impressment is a story of suffering; the facts that float to the surface reveal abuse and vulnerability. Grievance 17 asserts, in effect, that King George is the source not merely of irritations and annoyances; his agents violate people's fundamental rights.

Yet all the complaints allege what we would now call a rights violation. Each complaint helps to refine just that idea. The Declaration's definition of tyranny brings along with it a catalog of rights that should be considered sacred.

For each complaint, then, we need to figure out the specific nature of the rights violation. We've done that already with Grievance 3. We found that it belonged to a cluster. Similarly, it's easier to see the specific problem in Grievance 17 if we look at Grievances 14, 15, 16, and 18 at the same time.

Here they are again:

> 14. *He has abdicated Government here, by declaring us out of his Protection and waging War against us.*
>
> 15. *He has plundered our seas, ravaged our Coasts, burnt our towns, and destroyed the lives of our people.*
>
> 16. *He is at this time transporting large Armies of foreign Mercenaries to compleat the works of death, desolation and tyranny, already begun with circumstances of Cruelty & perfidy scarcely par-*

alleled in the most barbarous ages, and totally unworthy the Head
of a civilized nation.

17. He has constrained our fellow Citizens taken Captive on the
high Seas to bear Arms against their Country, to become the execution-
ers of their friends and Brethren, or to fall themselves by their Hands.

18. He has excited domestic insurrections amongst us, and has
endeavoured to bring on the inhabitants of our frontiers, the merci-
less Indian Savages, whose known rule of warfare, is an undistin-
guished destruction of all ages, sexes and conditions.

All of these grievances are complaints about war. King George has begun
to make war on the colonists. What's more, his approach to war is barbarous. Even in war there is room to respect rights, but the king infringes here,
too. He is an aggressor. He is conducting his war not only directly but also
by forcing some colonists, impressed or kidnapped, to fight against their
own people, by hiring foreign soldiers, mercenaries from distant Germany,
men who fight for the sake of money, not self-defense or honor, to direct the
full force of their professional arts of war against the colonial amateurs, and
by inciting Native American tribes and slaves to fight the colonists, a form
of conflict that could be expected to be particularly bitter, given the forms
of oppression employed by the colonists against the native populations and
African inhabitants of the colonies.

Grievances 1–6 are about the fact that the king was both undermining
the colonists' effort to pursue the common good through the rule of law
and refusing to take the will of the people seriously. Grievances 14–18 all,
in one way or another, charge that he has disturbed the peace and broken
the laws of war. Thus we add another detail to the definition of tyranny.
Tyrants do not respect the laws of war.

PLAGUES

EACH GRIEVANCE IN THE DECLARATION IS IN EFFECT A STORY IN miniature. Robbed of its original names, dates, and places, each ceases to be a historical story and becomes more like a myth or fable. Each little tale makes a general point. Taken together, all make the same two points: here is the definition of a tyrant; here is the kind of protection every human life needs.

The method behind this list stands revealed in Grievance 10. Here it is again:

> *10. He has erected a multitude of New Offices, and sent hither swarms of Officers to harass our people, and eat out their substance.*

If one had to sum up this complaint, what word would capture it? Perhaps "harassment"? This seems to be its central term. Like Grievances 11 and 12, which follow it, this complaint, Grievance 10, is basically about a situation of vulnerability, a situation where someone has power over you that you can't effectively combat. Here are Grievances 11 and 12:

> *11. He has kept among us, in times of peace, Standing Armies without the Consent of our legislatures.*
> *12. He has affected to render the Military independent of and superior to the Civil power.*

In Grievances 11 and 12 the concern is clearly that military power will make people vulnerable. It may at first seem as if the same kind of power is at stake in Grievance 10—after all, Grievance 10 talks about "swarms of Officers"—but the officers in this complaint are tax collectors, not military personnel.

Here we can see a touch of hyperbole in how the Declaration treats its complaints. While tax collectors and military personnel do both have the capacity to make a population vulnerable, they are not equivalent threats. What's more, there were only about fifty of the objectionable new customs officers throughout the colonies. Not exactly swarms. The word "swarms" is alarmist or incendiary. We are reminded that the document served also as propaganda; it had the job, among its other tasks, of firing colonial opinion against the British. And the signers were concerned not merely with their contemporaries. They thought about future generations, too. As John Adams put it, "Posterity must hear a Story that shall make their Ears to Tingle."

Yet there is more to say about the phrase "swarms of officers." Something recognizable reverberates in that phrase. Read slowly, listen closely, and you'll hear overtones of the Old Testament, of a tale from the Hebrew Bible. The relevant echo is a story about swarms of locusts.

Exodus relates how the Israelites escape from bondage in Egypt only after Yahweh inflicts ten plagues on the Egyptians to convince a tyrannical Pharaoh to let the Israelites go. The eighth plague is the swarm of locusts. Here's the story:

> Yahweh says to Pharaoh, "If you refuse to let them go, I will bring locusts into your country tomorrow. They will cover the face of the ground so that it cannot be seen. They will devour what little you have left after the hail, including every tree that is growing in your fields. They will fill your houses and those of all your officials and all the Egyptians—something neither your fathers nor your forefathers have ever seen from the day they settled in this land till now."

The swarms of tax collectors and the standing armies are like the locusts, and the Declaration's list of grievances is something like the collection of plagues in Exodus.

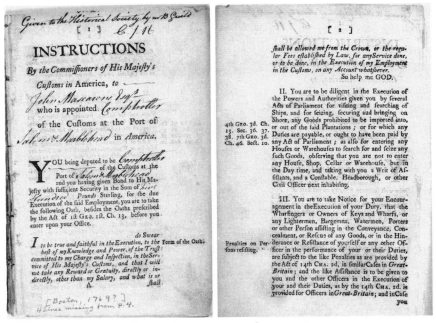

Instruction to customs officers, 1768.

There is a critical difference, of course. In Exodus the plagues are punishments visited on Pharaoh for being a tyrant; in the Declaration the plagues are instead the tyrant's own work.* Yet the stories nonetheless function in a parallel fashion. There is some connection to history in each set of tales, but that history is buried deep. Each set of stories more importantly describes the type of trouble that arises in a land when a tyrant reigns.

The stories are not really histories, then, but symbols, if not fables. They make it easy to remember general ideas. The general idea that we are asked to remember in Grievance 10 is that tyrants routinely harass their populations and make them vulnerable.

Grievances 10, 11, and 12 all have to do with King George unleashing powers on the colonists against whom the colonists have little defense—customs officers, tax collectors, and military personnel, all introduced through policies like the Sugar and the Stamp Acts, which imposed burdensome taxes on sugar and paper, and the Quartering Acts, which

---

* Thomas Paine explicitly refers to King George III as "Pharaoh" in *Common Sense*, as did a minister, a Mr. Duffil, whose sermon John Adams heard on May 17, 1776, as Adams reported to Abigail Adams in a letter of the same date.

required civilians to house military personnel. The crown's bureaucrats and soldiers, the Declaration warns, will fill the colonists' houses, devouring what they have.

Tyranny introduces vulnerability to our lives by overexposing us to state power. This is the next detail in the definition of a tyrant.

39

PORTRAIT OF A TYRANT

T HE PORTRAIT OF THE TYRANT SKETCHED BY THE DECLARATION'S
list of grievances is nearly complete. We have only four grievances
left to consider: Grievances 7–9 and 13. Grievance 13 is on its own nearly
as long as the rest of the list. Consequently, it will demand more of us. But
we can dispatch the others quickly enough. They suffice to complete the
portrait.

Here are Grievances 8 and 9:

> *8. He has obstructed the Administration of Justice, by refusing
> his Assent to Laws for establishing Judiciary powers.*
> *9. He has made Judges dependent on his Will alone, for the ten-
> ure of their offices, and the amount and payment of their salaries.*

With these grievances the colonists complain that King George is
destroying the judicial system. We can now see that with their complaints
the colonists have touched on all the functions of government: the legislative or lawmaking function, the executive function responsible for tax
collection and the military, and here the judicial function. In this picture
of tyranny we've cleverly been given an outline of constitutional theory.

And what about Grievance 7, our second-to-last complaint? Here
it is:

7. He has endeavoured to prevent the population of these States; for that purpose obstructing the Laws for Naturalization of Foreigners; refusing to pass others to encourage their migrations hither, and raising the conditions of new Appropriations of Lands.

King George, the colonists allege, was limiting immigration.

Why did they care? Did the colonists feel isolated and consequently desire larger communities? Even the largest colony, Virginia, had a population of only about half a million people. Although that was a large number for the time, it still meant that much of the colony was sparsely populated. Or perhaps they were trying to build up their numbers so that they could wield more power against Native Americans?

Both of these reasons mattered. But the colonists also cared about prosperity. They wanted to see more farming and more trading. These activities would bring them wealth. In brief, the colonists were interested in economic growth and, in order to have growth, they needed more people. They saw the king as robbing them of the opportunity to grow strong enough to come into their own as economies and societies. Societies under the thumb of tyrants do not grow prosperous. This is what they are telling us.

And this completes their portrait of the tyrant. According to the Declaration, tyrants

> undermine the common good (Grievances 1–2),
> undermine the rule of law and the sovereignty of the people in legislatures (Grievances 3–6),
> block material prosperity and growth (Grievance 7),
> undermine the judicial system (Grievances 8–9),
> harass and make their people vulnerable (Grievances 10–13),
> and even make war on their own people (Grievances 14–18).

That rounds out the definition of tyranny that the Declaration has been drawing up.

Yet we are not done. There is still Grievance 13 to consider. What could the colonists possibly have left to complain about after all that has already been said?

40

THE THIRTEENTH WAY OF
LOOKING AT A TYRANT

W E DON'T NEED THE THIRTEENTH GRIEVANCE IN ORDER TO grasp the Declaration's definition of tyranny, and yet it is the longest. It must serve some special function. To identify that function, we'll have to lay the grievance out again and look at it closely. Here it is:

13. He has combined with others to subject us to a jurisdiction foreign to our constitution, and unacknowledged by our laws; giving his Assent to their Acts of pretended Legislation:

13a. For Quartering large bodies of armed troops among us:

13b. For protecting them, by a mock Trial, from punishment for any Murders which they should commit on the Inhabitants of these States:

13c. For cutting off our Trade with all parts of the world:

13d. For imposing Taxes on us without our Consent:

13e. For depriving us in many cases, of the benefit of Trial by Jury:

13f. For transporting us beyond Seas to be tried for pretended offences:

13g. For abolishing the free System of English Laws in a neighbouring Province, establishing therein an Arbitrary government, and enlarging its Boundaries so as to render it at once an example and fit instrument for introducing the same absolute rule into these Colonies:

13h. For taking away our Charters, abolishing our most valuable Laws, and altering fundamentally the Forms of our Governments:

13i. For suspending our own Legislatures, and declaring themselves invested with power to legislate for us in all cases whatsoever.

In Grievance 13 many of the subparts repeat complaints that are also made about King George in the other grievances. In fact, they helpfully make explicit the principles of good government—for instance, no taxation without representation—that in the other grievances are largely implicit. They are not hard to understand.

Grievance 13 contains only two confusing details. Who are the "others" with whom King George has "combined"? And what is this jurisdiction to which King George, together with those "others," has subjected the colonists?

Some history here becomes necessary. King George, in addition to directly injuring the colonies, also handed power over them to other people who were treating the colonists in an equally tyrannical fashion. So the colonists argue. The "others" with whom King George combined were the members of the British Parliament, Britain's lawmaking body. Nine years earlier, in 1767, Parliament, with the King's approval, established the American Board of Customs Commissioners, whose members were to live in the colonies and regulate everything that had to do with trade and tax. This was the new jurisdiction about which the colonists complain.

The powers of this board and of the commissioners were sweeping, just as the colonists claim here. They were not constrained even by traditional English limits on governmental power. These new bodies were, for instance, doing away with the right to trial by jury.

This new jurisdiction, the colonists say, is foreign to their constitution. This is the only place in the Declaration where they directly reveal themselves to be thinking in terms of constitutions.

By "constitution" the colonists more specifically mean not a single document but the "free System of English laws," to which they refer in section h of Grievance 13. In that section, the colonists complain about the Quebec Act, by which the king enlarged Canada, established toleration of Catholicism, and restored French civil law to function alongside the British common law tradition in criminal law. The colonists considered the presence of French civil law an implicit threat to the endurance of the common law tradition, a customary constitution consisting of the "free System of English laws." (We are reminded, too, by this grievance how strong the anti-Catholic bias was in the new nation.)

In Grievance 13, which in effect combines all the grievances that precede it into one, we get the picture of a king who is not merely in his own inept and scattershot action—and perhaps merely accidentally—failing to meet the standards of good government; he is instead working systematically with others to establish entire legal regimes that, as the colonists see it, are opposed to good government. Their name for what they say King George destroys is constitutionalism.

Grievance 13 is not merely about the king but also about Parliament. Why don't the colonists explicitly name that body here? For some reason, even though Parliament was passing the laws to which they objected, they didn't wish for that body of men to stand formally accused. Once again the Declaration forces us to pay attention to its silences.

The colonists must have wanted to keep the focus on King George. In their choice, we discern their recognition of how much more rhetorically potent it is to concentrate on a single hated symbol of authority. The king himself thus becomes singly a figure for tyranny. He also becomes an emblem for the destruction of constitutions.

King George, Grievance 13 tells us, is the Anti-Constitution.

41

THE USE AND ABUSE OF HISTORY

THE LIST OF GRIEVANCES IN THE DECLARATION OF INDEPEN-
dence limns the nature of tyranny. We can and should judge that
general sketch. This the Declaration makes easy to do.

Does it count as tyranny if a ruler undermines the common good, the
rule of law, the sovereignty of the people, and the judicial system; hinders
material prosperity and growth; harasses the populace; makes people
vulnerable to injury; and makes war on his own people? Yes, indeed. It
also counts as an erosion of constitutionalism.

The signers of the Declaration did not, however, vote on a dictionary
entry by Jefferson about tyranny. They voted on a document charging,
specifically, that King George of Great Britain was becoming a tyrant.
Now that we know what a tyrant is, can we judge whether the Declaration
fairly applies the label "tyrant" to King George? This we can't do without
a deeper knowledge of the history.

Without historical knowledge, we can get a general idea of what the
colonists were complaining about, but each of those charges reflects a
response to some very specific policy action taken by King George. If we
are to judge King George, we must know what those policy actions were.

This presents us with a quandary.

I promised that one can successfully read the Declaration of Independence by using only the Declaration's own words, a willing mind, and life
experience. This minimal equipment, I suggested, should be enough to

make sense of the Declaration. But the expertise of a professional historian is necessary for a full understanding of the grievances. What, then, could possibly be the value in trying to make sense of the Declaration while drawing as little as possible on such expertise?

Here is the answer. If we put history to one side, we get an unrelenting focus on the structure of the Declaration's argument. And only by focusing on that structure can we see what is truly most important about this text. It is this: the Declaration teaches people how to do the very thing that it argues that everyone has the capacity to do, namely, make political judgments. By focusing on the structure of its argument—on *how* the Declaration says what it says and on *what* it makes happen for each reader—we can come to a very deep understanding of human equality.

The Declaration presents the claim that people are equal in all having the ability to judge whether they and their communities are on a course toward or away from happiness. It therefore lays claim to a certain kind of intellectual equality among us all. Not that all people are equally smart, but that all are equally engaged in a project of political judgment. What's more, there is good reason to take each person's judgment of the matter seriously—because each is the best judge of his own happiness.

Now, does the Declaration merely argue this point? Does it merely describe what makes human beings equal? Not at all. The Declaration also acts its main point out.

The Declaration shows us a group of people, the colonists, walking through the steps of making a judgment about whether their community is moving in a positive or a negative direction and, if the latter, what sort of action to turn things around is justified. Those people lay out some principles for judgment. They search the world for facts and patterns. They use their principles to judge the pattern of the facts. On the basis of that judgment, they determine a course of action.

The Declaration is, then, a model of political judgment. As such, it is a teaching tool. When we read the Declaration, we watch political judgment in action. Because we have been asked to judge, we also participate in that political judgment. Best of all, the text itself teaches us, by example, how to activate the kind of intellectual capacity that it claims we all have. That's the aspect of the Declaration that you don't need any history to understand. And this is fundamental.

If the Declaration is right that all people are created equal—in the sense of all being participants in the project of political judgment—then all people *should* be able to read or listen to the Declaration, understand the work that it is doing, and carry on similar work on their own account with no more help in unleashing their capacities than can be provided by the example of the Declaration itself. This is the hypothesis of the Declaration.

The Declaration tests its own hypothesis. It is constructed to prove that its claim about human equality is true. If all people can read or listen to it and understand how political judgment works in the Declaration without aids beyond the Declaration itself—which is to say, regardless of whether they have gone to school, or how much history they have learned—then the Declaration is right about human equality.

We don't want historical questions, important as they are, to obscure this fundamental feature of the text.

42

DASHBOARDS

T HE DECLARATION TAKEN AS A WHOLE IS A MODEL OF POLITICAL judgment. That is one of the most important things to remember about it.

The list of grievances is central to that work of judgment. This is true not merely because in that list we see the colonists judging the king. Their grievances are important for another reason, too. We're not yet quite done ferreting out the list's contribution to the Declaration's argument. We need to know what the list as a whole contributes, as distinct from what each individual grievance adds.

Above, I said the colonists were trying to prove four things:

(1) that King George had sponsored harms to them, in particular usurpations and injuries;
(2) that the pattern of these harms spelled "tyranny";
(3) that King George was not generating this pattern by accident but becoming a tyrant on purpose; and
(4) that the colonists were good anticipators; they knew how to spot the warning signs of tyranny.

We have seen how the list supports the first three points. But what about the fourth? How does the list prove that the colonists were good anticipators, that they could see the future?

First off, we have to admit that it's very hard to see the future. We all strain to see what is over the rise, ahead of us on our journey. How much better off we would be if we could tell that the road will soon drop down into a swamp, or simply turn off gently into a sunbathed meadow. When I brought up the need to see the future before, I said that the subject reminded me of the inhabitants of the village of Sighet in Elie Wiesel's book *Night*. They keep hearing reports that Germans are killing Jews but don't believe them. Because they don't believe the rumors—rumors that in their case conveyed something unimaginable—they are not able to assemble the puzzle that might have helped them see where things were headed. Consequently, nearly all the inhabitants of the village are killed.

When people are successful anticipators, they are able to identify all the different pieces of evidence that provide indications of what is coming and to bring these pieces of evidence together into a single, coherent picture. They put the puzzle together.

If the colonists are good anticipators, then they are good at doing such puzzles. In fact, their list of grievances is a puzzle successfully assembled. And we already know what picture it makes: the portrait of a tyrant.

Being a good anticipator involves more, though, than merely putting the pieces of the puzzle together. When you buy a jigsaw puzzle, someone else has already supplied the pieces, but real prognosticators have to figure out which details—which data points—amid the crush of human events are relevant to the puzzle in the first place.

This they do by asking questions.

If we know what a tyrant is, then good government must be the opposite. Good government must involve pursuing the common good, cultivating and protecting the rule of law and the sovereignty of the people, encouraging material prosperity and growth, and providing access to justice, security, and peace for the citizens.

Suddenly, when we see that the list of grievances implicitly contains a picture of good government, in addition to the picture of tyranny that's right on the surface, we realize that the list is something like a dashboard, say, in a car or an airplane.

The many different gauges on a dashboard indicate how the vehicle is faring with respect, for instance, to fuel, speed, heat, and tire pressure. As I drive, I keep checking all these gauges to make sure things are on track; it's the best method I have for getting ahead of serious trouble.

In just the same way, in providing this list of facts about what King George has done, the Declaration gives us readings from gauges that citizens can use to judge whether their society is humming along with good governance or plunging toward tyranny.

The colonists' gauges were questions like these:

Do our leaders pursue the common good?
Do they support the rule of law and the sovereignty of the people?
Do they cultivate material prosperity and growth?
Do they ensure access to justice?
Do they ensure access to security?
Do they ensure access to peace?

The colonists were asking questions such as these, and their answers took the shape of the complaints on their list. To know where our society is headed, we too could ask and answer such questions.

In addition to everything else it is, then, the list of grievances is a dashboard. We can use it to see where we are going if we remember to ask the questions that it is answering. This is how the Declaration proves that the colonists were good anticipators. They knew what sorts of questions to ask in order to figure out where they were headed.

ON POTLUCKS

THE COLONISTS ASKED QUESTIONS ABOUT WHERE THEIR COMMU-
nity was headed. The answers to those questions became their list
of grievances. The thought that behind the list of grievances lies a group
of people trying to see the future leads us to our final question about the
list: How exactly did it get made?

This may sound like a trick question—obviously, Jefferson just sat
down and wrote it out, no?—but, in fact, the answer is not so easy. The
answer will, however, bring us to the third facet of equality presented in
the Declaration.

When Jefferson sat down in June of 1776 to draft the Declaration,
he didn't at that point write to all the colonies to ask for their opinions
about King George. By the time the colonists tasked Jefferson with a first
draft, they had already, by talking to each other, completed their analysis
of the king.

How did the colonists come to understand their situation? This question merits some reflection.

Imagine again that husband and wife in the timber house with the
leatherwork shop in the Boston dusk. Remember how the wife said
to the husband, "I scarcely know which way to turn." Although she
responded strongly to the requirement that her husband travel to Salem
for general assembly meetings, the two of them were living through just

one piece of the puzzle. Only one of King George's actions was directly affecting them.

The lonely young wife in Nantucket whose husband was captured at sea and pressed into service in King George's navy lived in a different town. She didn't know the first couple. She too lived on a single puzzle piece. And I set these two stories both in Massachusetts. But what about the stories in New Jersey and Virginia and Georgia? Young men

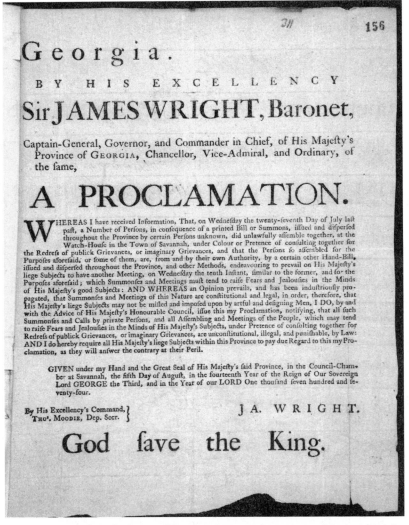

A 1774 Georgia broadside issued by Georgia's royal governor, Sir James Wright, baronet, promising punishment for those who assemble to discuss their grievances against the king.

THE Freeholders and other Inhabitants of the Town of *Boston*, qualified as the Law directs, are hereby notified to meet at *Faneuil*-Hall, on Wednesday the Twenty-first Instant, at Nine o'Clock in the Forenoon, being the Time to which the Town-Meeting held on the Sixth Instant stands adjourned, in Order to take the Sense of the Town relative to the following Bill, *Viz.*

Anno Regni Regis GEORGII *Tertii Tertio.*

An Act for making more effectual an Act, Intitled, An Act directing how Rates and Taxes to be granted by the General Assembly ; as also County, Town and Precinct Rates, shall be assessed and collected.

A 1763 call to the townspeople in Boston to assemble to discuss
their views of a new bill of King George III.

were pressed into service in the British navy when they set sail from those shores as well.

Only when people—each with an experience of one aspect of King George's rule—could gather to talk about how life was going could they, together, assemble the puzzle. And talk they did from north to south, even in Georgia, not generally thought of as a hotbed of revolution. Georgia's royalist governor, for instance, issued a proclamation to warn people against assembling to discuss their grievances against the king.

What's more, the Continental Congress encouraged this talk. In October 1775 it voted to gather up information about British hostilities. Its journal records this decision on October 18.

> Resolved, that a just and well authenticated account of the hostilities committed by the ministerial troops and navy in America since last March, be collected, with proper evidence of the truth of the facts related, the number and value of the buildings destroyed by them, also the number and value of the vessels inward and outward bound, which have been seized by them since that period, as near as the number and value can be ascertained; also the stock taken by them from different parts of the Continent.

Members of Congress began frenetically writing letters to their home "countries" to seek such information—John Adams, for instance, wrote four such letters in one day. Even more importantly, Congress put an ad in the paper. On November 6, 1775, the *Pennsylvania Packet* printed the texts of Congress's resolution and this additional notice: Congress "request[s] the Printers of the several public papers in the United Colonies to insert the above [resolution] for three or four weeks successively, and all persons possessed of any facts relative to, or that may throw light on the above subject, to transmit the same to them as early as possible."

This list of grievances was built out of much conversation. It reflects time spent comparing notes about experiences with the king's officers. This list, in other words, is an example of the kind of knowledge that a community produces, when a multitude of eyes and ears collect evidence and collaborate through conversation to figure out what it all means.

Everyone has a stake in the full picture. There is no one heroic private investigator behind this list. Only a greater community whose members are willing to share what they know with each other.

"When in the course of human events," the Declaration begins. The colonists worked together to discern the course of human events. Even more important, they were able to see the course of human events *because* they worked together. Their willingness to be in community with one another and to build a shared understanding out of the contributions of many people, who are equals in the collective work of coming to see and understand, preceded their ability to recognize themselves as a free people facing a tyrant. Community and equality came before independence.

I, however, respectfully solicit the correspondence of the learned and ingenious, such as think it not beneath them to communicate, through this humble but extensive channel, a little of that abundant knowledge they possess, for the instruction or entertainment of their less learned fellow-citizens. I also solicit all my readers to point out every thing they disapprove in this Almanac, and wherein it might have been more pleasing to them, that those defects may, if possible, be remedied in a future one. All communications intended for the improvement of my Almanac, may be addressed to me, and lodged with the publishers respectively early enough to come to my hands previous to the beginning of the year preceding that for which they are intended.

The author of this 1798 almanac seeks advice from both expert and lay readers.

In developing their list of complaints against King George and in coming to understand their situation, the colonists became the free people capable of self-government that, with their Declaration, they asserted themselves to be.

Wasn't the consolidation of this list guided, though, by leading men? Yes, there were leaders in these conversations. Yet each leader's understanding of the grievances in his community emerged from countless streams of conversation flowing together from every colony. Democratic conversations need experts, but in addition to expertise they need context and perspective. They need, in other words, social knowledge, which everyone possesses.

This list of grievances reminds me of a potluck, an age-old metaphor used by philosophers to explain why there can be wisdom in the crowd.*

Simple though it seems, think about how a potluck works. You're invited to bring your best dish. Someone brings brownies. Someone else brings fresh lettuce from a garden. Another person brings tomatoes and carrots. Someone else brings homemade ice cream. Another person brings tortillas and beans. Another person brings some roast chicken. Still another person brings a variety of cheeses. And then you have a menu that reads like this:

Appetizer: cheese tray
Main course: burritos with beans, chicken, and cheese; salad
Dessert: brownie sundaes

All the different ingredients can be organized into a menu with a clear structure. All the different ingredients are necessary to achieve a balanced meal. And the whole is excellent, though any part would not have sufficed.

Behind this list in the Declaration, we have to imagine conversations that have a similar effect. People pass complaints on to each other; there's

---

* I take this image from Aristotle, who in book 3 of the *Politics* (1281a40–b10) argues, "The many, of whom none is individually an excellent man, nevertheless can, when joined together, be better than those [the excellent few], not as individuals but all together, just as potluck dinners can be better than those provided at one man's expense. For, there being many, each person possesses a constituent part of virtue and practical reason, and when they have come together, the multitude is like a single person, yet many-footed and many-handed and possessing many sense-capacities, so it is likewise as regards to its multiplicity of character and its mind. This is why the many judge better in regard to musical works and those of the poets, for some judge a particular aspect, while all of them judge the whole."

a whole hodgepodge mess of them; these are sorted and organized; some are related to each other; some express the same problem in different ways. By focusing on the patterns in the complaints, the colonists come to see the core ideas underneath them: King George undermines the common good, undermines the rule of law and sovereignty of the people, blocks material prosperity and growth, denies justice, harasses and makes vulnerable, and wages war against the colonists. A jumble of complaints turns into a picture of tyranny clearly anatomized. All the perspectives are necessary to form the whole.

How this list of grievances was built is therefore yet another memorable, even moving, feature of the Declaration. To claim that there is beauty in this feature, too, may once again seem strange. Yet I think the beauty resides in two things: the conversion of particular, concrete details into general ideas, on the one hand, and on the other, the idea of equality inherent in the potluck approach to knowledge.

Instead of turning to experts to write a report, or asking a commission to review a situation, the colonists relied on ordinary citizens in conversational networks to generate analyses of the course of human events. This is a very democratic approach to knowledge and intelligence. That confidence in the capacity of ordinary people to know enough to see where their world is heading is jaw-dropping. Once again the text's optimism about human potential shines through.

All the colonists were equals in the project of coming to understand their situation. This is the third facet of equality: we can strengthen our individual and collective capacity to analyze the relation between present and future by drawing everyone into the work of understanding the course of human events. We can build a collective intelligence superior to what any individual or even a closed group of experts can achieve, by developing egalitarian approaches to knowledge cultivation.

Of course, to say everyone is an equal participant in the project of coming to see the course of human events does not mean that everyone is equally good at it. Only that everyone has the capacity to pick up some bit of information, some observation, which is relevant to the whole picture, and which no one else will have noticed. Some people will pick up more than others, but everyone picks up something. Experts have a crucial role to play within the larger democratic community, but the value of their contributions should not obscure the fact that contributions are needed from every quarter to achieve a complete view.

The Declaration's list of grievances rests on implicit recognition that human beings are sponges, taking in information about their environment. Some are better sponges than others, but all of us are absorbent.

All people are created equal, then, in that we are all born to absorb. Recognizing this fact, we can cultivate collective intelligence that is better than what any individual can achieve.

IF ACTIONS SPEAK LOUDER
THAN WORDS . . .

W E ARE DONE WITH THE LONG LIST OF GRIEVANCES AT THE
heart of the Declaration. We are done with the facts of the matter. Yet I find it hard to move on. Those grievances provoke in me a nagging question.

Here is the core of my difficulty. The list drives home the familiar
lesson that actions speak louder than words. But if the Declaration
teaches us to judge action and hear the language that it speaks, how can
we not apply that lesson to the signers themselves? This thought once
again conjures up the tragic shades whose lives are beyond the Declaration's reach.

What are we to make of the fact that the signers, who formally declared
a commitment to equality, also protected slavery and ruthlessly sought to
deracinate, if not exterminate, Native Americans? If we apply the lessons
of the Declaration to the signers themselves, don't we have to say that the
words of the Declaration don't acutally mean what they appear to mean?
That the signers didn't mean equality for everyone, since they didn't
practice it?

It might help to compare the signers of the Declaration to a group of
men whose words—and actions—inflexibly opposed equality. I have in
mind the men who founded the Confederate States of America (CSA)
and sparked the Civil War. The Confederates explicitly founded their

nation on the principle that white and black people were *not* equal. Their actions—fighting to keep slavery alive—matched their words.

In fact, the Confederates thought that they were correcting the errors of the Declaration of Independence. Alexander Stephens, the vice-president of the CSA, wrote that the original American Union "rested upon the assumption of the equality of races." He also wrote,

> Our new government is founded upon exactly the opposite ideas: its foundations are laid, its cornerstone rests, upon the great truth that the negro is not equal to the white man; that slavery is his natural and moral condition. This, our new government, is the first, in the history of the world, based upon this great . . . truth.

In other words, the slave owners who seceded from the United States and launched the Civil War thought that the words of the Declaration of Independence, and the phrase "all men are created equal," did pertain to everyone.

They were in a position to know. They chose to stake their lives on correcting the idea that the Declaration stood for general human equality. There must, then, be something to the idea that the Declaration did establish such a commitment. If the words of the Declaration had been obviously meaningless, the Confederates would not have needed to draw the contrast.

Perhaps we have to look more closely at the relation between the words and the deeds of the signers? After all, Jefferson's are not the only actions that matter.

In fact, after the Declaration was published, northern states did start abolishing slavery, beginning with Pennsylvania in 1780. (Vermont had abolished slavery in 1777, but it was its own country until 1791, when it joined the United States as the fourteenth state.)

Ten years later, in 1790, Benjamin Franklin helped submit a petition to Congress proposing the abolition of slavery for the whole country. He was, of course, a member of the Committee of Five and had worked on the first draft of the Declaration. Among the Philadelphia Quakers pursuing abolition, and pushing Franklin, was Timothy Matlack, engrosser of the Declaration.

Nearly a decade later again, George Washington emancipated many of his slaves in his will. He had used a letter some years earlier to make a public statement that he expected slavery to come to an end. In the letter he explained that he thought this end had to be pursued through legal means. With his will he meant to set an example.

Maybe the Confederates saw that the general drift of policy in the wake of the Declaration was indeed toward full human equality—that the course of human events was in fact now running toward emancipation.

Still, it's strange how even people like Washington, who became aware of a gap between their ideals and their social practices, accepted glacially slow movement of their practices toward their ideals. Why does this occur?

As we have seen, the things we come to know from abstract reflection and the things we know from force of habit can sometimes conflict. Sometimes our instincts and emotions side with the new ideas. At other times they lead us to cling to the familiar.

Is that really enough, though, to explain how very slowly people refashion their habits to conform with their ideals? There must be more to it than that.

Indeed, there is. In order to germinate and come alive in the world, ideas have to function as rules for action. This doesn't mean just that ideas tell you what you "ought" to do in some vague and general way. They need to take shape as a set of concrete actions that one can perform this morning, this evening, tomorrow, and next year. For ideals to grow into ordinary habits—to change material realities—one almost requires a script.

By the time the colonists affirmed the Declaration of Independence, they had already for over a century been scripting for themselves the set of actions that could bring the ideal of equality to life among themselves. Throughout the colonies—from Georgia to New Hampshire—they had been holding town meetings and colonial assemblies and forming fraternal societies for the free exchange of ideas and the construction of collective intelligence. They built specific new habits for interacting with each other at the same time that they were developing general ideas about political equality. They had scripts that made equality—in particular, equality with one another—real.

They had not similarly developed new scripts for interacting with slaves or Native Americans. They did not devise new actions that would reorganize these material relations.

There were exceptions. In 1782 a new law in Virginia allowed individual masters to emancipate their slaves, and some did. But this was only a first, low-risk step toward a new script—new material realities—for interactions among white and black Americans. As a first step, it was tiny and faltering. The law did not say anything about how white and black would interact after a slave was emancipated. It didn't say anything about what would happen to voting or employment or marriage or property ownership or memberships in fraternal societies.

In order for a moral idea to become real in the world, it must trail after it a multitude of concrete actions. The project of reimagining and reinventing the web of habits that bring ideas to life in the world is vast, even infinite.

An idea is weak until people can imagine in concrete terms the specific actions they will undertake under its ascendancy. Sometimes a vanguard intentionally models the new actions; sometimes those actions are discovered inadvertently. But the processes by which new scripts are invented are altogether different from those by which ideas are invented. They take place in a different cognitive register. And the actions those new scripts contain have to displace existing material realities.

Truth be told, new scripts are invented only as people begin to undertake new actions. Spaces must be ripped open in the existing web of human habits, which invariably have a tightly adhesive grip on the human spirit.

Sometimes those spaces are ripped open by those who are worst-off under present conditions. Think again of the slaves who liberated themselves from plantations during the Civil War and forced both North and South to change their policies toward runaway slaves and their military service.

Yet even when spaces are ripped open in the web of habit because some people have *pushed* others, both those who push and those who are pushed must also often be *pulled* forward. New actions must be attractive in themselves, intuitively, to people's spirits, even without reference to the ideal that gives them meaning, in order for people to break through old habits once and for all and adopt new ones, to relinquish old material realities and accept novel relationships.

Let me offer an example that will at first seem mismatched to our topic. Think about how fashion changes. If women have been wearing four-inch stilettos for several seasons, someone has to make flat shoes look really good before they'll take, even if doctors routinely dispense information about how bad the stilettos are for backs and knees. Similarly, since African Americans have straightened and textured and extended their hair for decades, someone has to give kinky curls some glamour, before they will be widely embraced; it doesn't matter that scholars and activists have equally long been saying that black is beautiful.

I introduce these seemingly out-of-place examples to pinpoint a key mechanism by which human habits change: we imitate what we find attractive. And although these examples may seem trivial, they are not. The discomfort so many women suffer in those shoes impinges on their scope of action, as well as their health, and I find it impossible to see the broad avoidance of kinky hair as anything other than a constant concession to the view, unconscious though it may be, that those with kinky hair are still somehow not equal. These examples underscore how minute are the habits that must evolve, when our ideas about freedom and equality change.

Yet we can also apply the idea that we must be attracted, as well as pushed, to issues that we more commonly consider politically serious, for instance, the American Revolution itself. Remember the script that Adams devised to make setting up new governments easy and appealing for his compatriots? He and Lee were taking them gently by the hand.

We can also find examples in our own day and age. We did not learn to spend our Sunday evenings sorting out our waste, recyclables, and compostables, until we were given separate containers in attractive colors, and precise and easily remembered schedules for when to put out what for pickup. Yet our habits have only just begun to change. Although we have acquired those sorting techniques, we still drive too much, fly too much, and buy too much with excessive packaging. On these fronts, most of us haven't yet internalized attractive alternatives.

What, then, about the issue of political equality? Perhaps the single most important thing we could do to reverse inequalities that abound in our society would be to repeal zoning laws and other measures that dramatically segregate people by income and ethnicity. Increased social connectedness across lines of socioeconomic and ethnic difference would generate egalitarian effects. Can we even imagine the neighborhoods that would look like that? Yet we need not merely to imagine them but even to find ways of bringing into being attractive examples worthy of imitation.

So let me put it this way. When we observe a person who says one thing and does another, we might be looking at a liar, but we might also be looking at a person who hasn't yet been able to turn her ideas into a script that is concrete enough to guide her actions.

What does it take for any given individual to change his basic day-to-day habits? This is the question one has to answer to understand why our ideas seem often to run so far on ahead of our habits.

Ideas don't change actions on their own. Our desires matter too. This, finally, is why a shadow of tragedy trails our Declaration.

Yet we can reasonably hope that our ideas, which wait up ahead, will make a clearing for desire.

45

RESPONSIVENESS

W E MAY NOT BE ABLE TO CLEAR THE SHADOWS THAT CLING TO the Declaration, but we have now put the list of grievances behind us. At last the time has come to turn to the seminal contribution made by Timothy Matlack to the Declaration. His most memorable contribution appears in the Declaration's ninth sentence, which, along with the tenth, will also bring us the Declaration's fourth facet of equality: the equality of agency that is achieved through practices of reciprocity.

Although the text now moves beyond the formal charges against the king, it does not yet dispense with complaint. Here are the ninth and tenth sentences:

> *In every stage of these Oppressions We have Petitioned for Redress in the most humble terms: Our repeated Petitions have been answered only by repeated injury. A Prince whose character is thus marked by every act which may define a Tyrant, is unfit to be the ruler of a free people.*

If the list of grievances is the heart of the Declaration, these sentences— the ninth and tenth—are its soul. The Declaration would not exist without the grievances, but these sentences provide the direction for the future that the colonists seize for themselves with the Declaration.

With the complaint that the colonists articulate in these sentences, they home in on the fundamental issue underneath their other charges against the king: the all-important connections among equality, freedom, and human responsiveness. All on its own, the ninth sentence—so very short—tells a powerful and important story. This is the story of the birth of a free people and the relationship of that birth to equality.

At the outset I said that the main purpose of reading the Declaration of Independence was to make the ideas of equality and freedom our own. We're at a point where we need to understand how freedom and equality are united.

What is happening in these sentences?

The colonists have petitioned for "redress"; King George has met their petitions with repeated injury. What exactly does "redress" mean? Here is the dictionary entry:

> *Noun*: Remedy or compensation for a wrong or grievance.
> *Verb*: Remedy or set right (an undesirable or unfair situation): as in "the power to redress the grievances of our citizens."

The colonists have asked King George to fix what he had done wrong, but he has responded only by making things still worse.

Yet in setting this out, the colonists do not merely complain. They also make a demand. They say that they are a free people and therefore deserve a special kind of treatment, a government befitting their free status. This is the first time we hear them demanding something specific.

What is this special treatment that a "free people" deserves and that they demand? Since King George isn't giving it to them, it must be the opposite of what he has done. Above I showed how the list of grievances is also an argument about good government. Good government requires pursuing the common good, cultivating and protecting the rule of law and the sovereignty of the people, encouraging material prosperity and growth, and providing access to justice, security, and peace for the citizens. This is what the colonists deserve.

Somehow, though, this sentence itself must also capture what they more specifically deserve as a *free* people. Indeed, it does.

In the ninth and tenth sentences the colonists describe not merely

King George's actions but also their own. Just as we were invited to understand tyranny by studying the king's actions, so now we are invited to understand freedom, by studying the colonists' actions.

What have they done? It's simple. They have responded to their oppressions by petitioning the king. This is an incredibly important action. We need to come to a full understanding of its significance.

To do that, we will have to pay even closer attention to the ninth sentence. It has some odd features. Here it is again:

> *In every stage of these Oppressions We have Petitioned for Redress in the most humble terms: Our repeated Petitions have been answered only by repeated injury.*

First of all, note the capitalized "We" in the middle of the sentence. Jefferson and the Committee of Five did not capitalize this word in the original rough draft. Nor did the capitalization emerge in the heat of congressional revision. Nor did it appear in the first broadside, printed by John Dunlap on July 6, and reprinted in newspapers throughout the land. The capitalization was added by Matlack when he engrossed the text on parchment for the Congress to sign. This particular detail illuminates, indeed like a lightening flash, the power of collective writing. It's as if the Declaration is telling a story about how "We, the people" was born. "We, the people" was born right here in the middle of the ninth sentence of the Declaration, when Congress signed a document in which its clerk had decided to capitalize this "We," thereby highlighting the arrival of a new character on the scene, as well as his membership in it.

How exactly was "We, the people" born, then? First, the colonists developed a shared understanding of their situation: they faced oppressions, and their oppression even had multiple stages. Then they decided to petition. "We, the people" was born when together the colonists developed a clear picture of their circumstances and then collectively, as a "We," decided what to do about it. The ninth sentence records for posterity the colonists' first action as a people—namely, their petition for redress. This brings into view what makes them not merely a people but a *free* people. It is this. They are committed to human responsiveness.

What exactly does that mean?

Two kinds of human responsiveness show up in this ninth sentence of the Declaration. First, there is the responsiveness of the colonists to their situation. Together, using egalitarian methods for building collective intelligence, they have figured out the course of human events; together, as a new "We," they responded to that course by asking King George to change.

The second kind of responsiveness is what they invited the king to participate in. They invited King George to respond to the picture that they saw, by correcting it, by putting a new picture in its place. They invited him to be responsive to them. This the king had refused to do. (Yet even as late as July of 1776 some members of the Continental Congress still hoped for reconciliation and went along with independence quite reluctantly.)

The ninth sentence is emphatic in drawing a connection between the responsiveness of the colonists and the nonresponsiveness of the king. Here we come to the second odd feature of this sentence. Notice that the two main clauses of our sentence are separated by a colon, not a period or semicolon.

In general, a colon indicates that what comes after the colon follows from, or is an element of, or somehow directly relates to what comes before the colon. The sentence is directing our attention precisely to the question of how the unresponsiveness of the king relates to the responsiveness of the colonists. And how do they relate? Look at this:

1	2	3	4	5	6	7	8	9	10
We	have	Petitioned	for	Redress	in	the	most	humble	terms
Our	repeated	Petitions	have	been	answered	only	by	repeated	injury

The colonists' action and the king's response are both described with ten words. These two actions balance each other out. The colon serves as a fulcrum. Franklin suggested the word "only" in the second clause, thus bringing the clauses to their ten-word symmetry. Someone, possibly Adams, changed Jefferson's "injuries" to "injury," achieving a better balance with "Redress." As a group, the Committee of Five constructed this sentence to stress a certain symmetry or equality between the two actions.

In physics, Newton's third law of motion—that for every action, there is an equal and opposite reaction—means that, for instance, if you're not careful, if you push off a boat to step onto land, the boat will move away going the opposite direction from you. Something similar is captured here. The colonists act, and then the king reacts. The symmetry of the sentence and the use of the colon suggest that the two actions should achieve a kind of balance. There should be a kind of equality between them. The colonists petitioned reasonably; they wanted a reasonable action in response. Even in the fall of 1775, many members of the Continental Congress still genuinely desired reconciliation.

Yet the king did not act as the colonists hoped he would. He did not change; he was unreasonably implacable. His reaction was equal but opposite. The colonists are like people who stepped onto a battlefield waving a white flag and found themselves being shot at anyway. The king's action did not harmonize with theirs.

And this is the problem. The colonists sought a certain kind of equality from the king—an action equally reasonable, equally responsive to the one they had offered him—not one that was equal but opposite. Somehow what they sought marks them out as a free people, while the king's refusal to provide it marks him as unfit to be the ruler of such a people.

We will have to probe the nature of the equality at stake in this ninth sentence of the Declaration and its connection to freedom. After all, what kind of equality can the colonists hope for between themselves and a king?

Let's pretend that the sort of exchange that took place between the colonists and the king had occurred between two friends. This should help make clearer the kind of equality at stake.

Friend A, Amy, says to Friend B, Betty, "I can't believe that (1) you forgot my birthday; (2) you still haven't returned the bike you borrowed from me; and (3) you keep interrupting me in this conversation when I try to explain what is wrong in our friendship!"

How do we expect Betty to respond? What does a good friend say in response to such a list of complaints?

The answer is pretty straightforward. Betty should say something like, "First, I'm sorry I forgot your birthday; I'm sorry I still have your bike; and I'm sorry I keep interrupting you. Why don't I go get your bike right now, and then let's sit down to talk. I keep interrupting you because, standing here on the porch, makes me feel like I need to get on to the next thing. I feel like I'm in a hurry. Clearly, we need to give this conversation some space and time. And about your birthday, well, how can I make it up to you? You name it and I'll do it."

That seems like a reasonable set of responses.

But what if Betty doesn't respond in that open and responsive way? What if she says instead, "Geez, Amy, I just don't have time to deal with this right now"?

Whether a person is responsive tells us whether she is our friend. If a friend of mine isn't responsive, I wouldn't think of that person as a friend anymore.

So why do we require our friends to be responsive?

We could put that question another way: when Betty doesn't respond to Amy, what do we think has gone wrong? Is the problem that Betty is selfish? Not necessarily. Maybe Betty has her own good reasons for saying these things to Amy. Maybe, for instance, she says that she doesn't have time to deal with Amy's issues because her mother has just gone to the emergency room. Would the problem with her unresponsiveness still be that she was selfish? I don't think we would say it was.

In fact, if Betty's mother were in the emergency room, we would expect Amy to overlook the problem, wouldn't we? But if it makes sense to say that Amy should "overlook the problem," then there's still something that she would be overlooking. Not selfishness. Betty is not selfish. But something else. We should try to figure out just what Amy needs to overlook because it is the actual core of the problem here.

I think we would basically ask Amy to overlook the fact that Betty is not taking her interests to heart. Our friends are supposed to take our interests to heart; that's why we look for responsiveness from them. Since we are the only ones who can tell them what our interests are, if they don't listen to us, if their actions aren't affected, or don't change direction, on account of what we say to them about our interests, then we know they aren't taking our interests to heart. When that happens, we can't count them as friends anymore, unless, like Betty, they have a good excuse so that we should overlook the problem. We are used to thinking about reciprocity this way in the context of friendship; yet the same dynamic applies to politics.

Why should the colonists expect King George to take their interests to heart? Although the colonists and the king are not friends, a king, or at least a good one, is supposed to have the interests of his subjects in mind. If a king doesn't take his subjects' interests to heart, he's not really doing his job. Reciprocity—or mutual responsiveness—is at the heart of justice.

Still, this is only part of the problem with King George's behavior. To see the problem in full, we will have to think more about Amy and Betty. How do we talk about it when one of our friends ignores what we say? If Betty didn't have a good excuse, what would Amy say about her? That Betty had treated her like dirt. That Betty had made her feel small.

In a friendship, we expect, ideally, to be equal with our friends. We expect, in essence, to take up the same amount of space. Each of us should have the same degree of agency in the friendship. Neither should be sacrificing more for the other, or being dominated by the other.* We achieve that by talking. This is one of the most important things in life that we can do with words.

When something seems out of balance, we say so. And if the person to whom we make our complaint is a friend, then she will try to fix her actions, to recalibrate the relations between us, so that each of us has an equal sphere of agency and so that our distinct spheres of agency support one another's spheres of agency. We expect responsiveness from our friends because an ideal of equality rules in our relations. We know that over time we will have to use conversation constantly to recalibrate the balance between us because it is, after all, relatively easy to let things get out of whack.

This is the sort of responsiveness for which the colonists tested King George when they made their petitions. This is the kind of responsiveness the king failed to exhibit. And this leads us to a critical question: What does it mean to test for this sort of responsiveness in politics, instead of in personal relations?

The role of talk in politics is no different from its role in friendship. The same sorts of notions of fairness that apply to our friendships also apply to our political relationships. If we expect to recalibrate relations among ourselves and rulers or among ourselves and fellow citizens on the basis of conversation, then we expect that the person to whom we speak participates with us in a world where we try to protect equal spheres of agency by using conversation to identify where the balance has gone wrong and needs to be recalibrated. In other words, the ideal of equality

* Sometimes one friend is more wounded, vulnerable, or depressed than the other. In such cases, Friend A, who is stronger, may well end up sacrificing more in order to help Friend B. The way of understanding the equality sketched here is as involving the ideas that (1) A ought to be willing to make the same level of sacrifice for B that B is willing to make for A, under circumstances where such sacrifice is necessary; and (2) B ought to be willing to give what is within B's capacity to give, even if, in those circumstances, it is less than what A gives. My thanks to Jeff Stout, author of *Blessed Are the Organized*, for this formulation.

THE GOOD NEIGHBOR.

THE duties and the comforts of good neighborhood confift in the fuppreffion of the felfifh, the irafcible, and the malevolent paffions, and in the cultivation and exercife of thofe that are generous and friendly.   He that is attentive only to his own concerns and intereft, and cares not what becomes of others ; he that is eafily provoked and ready to refent ; he that is envious at the profperity of others, or wifhes their hurt, or is glad of their calamity, cannot be a good neighbor.   He only is deferving of the character, who is kind, obliging, who is as willing to do a good turn, as to receive one ; willing to lend as well as to borrow ; who is tender of the characters and of the interefts of thofe among whom he lives ; who, being a fallible creature himfelf, is difpofed to make all reafonable allowances for the failings of others ; in fhort, who is obfervant of the golden rule, *to do to others whatfoever he would have others to do to him.*

This 1799 almanac spells out the rule of reciprocity.

that lies behind the ninth sentence of the Declaration is an equality of agency, and a commitment to participate in the conversational modes that allow friends, or groups of citizens, to restore balance in the distribution of agency.

By trying with their petitions to engage King George in this process of recalibration, the colonists show themselves to be reasonable people. Violence will be a last resort for them. Their commitments to equality and peace are deeply linked to one another. They can be committed to peace because they are committed to equality, which sustains peaceable modes of conflict resolution, peaceable modes for restoring equal spheres of agency. By refusing to engage in this process of recalibration, King George has shown himself to be unreasonable.

Here, in this part of the Declaration, we have a powerful example of what it means to say that all men are created equal. Each wants a sphere of agency unfettered by others. Each has the capacity to engage, through talk, in a project of responsiveness to make sure that none is encroaching on the sphere of agency of another. The achievement of freedom depends on this egalitarian engagement in a constant recalibration to undo, or redress, or fix encroachments. A free people grounds its problem-solving methods on this sort of egalitarian basis, in habits of reciprocity. Doing things with words is at the heart of those egalitarian problem-solving methods and mutual responsiveness.

Those who do not wish to participate in an egalitarian project of responsiveness through talk are the enemies of freedom. They pursue instead a path of domination. The king has shown himself to be such an enemy.

King George is not fit to be a ruler of a free people because, it turns out, he does not understand the only practice that secures freedom: the engagement of the relevant parties in practices of responsiveness that permit the ongoing recalibration of relations in order to preserve the equal spheres of agency that each wants, regardless of what different things each may do with it.

There is here the remarkable idea that freedom depends on our entangled relations with others. It grows not from the absence of those relations but rather from the egalitarian commitment of all participating parties to respond to each other's complaints about encroachment.

In short, the ninth and tenth sentences of the Declaration very carefully define the kind of equality that needs to be in play in relations between people in order for freedom to obtain. This is an equality in which, when one person does injury to another, the other person can push back and achieve redress so that there can be a balancing of agency in their relations. This, an egalitarian principle of reciprocity, is the fourth facet of equality presented in the Declaration. An egalitarian principle of reciprocity is integral to the capacity of individuals to establish freedom. For this reason, equality is the ground of freedom.

This is how equality and freedom are united.

DRAWING
CONCLUSIONS

This 1775 almanac cover concludes an annual
sequence that treats time as a river with
the conclusion "But bears down Kings and
Kingdoms in its Way."

46

WE MUST, THEREFORE, ACQUIESCE...

*How doth the little busy bee
Improve each shining hour,
And gather honey all the day
From every opening flower!*

THE VOICE OF ISAAC WATTS (1674–1748), WHO WROTE THOSE WORDS about the busy bee, is strangely present in American culture. An English theologican, logician, and author of some 750 hymns, Watts is familiar to contemporary churchgoers; hymnals are still full of his hymns. Watts also wrote what was perhaps the eighteenth century's most popular handbook on logic.

First published in 1724, *Logic; or, The Right Use of Reason in the Enquiry after Truth with a Variety of Rules to Guard against Error in the Affairs of Religion and Human Life* went through twenty editions. Its sixteenth was published in Philadelphia in 1789. Many in the founding generation would have read it in one of its earlier editions.

Watts had a lot to say about how perception, judgment, and reasoning operate to generate syllogisms that support the drawing of inferences from more evident to less evident truths. For instance, he wrote,

> As the first work of the mind is *Perception*, whereby our *ideas* are framed, and the second is *Judgment*, which joins or disjoins our ideas, and forms a Proposition, so the third operation of the mind is *Reasoning*, which joins several propositions together, and makes a Syllogism, that is, *an argument whereby we are wont to infer something that is less known, from truths which are more evident.*

He also had things to say, more specifically, about the vocabulary to be used for the construction of syllogisms and for drawing conclusions. For example,

> The *Act of reasoning*, or inferring one thing from another, is generally expressed and known by the particle *therefore,* when the argument is formed according to the rules of art; though in common discourse or writing, such *causal* particles as *for, because,* manifest the act of reasoning as well as the *illative* particles *then* and *therefore*: And wheresoever any of these words are used, there is a perfect Syllogism expressed or implied, though perhaps the three propositions do not appear, or are not placed in regular form.

We have followed the Declaration sentence by sentence as it set out principles, among them the proposition, as Lincoln called it, that all men are created equal. We have tracked it through its presentation of an important syllogism about equality, rights, and government. We then pursued the argument as the Declaration laid out matters of fact to generate propositions about tyranny and good government. Along the way, we have mastered four out of the five facets of equality presented in the Declaration. The ideal of equality designates freedom from domination, equality of the opportunity to use the tool of government, the use of egalitarian methods to generate collective intelligence, and an equality of agency achieved through practices of reciprocity. The time has come to draw some conclusions.

Indeed, we are on the cusp of the sentences in which the Declaration draws its own conclusions. As Watts recommended, it will announce these with the word "therefore." And as the Declaration concludes, it also presents its fifth and final facet of equality: equality as co-creation and co-ownership of our shared world. Once we have mastered this idea, we will be in a position to draw conclusions too—about the ideal of equality, and also about our contemporary relationship to the Declaration of Independence.

47

FRIENDS, ENEMIES,
AND BLOOD RELATIONS

WE ARE READY, AT LAST, FOR THE DECLARATION'S RESOUND-ing conclusions. Here are sentences eleven through sixteen:

Nor have We been wanting in attentions to our British brethren. We have warned them from time to time of attempts by their legis-lature to extend an unwarrantable jurisdiction over us. We have reminded them of the circumstances of our emigration and settle-ment here. We have appealed to their native justice and magnanim-ity, and we have conjured them by the ties of our common kindred to disavow these usurpations, which, would inevitably interrupt our connections and correspondence. They too have been deaf to the voice of justice and of consanguinity. We must, therefore, acquiesce in the necessity, which denounces our Separation, and hold them, as we hold the rest of mankind, Enemies in War, in Peace Friends.

Earlier I said the colonists were like people waving a white flag in King George's direction. Isn't the Declaration saying here that they also waved the white flag in the direction of, as the text puts it, their "British brethren"?

"Consanguinity" is not a word we hear often these days. It too comes from Latin. It identifies a blood relation, someone with whom we share a lineage (*sanguinis* means "blood"; and *con* means "with"). Why do the signers care to stress their status as blood relations to the British population?

Thus far the Declaration has sounded like a legal case. As if, thanks to a presentation of principles and facts, pure reason should show that right is on the side of the colonists. Now the Declaration brings in an additional reason for the British, in particular, to support the colonists. Not just because they're right but also because they're blood relations. Here the Declaration adds a different emphasis to the argument for independence and invokes a tale of love betrayed.

Although the Continental Congress cut more words out of this section than any other, it didn't edit out all the heartbreak that Jefferson crammed into the draft. The signers go along with Jefferson's desire to stress that the colonists feel a different sort of connection to the British people generally than they do to the king. They have, after all, asked their British "brothers" to disavow the king's usurpations. The colonists want their British brothers and sisters to help them resist King George.

This fits with another detail. As we saw, in the list of grievances, the Declaration kept Parliament's name out of its complaints, even when Parliament was involved. We realized that they were trying to keep the focus on King George to turn him singly into a symbol of tyranny. Now we can see a second reason why they do that. The colonists are trying to bring Parliament around to their side. They are trying to drive a wedge between the British people and their king. They are politically canny, and the text reveals their canniness.

That the British people have not been responsive is the final complaint. Having made it, the colonists are at last ready to round the corner and announce their dramatic conclusions. The sixteenth sentence deserves close attention:

> *We must, therefore, acquiesce in the necessity, which denounces our Separation, and hold them, as we hold the rest of mankind, Enemies in War, in Peace Friends.*

"Therefore" is a very important word. "Therefore" means that, on the basis of what has come before and for the reasons just laid out, the conclusion now follows. It leads an argument into the home stretch, shifting us from premises to conclusion.

The Declaration has been telling a story about King George. In its shortest version, it goes like this:

> *King George had undermined the common good, undermined the rule of law and the sovereignty of the people, blocked material prosperity and growth, denied justice, harassed and made the colonists vulnerable, and made war against them. In response, they first tried a stage-one response; they brought King George's wrongs to his attention and asked him to fix them. He refused. So they tried a stage-two response. They appealed to the ordinary citizens of Britain for help. They too refused their help.*

And then the text rounds the corner.

The signers say, "We must, *therefore*, acquiesce in the necessity which denounces our Separation, and hold them, as we hold the rest of mankind, Enemies in War, in Peace Friends." This is the first of two "therefore's" that, like trumpet blasts, announce that we have, at long last, reached the grand finale of the Declaration.

The colonists do not wish to separate from King George and from their British brothers and sisters, but they must. It is a matter of necessity, of last resort. Because it is a matter of last resort, the step they now take must be recognized as a failure. This is why Jefferson uses the word "denounces."

In particular, two free peoples, the British and the colonists, have failed to engage with each other to solve common problems, as friends do, by means of conversational responsiveness and egalitarian reciprocity. King George and the British people have failed a test put to them by the American colonists—they were unwilling to engage a free people as free people themselves—and so they must be treated as enemies.

At the beginning of the Committee of Five's draft of the Declaration, the group wrote, "We hold these truths to be self-evident." Now, here at the end, the Continental Congress writes, "[we] hold them, as we hold the rest of mankind, Enemies in War, in Peace Friends." The colonists have not been told by someone else that King George is now an enemy.

They themselves judge him to be such. As a community, they grasp and hold this fact through their own collective interpretation of their present circumstances. On its account, they must now act differently.

What does it mean to hold mankind "Enemies in War, in Peace Friends"? This is another of the Declaration's lovely symmetrical phrases. The colonists can tell that King George is an enemy because he is already making war on them. It's as if the phrase means, "When you act in a warlike way, we'll count you as an enemy, and when you act in a peacelike way, we'll count you as a friend."

The colonists are saying people have to prove whether they come in peace or in war. The colonists will react differently depending on which it is. Think of the phrase "We come in peace," from the movies. It's present here, too, as an invisible clause in Jefferson's formulation. If he'd written out the full thought captured in this sentence, it would be this:

> *We hold them, as we hold the rest of mankind, Enemies <u>when they come</u> in war; and <u>when they come</u> in peace, friends*

A blood relationship is not enough to guarantee that someone comes in peace. We should count as friends, the Declaration tells us, only those who are responsive to our petitions for redress. This means that even blood relations can end up as enemies. And when they do, we have to let them go.

Equality and freedom are that important.

48

ON OATH

A SECOND DRAMATIC TRUMPET BLAST—*THEREFORE!*—ANNOUNCES the grand finale for which we have been waiting:

> *We, therefore, the Representatives of the united States of America, in General Congress, Assembled, appealing to the Supreme Judge of the world for the rectitude of our intentions, do, in the Name, and by Authority of the good People of these Colonies, solemnly publish and declare, That these united Colonies are, and of Right ought to be Free and Independent States, that they are Absolved from all Allegiance to the British Crown, and that all political connection between them and the State of Great Britain, is and ought to be totally dissolved; and that as Free and Independent States, they have full Power to levy War, conclude Peace, contract Alliances, establish Commerce, and to do all other Acts and Things which Independent States may of right do.*

That is the crux of the whole affair. This second "therefore" announces the actual declaration of independence itself.

So where are we?

We have ended up at the sentences that the Virginian Richard Henry Lee—our cunning strategist who worked so hard with John Adams to bring about independence—delivered to the Continental Congress in early June to propose that the colonies declare their independence. What was in Lee's text?

> *Resolved, That these United Colonies are, and of right ought to be, free and independent States, that they are absolved from all allegiance to the British Crown, and that all political connection between them and the State of Great Britain is, and ought to be, totally dissolved.*
>
> *That it is expedient forthwith to take the most effectual measures for forming foreign Alliances.*
>
> *That a plan of confederation be prepared and transmitted to the respective Colonies for their consideration and approbation.*

Notice how close the final, official actual Declaration of Independence was to the original Lee resolution. This is another detail that underscores the extent to which the text resulted from group writing and is the product of democratic art. The job of Jefferson's committee was in effect to cut and set Lee's rough diamond.

Jefferson hadn't intended to use Lee's actual words—in fact, Congress put them in during the editing session—but those words were, after all, the reason Jefferson had a declaration to write. Jefferson's job was to provide the supporting argument for Congress's chosen action. This task—to support action—explains the nature of the text's conclusions. Here they are again:

> *We must, therefore, acquiesce. . . .*
> *We, therefore, . . . solemnly publish and declare. . . .*

Neither of these conclusions tells us, for instance, that now we know something we didn't know before. Instead, both lay out actions. First, the Continental Congress will begin to treat Great Britain like any other nation on earth, not as a special relation. Second, the Congress declares the existence of the newly united States of America, and lays claim for those states to the rights that pertain to independent states under the law of nations.

We were right, then, when we originally divided the Declaration into actions, not sections. Although the Declaration is a profound philosophical document, it is indeed, speaking roughly, merely a memo. Philosophical treatises conclude with summary statements of the new things we have come to know thanks to the philosopher's arguments. But memos conclude with recommended actions. The arguments of memos are what philosophers would call practical syllogisms.

Earlier we used the structure of a syllogism to look at how the Declaration laid out its three self-evident truths—one about people, one about governments, and one about the relation between the two. Now the time has come to figure out the syllogistic structure for the Declaration as a whole.

As a practical syllogism—a syllogism concluding in a recommended action instead of in an idea—the argument of the Declaration goes like this:

PREMISE 1: When a long train of abuses and usurpations, pursuing invariably the same Object evinces a design to reduce [a people] under absolute Despotism, it is their right, it is their duty, to throw off such Government, and to provide new Guards for their future security.—

PREMISE 2: The history of the present King of Great Britain is a history of repeated injuries and usurpations, all having in direct object the establishment of an absolute Tyranny over these States.

CONCLUSION: *Therefore*, it is our right and duty to throw off our old government and set up a new one, and so we hereby acquiesce in our separation from Britain and publish and declare our independence.

The wizardry of the actions with which the Declaration concludes is that they are themselves made out of words.

When the Declaration opens, one situation obtains in the world: the colonists are King George's subjects. By the end of the Declaration, they have renounced that relationship and declared the existence of a new one among themselves. The words of the Declaration itself are the action that brought about these changes.

Yet the colonists do not in the end depend on words alone. They are not, after all, like a person who simply declares himself divorced and remarried without going to a judge. As we have seen, the colonists present themselves "to the Supreme Judge of the world for the rectitude of [their] intentions." And the Supreme Judge will make a judgment known only in the war the colonists are about to fight.

We really should look more closely at the colonist's appeal to the Supreme Judge. They do not appeal to the Supreme Judge of the world to evaluate the rightness of their actions. They appealed to the candid world for that. They think that ordinary human beings are in a position to judge whether their reasoning is right or wrong, whether their course qualifies as reasonable and fair. They appeal to the Supreme Judge to evaluate their intentions.

Are they honest? Do they act with pure hearts? Or with mixed intentions? Are their pretty arguments a cover for a dastardly purpose? How guileful are they? We cannot see into their hearts. Only the Supreme Judge, the judge of people's consciences, knows the answer.

Yet we, the readers of their words, are meant to take heart from the fact that they wish to be judged by the Supreme Judge of the world. By this means, they tell us they care that their intentions be pure. This, at the very end of the Declaration, at last gives us some basis for judging the probable validity of their allegations against King George in the list of grievances at the heart of the Declaration.

The colonists believe in their allegations so totally that they are willing to stake their lives on them and to answer for the honesty of their intentions before God. This gives us grounds to believe, even without undertaking a research project, that there is substantial truth in their account and that their declaration is just. They have, in other words, presented their grievances against the king on oath.

We asked at the beginning how 1,337 words could turn a group of thirteen dependent colonies into thirteen independent states.

We saw that those words had behind them very elaborate rituals of consensus making. These rituals gave the colonists as a group a reason to consent to the divorce of the colonies from Britain and their remarriage to themselves.

Now we can see that their words are backed not only with rituals but also with an oath. The oath gives the candid world a basis to believe in their allegations against King George III.

In this way—with rituals and oaths—the colonists backed up their words.

REAL EQUALITY

THE DECLARATION AS A WHOLE SHOWS US WORDS IN ACTION. IT shows us words *as* actions. But for all the power of those words, it also shows us their limits. They are a start. Nothing less. But also nothing more.

Words must be backed up with actions. With rituals. With oaths. And in order to make real change in the world, words must eventually be backed up with new habits.

The Declaration itself must therefore end with action. And so it does:

And for the support of this Declaration, with a firm reliance on the protection of divine Providence, we mutually pledge to each other our Lives, our Fortunes and our sacred Honor.

Clearly, the colonists do not think that merely declaring themselves independent is enough to make it so. They have found a way to support their words. They are ready to fight beside and for one another. Their final pledge reinforces the idea that they back their words with their bodies and their souls.

By pledging themselves to one another, the colonists establish a bond with real force—with the power of people, money, and passion—that in its material consequence trumps the previous bond that each of them had independently with England. They are building their new country, their peoplehood, on a notion of shared sacrifice.

When I began describing the Declaration, I compared it to the marriage vows a couple exchanges. Now that the whole Declaration has unfolded for us slowly and intensely, what more can I say?

The Declaration concludes in a remarkably poignant moment. Much of the text has been quite dry. Abstract arguments about politics and good governance. But in this conclusion we can feel the fragility of the signers' venture. Everything is at stake. Everything may be lost.

The signers themselves felt their vulnerability directly. Once the Continental Congress had voted in favor of declaring independence, it also required any member of Congress who had abstained or voted against the Declaration to resign. For reasons of trust and security, the signers needed a 100 percent commitment to the chosen course.

The power of their bond comes from their embrace of their equality to one another. They all pledge everything to each other. Since the signers made their pledges as representatives of their states, they were also pledging their states and everything in them. They staked their claim to independence on the bedrock of equality.

It is time, then, to spell out the complete content of the ideal of equality that guided the thinking of the signers of the Declaration of Independence.

In reading the Declaration slowly, we have encountered five facets of this ideal.

First, the colonists wanted to establish that their new states were separate from and equal to the other powers on the earth. They wanted to be equal *as* powers. This means they did not want any other state to try to dominate them. For them, the ideal of equality required securing conditions free from domination.

Second, there was the phrase "that all men are created equal." Here the idea is that each human being is the best judge of her own happiness and all are therefore participants in the project of political judgment, which entails considering whether one's community fares well or ill. The ideal of equality, in this dimension, involves recognizing and enabling the general human capacity for political judgment. Moreover, recognition of this fact of human equality requires that each of us have access to the single most important tool available for securing our happiness: government. This is an idea of equality of opportunity where the opportunity that we all need is access to the tool of government.

Third, we considered the list of grievances and reflected on how that list came to exist. We saw in it the use of a "potluck method" for developing a community's knowledge stock. Now we would call it "crowd sourcing." Instead of relying on experts alone, Jefferson and his colleagues drew on extensive conversational networks among ordinary people to develop a clear picture of the course of human events. The ideal of equality here entails finding what each member of the community can contribute to the collective supply of knowledge, for the sake of maximizing the community's knowledge capacities.*

Fourth, we focused on the importance of reciprocity or mutual responsiveness to achieving the conditions of freedom. Securing conditions in which no one dominates anyone else requires a form of conversational interaction that rests on and embodies equality in the relationships among the participants. It is not merely that the ideal of equality requires securing conditions free from domination—the first facet of equality that we looked at—but also that equality of agency, achieved through reciprocal responsiveness, itself provides the means for securing freedom.

And now, here at the very end of the Declaration, we are presented with a final, fifth facet of the ideal.

In pledging to one another their lives, their fortunes, and their sacred honor, each signer of the Declaration anted up, on behalf of both himself personally and his state, an equal stake in the creation of a new political order. Each thereby claimed an equal ownership share. This is an ideal of equality as co-creation, where many people participate equally in creating a world together. They do so under conditions of mutual respect and accountability by sharing intelligence, sacrifice, and ownership. The point of political equality, then, is not merely to secure spaces free from domination but also to engage all members of a community equally in the work of creating and constantly re-creating that community.

Equality is the foundation of freedom because from a commitment to equality emerges the people itself—we, the people—with the power both to create a shared world in which all can flourish and to defend it from encroachers. On the basis of the Declaration's five facets of equality—and for the freedom secured by them—the colonists were willing to risk everything.

Equality & freedom.

The colonists judged them worth all they had.

---

* I call this epistemic egalitarianism. "Epistemic" just means "having to do with knowledge."

WHAT'S IN A NAME?

THERE'S STILL ONE MORE SECTION OF THE DECLARATION OF Independence. Here are its final words:

NEW HAMPSHIRE:

Josiah Bartlett, William Whipple, Matthew Thornton

MASSACHUSETTS:

John Hancock, Samuel Adams, John Adams, Robert Treat Paine, Elbridge Gerry

RHODE ISLAND:

Stephen Hopkins, William Ellery

CONNECTICUT:

Roger Sherman, Samuel Huntington, William Williams, Oliver Wolcott

NEW YORK:

William Floyd, Philip Livingston, Francis Lewis, Lewis Morris

NEW JERSEY:

Richard Stockton, John Witherspoon, Francis Hopkinson, John Hart, Abraham Clark

PENNSYLVANIA:

> Robert Morris, Benjamin Rush, Benjamin Franklin, John Morton, George Clymer, James Smith, George Taylor, James Wilson, George Ross

DELAWARE:

> Caesar Rodney, George Read, Thomas McKean

MARYLAND:

> Samuel Chase, William Paca, Thomas Stone, Charles Carroll of Carrollton

VIRGINIA:

> George Wythe, Richard Henry Lee, Thomas Jefferson, Benjamin Harrison, Thomas Nelson, Jr., Francis Lightfoot Lee, Carter Braxton

NORTH CAROLINA:

> William Hooper, Joseph Hewes, John Penn

SOUTH CAROLINA:

> Edward Rutledge, Thomas Heyward, Jr., Thomas Lynch, Jr., Arthur Middleton

GEORGIA:

> Button Gwinnett, Lyman Hall, George Walton

These are the names of the men who signed the Declaration.

What are these names worth?

In our answer to this question, our starting point must be that nearly every human being has a first and a last name, or a personal and a family name. The former is also sometimes called a "given" name or a "bestowed" name. The latter is sometimes a clan or tribal name. Different cultures put them in different orders—or organize those two functions of naming differently—but the basic pattern is there. Perhaps here we can spot yet another aspect of human equality?

We give our pets names, of course, but in so doing we draw them into our human community. While our animals may recognize their names, they cannot distinguish a personal from a family name, nor understand the important difference between them. This double naming is specifically human.

Although as English speakers we call our family name our "surname" or "last name," in reality it comes first, preexisting us and marking the histories out of which we emerge. Our first or personal, given name, in contrast, comes last, a gift from our parents, barely older than ourselves, really, who hope for us a full human flourishing along our own distinctive path.

Names are an ancient and core technology for acknowledging aspiration and maintaining accountability. With our names, we are held accountable by others and we take credit for what we have done. Our names fix each and every one of us equally as creatures who aspire and can be held responsible.

Whereas our last names bind us to specific traditions and broader histories, our first names mark our potential to break from the past. The idiosyncratic patterns of our predecessors prepare the moment of our entrance into the world but do not determine our passage through it. Each of us will extend the particular tradition from which we emerge in ways that our forebears can neither predict nor predetermine. Only we

AMERICA is a Subject which daily becomes more and more interesting :—I shall therefore fill these Pages with a Word upon its Past, Present and Future State.

even those who shall now save their Country. ——— O ! Ye unborn Inhabitants of America ! Should this Page escape its destin'd Conflagration at the Year's End, and these Alphabetical Letters remain legible,—when your Eyes behold the Sun after he has rolled the Seasons round for two or three Centuries more, you will know that in AnnoDomini 1758, we dream'd of your Times.

NATH. AMES.

This 1758 almanac imagines readers three hundred years on. Nathaniel Ames writes, "[Y]ou will know that in Anno Domini 1758, we dream'd of your Times."

are accountable for our passage, regardless of the aspirations our progenitors have on our behalf or the history they left behind. In this we are all equal, even though our courses through this world are infinitely diverse. No matter where one starts in life, one can, from that starting point, conduct one's life well, or badly too.

It is because all human beings aspire and can be held accountable that all play a role in shaping our collective lives, regardless of how well that role is played. Every life counts—contributes to the whole—no matter its shape. No life is altogether accidental. The proposition of human equality designates a fact of human life, as well as an ideal. In signing each his name to the Declaration, the signers acted out this fact of equality—of the equal engagement of each of them in aspiration and accountability. They did so to found a political system that would give their equality institutional form and, by doing that, secure the basis of freedom for each and all.

To dedicate oneself to the proposition of human equality is a two-step act. It is, first, to recognize that all people aspire—that is, they pursue happiness—and that all people can and should be held accountable for how they act on their aspirations. It is, second, to build a political order that puts this recognition of human equality front and center.

How can such a political order be built? The political institutions of the United States have evolved constantly as the result of efforts to answer that question.

As it was for past generations, this question is ours to answer anew.

EPILOGUE

THE DECLARATION OF INDEPENDENCE MAKES A COHERENT PHILO-
sophical argument from start to finish. It is this: equality has prece-
dence over freedom; only on the basis of equality can freedom be securely
achieved.

That the Declaration is centrally about freedom and equality is
clear from two basic facts. The title—a declaration of *independence*—
establishes that the text is about freedom. But the first sentence, the
most memorable sentence, and the concluding sentence are all about
equality. The most important question to ask about the Declaration,
then, is how it helps us understand the relationship between freedom
and equality.

Political philosophers have generated the view that equality and freedom are necessarily in tension with each other. As a public, we have swallowed this argument whole. We think we are required to choose between
freedom and equality. Our choice in recent years has tipped toward freedom. The vocabulary of presidential candidates routinely places far more
emphasis on freedom than on equality. As I said at the start, such a choice
is dangerous. If we abandon equality, we lose the single bond that makes
us a community, that makes us a people with the capacity to be free collectively and individually in the first place.

What exactly does the Declaration have to say about equality? First of
all, the text focuses on political equality. In the twentieth century we came
to understand political equality as meaning primarily formal civic rights:
the rights to vote, serve on juries, and run for elected office. These polit-

ical rights are, of course, fundamental, but civic rights are only a part of the story about political equality. The Declaration has much more to say.

As it moves from its opening salvo for divorce to its closing recommitment of the colonists to one another, the Declaration first sets its sights on achieving freedom from domination for the polity as a whole, and for individual citizens. It lays out egalitarian access to the instrument of government as crucial to the pursuit of happiness. There we find the familiar emphasis on civic rights. Then the Declaration moves on to argue for an egalitarian cultivation of collective intelligence as well as for an associational egalitarianism that establishes norms and practices of genuine reciprocity as the baseline for decent interactions with one's fellow citizens. Finally, the Declaration shows us the egalitarianism of co-creation and co-ownership of a shared world, an expectation for inclusive participation that fosters in each citizen the self-understanding that she, too, he, too, helps to make, and is responsible for, this world in which we live together. That rich and expansive notion of political equality is the ground of independence, personal and political.

That the achievement of equality is the sole foundation on which we can build lasting and meaningful freedom is a fundamentally antilibertarian argument. Since libertarianism currently dominates our political imaginations, this first argument runs against the grain of our contemporary culture.

Importantly, the Declaration gives us a reason to believe its argument about human equality and the capacity of all of us to participate in political judgment. If the Declaration is right that all people are created equal—in the sense of all being participants in the project of political judgment—then all people *should* be able to read or listen to the Declaration, understand the work that it is doing, and carry on similar work on their own account, with no more help in unleashing their capacities than can be provided by the example of the Declaration itself. And this, in fact, seems to be true. The Declaration and its import are accessible to any reader or hearer of its words.

My second argument, conveyed through my expression of love for the Declaration, is that I endorse its egalitarian case. I judge it valid and worthy. It is in the hopes of conveying the Declaration's egalitarian argument as clearly and succinctly as possible that I have written this book.

With my reading of the Declaration, then, I hope to have brought us into awareness of our own democratic powers. I hope to have inspired the conviction that their source is inside us, all of us. I hope I have made visible the democratic art of doing things with words. I hope, in sum, to have brought the Declaration to life and at the same time to have brought all of us together into a different kind of shared life—as citizens and thinkers, as political deliberators and decision makers, as democratic writers and group artists. I hope that collectively we will reclaim this text as *ours*.

I also, however, understand the limits of words; I understand the entanglements of desire. When articulated in 1776, these words made only modest inroads against the desires of white Americans to dominate Americans of color, whether native or non-native. They made scant inroads against the desires of men to maintain patriarchal social structures, or against the desires of communitarian monitors to regulate private intimacies.

Yet these words also supported the cultivation of solidarity among people committed to their principles, people who could see new ways of being in a world that more fully embodied these ideals. And in supporting the cultivation of solidarity, the text built roads to action that changed worlds. Hosts of abolitionists were, for instance, inspired by the Declaration. Members of the Indian Congress Party took it as a model when they decided to launch their own independence struggle against Britain in 1930.

In an important way, the Declaration itself acknowledges the complex entanglement of ideals with desire. Human beings, it argues, are masters enough of their own fate to inch their way toward happiness—this is a supremely optimistic document. At the same time, though, it makes clear that the best we all can do is *inch* in that direction. Humans are long-suffering; evils are long suffered. The Declaration reins in its own optimism. On its own, it admits the halting, partial nature of human progress. This is another reason it is worth reading. The Declaration tells the truth about itself.

Given all these good reasons to read the Declaration, how astonishing, then, that such readings occur so very infrequently. My casual survey of undergraduates at the most selective universities in this country suggests that, at best, half—pause on that, *half*—of them have ever read from start to finish the 1,337 words of the Declaration. How can it be that so few of our students, coming out of the best public and private high schools in the country, have, by age eighteen, read the 1,337 words of the Declaration?

It is not, to be sure, the young people alone who are not reading the Declaration. We, the adults, have not done so either. Let me provide one critical example, by diving for a final time, into textual particulars.

As this book went to press, the National Archives was still printing on its website a transcript of the Declaration that contains a significant error. Here is the relevant section of the National Archives transcription:

> *We hold these truths to be self-evident, that all men are created equal, that they are endowed by their Creator with certain unalienable Rights, that among these are Life, Liberty and the pursuit of Happiness.—That to secure these rights, Governments are instituted among Men, deriving their just powers from the consent of the governed,—That whenever any Form of Government becomes destructive of these ends, it is the Right of the People to alter or to abolish it, and to institute new Government, laying its foundation on such principles and organizing its powers in such form, as to them shall seem most likely to effect their Safety and Happiness.*

Having now read the Declaration closely, you should notice the error. This transcription prints a period after "Life, Liberty, and the pursuit of Happiness." This period breaks up a well-formed syllogism. It interrupts an argument that leads from a recognition that individually we all pursue happiness to a subsequent recognition that our best instrument for doing that is what we make together: our government. The rights to life, liberty, and the pursuit of happiness lead directly to a right to government.

Jefferson's first draft did not have this period, nor did any of the copies that he and Adams produced. As we have seen, in every draft that Jefferson copied out and in the draft that Adams copied out, each of the five truths is separated equally from the others with the same punctuation mark. The manuscript in the "corrected" journal, as Congress's official record of its work was called, does not have the period. Nor does the Dunlap broadside, the first printed text of the Declaration. Most major scholarly books about the Declaration published in the twentieth century do not print this period either. Those who etched these phrases on the Jefferson monument also did so without a period. All agree: this well-formed syllogism is a single sentence.

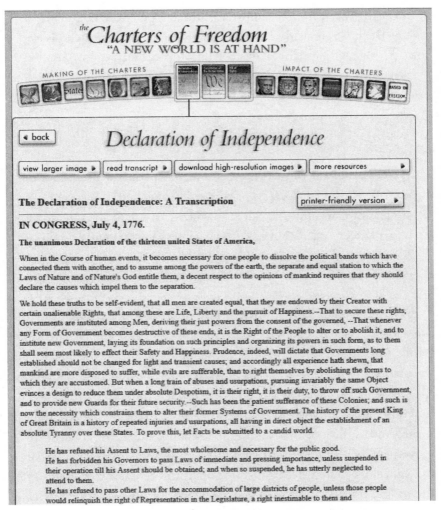

A screenshot of the National Archives text of the Declaration, March 12, 2013.

How, you might well ask, did this period—an interruption in the argumentative logic—get into the authoritative text published in print and online by the National Archives? In October 2012 I wrote to the archive and was told,

I assume the online transcription on our web site was taken from an earlier National Archives publication, *Milestone Documents in the National Archives: The Declaration of Independence* (1992). Since the engrossed parchment is so badly faded, I think it's safe to also assume that the transcription for that publication was probably taken from an imprint of the copper plate engraving of the Declaration made by William Stone in 1823, which shows a period, followed by a dash, while the earlier typeset Dunlap broadside version shows only a dash. Some transcriptions show a period, while others don't.

My correspondent then continued,

> It's very difficult to read the parchment document itself, and in our office's digital scan (cropped portion attached), I believe I can see a faint mark, but I'm not sure whether it's actually a period, a paper defect, or a comma. We're checking to see whether our conservation staff can magnify this section for us, and I'll let you know what we find out.

What happened between the printing of the Dunlap broadside and the 1823 copperplate? As we have seen, Congress commissioned three public texts: the Dunlap broadside, the engrossment on parchment, and the broadsides distributed to the thirteen state governments. In each case, the craftsmen made changes. The first printer, John Dunlap, added the first dash after "pursuit of Happiness." The engrosser, Timothy Matlack, turned one dash into two, adding the second one after "consent of the Governed." Their work brought out the underlying argumentative structure and showed how five truths were really three. Then, in January 1777, the second printer, Mary Katherine Goddard, produced the authenticated versions sent to all the states. She printed a clear period after "pursuit of Happiness." Why? Was she copying a period that had been added by Matlack to the parchment but which we can no longer see clearly? What, in other words, should we make of the now obscure mark after "pursuit of Happiness" on Matlack's parchment? Was it a period or a comma?

In all probability, Matlack used a comma. The second dash, after "consent of the Governed," is visibly preceded by a comma. Reading a comma after "Happiness" would make these two dashes parallel to each other as they are clearly meant to be since they track parallelism in the syntax.

If this is right, then Goddard is responsible for the errant period. Perhaps she was helped along by time. We cannot know how quickly that now obscure mark on Matlack's parchment became difficult to read. Or perhaps this was another of her innovations, like the use of uppercase for all the words for God in the Declaration. Whatever the explanation, the 1823 copperplate probably took the period from her broadside and then the National Archives took it from the copperplate. Thus the bizarre truncation of the well-formed single-sentence syllogism entered the official record of the digital age, the textual equivalent of an antique statue whose head has been severed from its body and now, in a museum, rests alongside but separate from the torso. Stunningly, too few adults have read the Declaration closely enough of late for this error to have come to light.

The democratic author has, therefore, one more move to make. It's time to ask the National Archives to remove that period. This reading of the parchment would respect the Jeffersonian syntax, instead of doing it violence. It would respect the endorsements of that syntax by Adams in his manuscript and by Congress in the official record. It would also respect the layers of emphasis rightly added to the document by Dunlap's and Matlack's dashes. This approach is the best way of conveying the structure of the argument. It is the best way of synthesizing the multi-headed work of the democratic author.

But why not simply consider Goddard's addition another laudable example of the democratic author at work? The practice of democratic writing includes the work of mutual critique. Congress rejected some of Jefferson's contributions. Goddard's contribution, I would argue, was ill-judged and should be corrected. You, in turn, should judge the case that I have made against it.

This affair of the errant period is no trivial matter, no arid scholastic debate about angels on the heads of pins. That extra bit of punctuation in the National Archives' transcription generates a routine but serious misunderstanding of our founding document. Over and over, those who gloss the text's self-evident truths stop at "pursuit of Happiness." As if the sentence ended there. As if the Declaration celebrated only individual rights. But the phrase "Life, Liberty and pursuit of Happiness" is meant to lead us directly, and without interruption, in this single sentence through "consent of the Governed," and to the phrase "most likely to effect *their* Safety and Happiness [emphasis added]." The sentence laying out the self-evident truths leads us from the individual to the community—from our separate and equal rights to what we can achieve only together. The Declaration really is *ours*, not *mine*.

There are no silver bullets for the problem of civility in our political life. There are no panaceas for educational reform. But if I were to pretend to offer either, it would be this: all adults should read the Declaration closely; all students should have read the Declaration from start to finish before they leave high school. Doing this would help our own powers of reading; it would help our children with their reading. It would strengthen our writing and theirs. It would nourish everyone's capacity for moral reflection. It would prepare us all for citizenship. Together we would learn the democratic arts.

I have sought to reach my own generation and that of my parents, then, to remind us of the Declaration; I have sought to reach the generations that follow us to introduce them to the Declaration. My goal in this twinned endeavor has been very simple. The time has come to reclaim our patrimony and also to pass it on—to learn how to read this text again—and to bring back to life our national commitment to equality. It is time to let the Declaration once more be ours, as it was always meant to be.

NOTES

PART I: ORIGINS

27   **The unanimous Declaration:** The text of the Declaration reproduced here is that of the engrossed parchment. The punctuation mark preceding the dash following "pursuit of Happiness" is under dispute. My view is that it is a comma. I argue for that position in the epilogue.

Chapter 1: Night Teaching

32   **She is autonomous:** Sophocles, *Antigone*, line 821 in the Greek.

32   **They that have the power to hurt:** Shakespeare, Sonnet 94.

32   **That time of year thou mayst in me behold:** Shakespeare, Sonnet 73.

Chapter 3: Loving Democracy

41   **"there was a new king of Egypt":** Exodus 1:8.

Chapter 4: Animating the Declaration

42   **clothes made out of North American products:** Ron Chernow, *George Washington: A Life* (New York: Penguin, 2010), Kindle location 11625.

45   **seven razors:** According to a tour guide at the Rockingham Historic Site in Kingston, NJ, George Washington's final revolutionary headquarters, autumn 2012.

Chapter 5: The Writer

48   **had come to view independence . . . as inevitable:** See, e.g., the July 6, 1775, letter from John Adams to James Warren (misdated by Adams June 6, 1775), in *LDC*.

48   **"instrumental of touching some Springs:** John Adams to Abigail Adams, May 17, 1776, in *LDC* and *AFP*.

48   **the suffocatingly hot summer of 1775:** "suffocating heat" in a letter from John Adams to Abigail Adams, July 17, 1775, in *LDC* and *AFP*.

48   **smallpox-plagued Philadelphia:** Josiah Bartlett to Mary Bartlett, Sept. 16, 1775, in *LDC*.

48   **meeting in Congress:** John Adams to Abigail Adams, Dec. 3, 1775, in *LDC* and *AFP*.

49   **"I have set apart nearly one day:** Thomas Jefferson to John Page, Oct. 31, 1775, in *LDC*.

49   **his fashionable horse-drawn carriage:** Ellis, pp. 21–22.

50   **instructions delivered to his compatriots:** Meacham, p. 74.

50   **"strong independent":** The phrase was used to describe John Adams and Benjamin Franklin. Richard Henry Lee to Patrick Henry, Philadelphia, Sept. 15, 1776, in *LDC* and *RHL*.

51   **Together Jefferson and Dickinson drafted a text:** Editorial note on "Declaration of the Causes and Necessity for Taking Up Arms," in *PTJ*.

51   **Eventually he would be assigned the job:** *JCC*, July 17, 1776: "Resolved, That a committee of three be appointed to revise the journals, and direct what part of it ought to be published: The members chosen, Mr. [Thomas] Jefferson, Mr. [Thomas] Lynch, [jun.] and Mr. [Francis] Hopkinson."

51   **Congress's "draftsman":** Ellis, p. 46.

Chapter 6: The Politicos

52   **John Wentworth, the royal governor:** James K. Martin, "A Model for the Coming American Revolution: The Birth and Death of the Wentworth Oligarchy in New Hampshire, 1741–1776," *Journal of Social History* 4, no. 1 (Autumn 1970): 41–60.

52   **the governor controlled the whole:** Ibid., p. 45.

53   **"We would have you immediately use":** Oct. 18, 1775, *JCC*.

53   **petition to court only in late August:** Maier, Kindle location 711.

53   **"We are in hourly Expectation:** John Adams to Joseph Palmer, Oct. 19, 1775, *LDC*.

53   **Two weeks earlier, a British naval captain:** Maier, Kindle location 743; Oct. and Nov. 1775, *JCC*.

54   **the British navy had been harassing:** John E. Selby, *The Revolution in Virginia, 1775–1783* (1988; repr., Williamsburg: Colonial Williamsburg Foundation, 2007), p. 62. On Oct. 12 Dunmore launched broad attacks in Norfolk County, but the first aggressive act, the destruction of a newspaper in Norfolk, occurred on Sept. 30, 1775. Members of Con-

gress referred to months of harassment by Dunmore in early October: notes from debates Oct. 6, 1775, in *JCC*.

54   **"the last Advices from London":** New Hampshire delegates (Josiah Bartlett and John Langdon) to Matthew Thornton, Oct. 7, 1775, in *LDC*.

54   **"Resolved, That it be recommended":** Nov. 3, 1775, *JCC*.

55   **"Although this Committee":** John Adams autobiography, pt. 1, "John Adams," through 1776, sheet 29 of 53 [electronic edition], Diary entry for Oct. 26, 1775, in *AFP*.

55   **"open and avowed" rebellion:** Dec. 6, 1775, *JCC*. The text of the king's Proclamation of Rebellion is available in William MacDonald, ed., *Documentary Source Book of American History, 1606–1913*, new ed. (New York: Macmillan, 1918), available at http://www.archive.org/details/documentarysour03macdgoog.

55   **the news from London had begun to arrive:** *JCC*, Nov. 9, 1775.

55   **"All the other letters from London:** Richard Henry Lee to George Washington, Nov. 13, 1775, in *LDC* and *RHL*. In his letter, Lee forwarded to Washington a letter from London dated Sept. 4 referring to both of these events.

56   **An estimated sixty thousand Londoners:** McCullough *1776*, Kindle location 81–95.

56   **"colonial vessels and their cargoes:** Maier, Kindle location 733.

56   **Dunmore declared martial law:** Meacham, p. 95.

56   **This proclamation instantaneously radicalized:** Dec. 4, 1775, *JCC*.

56   **news began to filter into Philadelphia:** Nov. 29, 1775, *JCC*.

56   **"The act of Parliament has to every legal intent":** Richard Henry Lee to Patrick Henry, April 20, 1776, in *LDC* and *RHL*.

57   **"As you was the last Evening":** John Adams to Richard Henry Lee, Nov. 15, 1776, in *LDC*.

59   **"above all to set an example:** Richard Henry Lee to Patrick Henry, April 20, 1776, in *LDC* and *RHL*.

59   **In February, Lee prepared a poster:** Selby, pp. 393–94.

59   **Adams's writing arm was exhausted:** Ibid., p. 395.

60   **Lee began to circulate:** Ibid.

60   **Adams drew up an address list:** Scholars have tentatively dated the address list to April 1776. See John Adams diary, Oct. 25, 27, 1775, Oct. 13, 1776, in *AFP*. Source of transcription: L. H. Butterfield, ed., *Diary and Autobiography of John Adams*, vol. 2 (Cambridge, MA: Harvard University Press, 1961).

60   **"I have made it my Business:** John Adams to John Warren, July 6, 1775, in *LDC*.

61   **"I am so hurried that I scarcely know:** Richard Henry Lee to Charles Lee, April 22, 1776, in *RHL* and *LDC*.

62   **"uncommonly hot":** McCullough *Adams*, Kindle location 1833.

62   **two British battleships had tried:** Ibid., Kindle location 1790.

62   **Resolved, That it be recommended:** May 10, 1776, *JCC*.

63   **"storm and thunder":** John Adams to Abigail Adams, May 12, 1776, in *LDC* and *AFP*.

63   **a six weeks' battle with migraines:** Ellis, pp. 43–44.

63   **He would arrive only on May 14:** McCullough *Adams*, Kindle location 1835.

63   **"Whereas his Brittanic Majesty":** May 15, 1776, *JCC*.

64   **"This Day the Congress has passed:** John Adams to James Warren, May 15, 1776, in *LDC*.

64   **"this piece of mechanism":** Notes of debates, May 10, 1776, *JCC*.

64   **"a machine for the fabrication of independence"; "independence itself":** McCullough *Adams*, Kindle location 1821; entry of May 15, 1776, in John Adams autobiography, pt. 1, "John Adams," sheet 35, *AFP*.

64   **"I have Reasons to believe":** John Adams to Abigail Adams, May 17, 1776, in *LDC* and *AFP*.

64   **"Government to be assumed:** John Adams diary, Feb. [?] 1776, *AFP*.

CHAPTER 7: THE COMMITTEE

65   **On June 7 Lee rose:** The National Archives provides a good basic history: http://www.archives.gov/exhibits/charters/declaration_history.html. One can find the same history in the books listed under "Resources."

66   **"Resolved, That these United Colonies are:** June 7, 1776, *JCC.*

66   **committee of five individuals:** The National Archives provides a good basic history: http://www.archives.gov/exhibits/charters/declaration_history.html.

66   **Adams worked the hustings:** John Adams to Thomas Pickering, Aug. 6, 1822, quoted in Meacham, p. 102. See also Adams's autobiographical notes on the June 11, 1776, resolution of Continental Congress to establish the drafting committee, in John Adams autobiography, pt. 1, "John Adams," sheet 37, *AFP.*

67   **Livingston had written:** The *New York Times* reported the discovery of a manuscript of the letter in Livingston's hand on Jan. 1, 2014. Authorship had previously been attributed to Richard Henry Lee. See James Brown, "Found in Museum's Attic: Lost Document Linked to Fight for Independence," *New York Times,* January 2, 2014, New York edition, A12.

67   **Livingston and Sherman would be far too busy:** Interestingly, by 1779 Adams would have forgotten that these two men had served on the committee, as indicated by his diary entry of June 3, 1779, *AFP.*

67   **According to Adams:** John Adams to Thomas Pickering, Aug. 6, 1822, in *The Works of John Adams,* ed. Charles Francis Adams, vol. 2 (Boston, 1850), p. 514.

67   **Jefferson's story about what happened:** Thomas Jefferson to James Madison, Aug. 30, 1823, in *Thomas Jefferson Papers Series 1, General Correspondence, 1651–1827,* http://hdl.loc.gov/loc.mss/mtj.mtjbib024747.

68   **finishing a third draft for the Virginia constitution:** Ellis, p. 45.

68   **bill of rights drafted for Virginia by George Mason:** The text is available at http://www.archives.gov/exhibits/charters/virginia_declaration_of_rights.html.

69   **"Dish for the palates of Freemen":** Richard Henry Lee to Thomas Jefferson, July 21, 1776, in *RHL.*

69   **instructions that the delegation had from home:** Maier, Kindle location 1115.

69   **Yesterday the greatest Question was decided:** John Adams to Abigail Adams, July 3, 1776, in *LDC* and *AFP.*

70   **Timothy Matlack, one of Congress's clerks:** "Agreed, That the Secy. be allowed to employ Timothy Matlack as a clerk he having first taken an oath or affirmation to keep secret and not to reveal any of the transactions [or secrets] of the Congress, that may be intrusted to him, or may come to his knowledge." See *JCC,*: May 15, 1775. On Oct. 5, 1775, Congress hired him additionally as a storekeeper "that the implements provided for the hussars be put under his care, also the tents and linen, &c. purchased for the army some time since." Oct. 28 finds him supplying wood to Congress. His entrepreneurial energies led to rapid expansion of his role. On Jan. 20, 1776, after Matlack had been asked by Congress to supply ball or lead and powder to New Jersey, John Hancock wrote to him, "Mr. Matlack, The Congress desire you would please to purchase a sufficiency of Ball, which it was said was to be Sold in this City, & your Bill shall be immediately paid. They look on you as their Commis[sar]y. Yours, J. Hancock." (New Jersey Letters, NjR. Matlack [173S1829]). In June 1776, we find this resolution concerning him, in the wake of a decision to hire Thomas Bates, a blacksmith, to supply the continental troops with a quantity of camp kettles, of sheet iron at one and 1/3 dollar each: "Resolved, That Timothy Matlack, Esq.r be directed to write to Thomas Mayberry, of Mount holly, the manufacturer of sheet iron, to send down to him five tons of sheet iron, for which he will be paid on the delivery; and, that T. Matlack be directed to receive said iron, and deliver it out, as it may be wanted, to Thomas Bates, and receive the kettles as fast as made." The kettles were delivered to Matlack in August. Between June 14 and June 27, 1776, he acquired the title of colonel at the head of a Pennsylvania battalion. By June 1777 he was secretary of the state of Pennsylvania. All from *JCC* on relevant dates.

70   **asked to inscribe the Declaration on parchment:** John C. Fitzpatrick, ed., *Calendar of the Correspondence of George Washington: Commander-in Chief of the Continental Army, with the Continental Congress* (Washington, DC: Library of Congress, Manuscript Division, 1906), p. 72. The Calendar also identifies other documents as in the handwriting of Timothy Matlack (see, e.g., pp. 11, 12, 13, 25, 28, 32, 36, 55, 57, and 71). One can find facsimiles of those documents through the Library of Congress website and compare them with the handwriting on the Declaration to confirm the identification.

CHAPTER 8: THE EDITORS

72   **first draft as worked over by Adams, Franklin, and Jefferson:** Thomas Jefferson to James Madison, Aug. 30, 1823, in *The Thomas Jefferson Papers Series 1, General Correspondence, 1651–1827,* http://hdl.loc.gov/loc.mss/mtj.mtjbib024747.

73   **we hold these truths to be sacred and undeniable:** "The phrase 'sacred & undeniable' was changed to 'self-evident' before Adams made his copy," Boyd writes. "This change has been attributed to Franklin, but the opinion rests on no conclusive evidence, and there seems to be even stronger evidence that the change was made by Thomas Jefferson or at least that it is in his handwriting." See Julian P. Boyd, *The Declaration of Independence: The Evolution of the Text* (Princeton: Princeton University Press, 1945), pp. 22–23.

74   **what Congress did to that passage:** Boyd; Maier, Appendix C.

76   **"an expert and correct compositor of types":** Isaiah Thomas, *A History of Printing in America: With a Biography of Printers and Account of Newspapers,* 2 vols. (Worcester, MA, 1810), 1:329.

77   **in all probability Adams:** The entry in *JCC* for July 4 records a decision: "That the committee appointed to prepare the declaration, superintend and correct the press." Scholars have long speculated about which committee member did this work. The alignment between the capitalization in the broadside and in the manuscript copy prepared by Adams gives us a good basis for attributing to Adams the performance of that duty.

77   **seven pairs of ladies gloves:** Meacham, p. 106.

77   **When not working in Congress that summer:** George Washington's correspondence contains evidence of his handiwork in writing up Congress's resolutions from June 19, June 27, July 24, Nov. 6, Nov. 25, and Dec. 26, 1775, and Jan. 20, Jan. 29, June 12, June 14, July 17, July 19–Aug 2, and Oct. 2, 1776. A resolution of July 24, 1776, is not in his hand but in that of Jacob Rush, younger brother of Benjamin Rush, who often wrote letters for John Hancock. See John C. Fitzpatrick, ed., *Calendar of the Correspondence of George Washington: Commander-in Chief of the Continental Army, with the Continental Congress* (Washington, DC: Library of Congress, Manuscript Division, 1906).

CHAPTER 9: THE PEOPLE

79   **dozens of committees:** When Adams was assigned to the drafting committee for the Declaration of Independence, he was already serving on twenty-three committees, and he was assigned to an additional three that same week. See McCullough *Adams,* Kindle location 2014.

80   **Abigail particularly liked to analogize time:** Here are a few examples from Abigail and one from John, all in *AFP.*

> The great distance between us, makes the time appear very long to me. It seems already a month since you left me. The great anxiety I feel for my Country, for you and for our family renders the day tedious, and the night unpleasent. The Rocks and quick Sands appear upon every Side. What course you can or will take is all wrapt in the Bosom of futurity. Uncertainty and expectation leave the mind great Scope. Did ever any Kingdom or State regain their Liberty, when once it was invaded without Blood shed? I cannot think of it without horror.
> —Abigail Adams to John Adams, Braintree, MA, Aug. 19, 1774.

> *"Extremity is the trier of Spirits—*
> *Common chances common men will bear;*
> *And when the Sea is calm all boats alike*
> *Shew mastership in floating, but fortunes blows*
> *When most struck home, being nobly bravely warded, crave*
> *A noble cunning."* <u>*Shakespear.*</u>
> —Abigail Adams to John Adams, June 25, 1775.

I cannot Bear to think of your continuing in a State of Supineness this winter.

"*There is a tide in the affairs of Men*
Which taken, at the flood leads on to fortune;
omitted, all the ~~voiyage~~ voyage of their life
is bound in shallows and in miseries.
On such a full sea are we now afloat;
And we must take the current when it serves,
or lose our ventures." Shakespear.

—Abigail Adams to John Adams, March 2–10, 1776.

In this Dilemma I have taken Belcher into pay, and must secure him for the Season, as I know not what better course to steer. I hope in time to have the Reputation of being as good a *Farmeress* as my partner has of being a good Statesmen.

—Abigail Adams to John Adams, April 11, 1776.

I have this Morning heard Mr. Duffil upon the Signs of the Times. He run a Parrallell between the Case of Israel and that of America, and between the Conduct of Pharaoh and that of George.

Jealousy that the Israelites would throw off the Government of Egypt made him issue his Edict that the Midwives should cast the Children into the River, and the other Edict that the Men should make a large Revenue of Brick without Straw. He concluded that the Course of Events, indicated strongly the Design of Providence that We should be seperated from G. Britain, &c.

—John Adams to Abigail Adams, May 17, 1776.

Chapter 10: On Memos

86   **An informal diplomatic message:** "memorandum, int. and n," *OED Online*, http://www .oed.com/view/Entry/116345?rskey=MGJmTt&result=2&isAdvanced=false, accessed May 31, 2013.

86   ***Memorandum, That it is hereby declared:*** The OED offers this example from 1820: "J. Gifford Compl. Eng. Lawyer (ed. 5) 664   An Agreement for letting a First and Second Floor, Garret, and Kitchen, unfurnished. Memorandum, That it is hereby declared and agreed by and between [etc.]."

87   **Charles Prince, CEO of Citigroup:** The *New York Times* printed this memo as part of its reporting on his resignation in 2007. The memo is no longer available on the newspaper website. A copy is on file with the author.

Chapter 11: On Moral Sense

89   **"Candid" means honest:** This is a point made by Wills, pp. 190, 302.

Chapter 12: On Doing Things with Words

92   **"[T]he Declaration can be divided":** Lucas.

93   **As philosophers have shown:** J. L. Austin, *How to Do Things with Words* (Cambridge, MA: Harvard University Press, 1962).

94   **"[I]t was *decreed* that the marriage":** See http://articles.cnn.com/1996-08-28/world/9608 _28_royal.divorce_decree_1_prince-charles-matrimonial-family-division?_s=PM:WORLD, accessed March 12, 2013.

97   **"Both read the same Bible:** Abraham Lincoln, second inaugural address, March 4, 1865.

97   **discussion about what to pledge:** I owe this point to Jill Frank at the University of South Carolina.

99   **bonfires were lit, candles glowed:** Maier, Kindle location 5880.
99   **"The Bells rung all Day:** John Adams to Samuel Chase, July 9, 1776, in *LDC*.
99   **"inflexible in their Zeal; "all fallen, like Grass":** John Adams to Abigail Adams, July 10, 1776, in *LDC* and *AFP*.

CHAPTER 13: ON WORDS AND POWER

100   **original rough draft:** See the notes on sources for information on this and other manuscripts of the Declaration.
102   **Washington . . . prevailed on Madison to ghostwrite:** William B. Allen, ed., *George Washington: A Collection* (Indianapolis: Liberty Classics, 1988), p. 530.
102, 103   **"enlightened maxims"; "Your very affectionate address":** May 5 and May 8, 1789. U.S. *House Journal*, 1st Cong., 1st sess., April 30–May 18, 1789.
103   **As my father once quipped:** Ibid.

CHAPTER 14: WHEN IN THE COURSE OF HUMAN EVENTS . . .

108   **neither of two parties can dominate:** On the political philosophy of nondomination, see Philip Pettit, *Republicanism: A Theory of Freedom and Government* (Oxford: Oxford University Press, 1999).
108   **equal access to the tool of government:** On political access as a basic right, see Amartya Sen, *Development as Freedom* (New York: Knopf, 1999).
109   **policy outcomes routinely track the stated preferences:** Larry M. Bartels, *Unequal Democracy: The Political Economy of the New Gilded Age* (Princeton: Princeton University Press, 2008); Martin Gilens, *Affluence and Influence: Economic Inequality and Political Power in America* (Princeton: Princeton University Press, 2011).
109   **egalitarian approaches to the development of collective intelligence:** On this subject, see Josiah Ober, *Democracy and Knowledge: Innovation and Learning in Classical Athens* (Princeton: Princeton University Press, 2010).
109   **egalitarian practices of reciprocity:** On this, see Axel Honneth, "Integrity and Disrespect: Principles of a Conception of Morality Based on a Theory of Recognition," *Political Theory* 20, no. 2 (1992): 187–201; W. E. B. DuBois, "Of Our Spiritual Strivings," *Souls of Black Folk* (1903), 1, in *W. E. B. DuBois: Writings* (New York: Library of America, 1987); and Danielle Allen, *Talking to Strangers: Anxieties of Citizenship since* Brown v. Board of Education (Chicago: University of Chicago Press, 2004).
109   **co-creating our common world:** DuBois, "Of Our Spiritual Strivings."

CHAPTER 15: JUST ANOTHER WORD FOR RIVER

111   **The city of Chicago:** "The reversal of the Chicago River was the largest municipal earth-moving project ever completed, and was hailed as a monumental engineering achievement," according to the American Public Works Association. See http://www.apwa.net/Resources/Reporter/Articles/2001/7/Top-Ten-Public-Works-Projects-of-the-Century, accessed March 12, 2013. The project was also identified as one of the seven wonders of the modern world by the American Society of Civil Engineers. See http://www.asce.org/People-and-Projects/Projects/Monuments-of-the-Millennium/Chicago-Wastewater-System/, accessed March 12, 2013. For an account of the significance of the reengineering of the river and its significantly *negative* environmental impact, see a series of articles in the *Milwaukee Journal Sentinel* by Dan Egan (Aug. 19, 22, and 26, 2012; Dec. 16 and 17, 2012). Egan was a 2013 Pulitzer Prize finalist for these articles.
112   **John Locke . . . argued:** *Second Treatise of Civil Government.*
112   **"If all the World shall observe pretences":** John Locke, *Second Treatise*, section 20, paragraph 210. Emily Nacol drew my attention to this as a crucial passage in Locke. On Locke's involvement in colonial policy, see Holly Brewer, "Subjects by Allegiance to the King? Debating Status and Power for Subjects—and Slaves—through the Religious Debates of

the Early British Atlantic," in P. Onuf and P. Thompson, eds., *State and Citizen: British America and the Early United States* (Charlottesville: University of Virginia Press, 2013). On Locke and his mix of "ameliorative" and "exploitative" stands on African slavery, see also Jack Turner, "John Locke, Christian Mission, and Colonial America," *Modern Intellectual History* 8 (2011): 267–97.

113   **"instinctive mistrust":** Samantha Power, *Problem from Hell: America and the Age of Genocide* (2002; repr., New York: Harper Collins, 2007), p. 36.

113   **"U.S. ambassador Henry Morgenthau Sr. examined":** Ibid., p. 13.

CHAPTER 16: ONE PEOPLE

116   **long been a very fractious set:** Bernard Bailyn, *The Barbarous Years: The Peopling of British North America: The Conflict of Civilizations, 1600–1675* (New York: Knopf, 2012).

117   **"the people" could mean:** Danielle Allen, *Talking to Strangers: Anxieties of Citizenship since* Brown v. Board of Education (Chicago: University of Chicago Press, 2004), pp. 70ff.

CHAPTER 17: WE ARE YOUR EQUALS

119   **more than three times as many people:** Gordon Wood, *The American Revolution: A History* (New York: Modern Library, 2002), Kindle location 1124.

120   **France had the third-largest population:** Some 25 million in 1778. See Ian Barnes, *The Historical Atlas of the American Revolution* (New York: Routledge, 2000), p. 65.

122   **how states are equal to each other:** Derek Croxton, "The Peace of Westphalia of 1648 and the Origins of Sovereignty," *International History Review* 21, no. 3 (Sept. 1999): 569–91.

CHAPTER 18: AN ECHO

124   **segregation was used:** Charles Wollenberg, *All Deliberate Speed: Segregation and Exclusion in California Schools, 1855–1975* (1976; repr., Berkeley: University of California Press, 1978).

CHAPTER 20: THE LAWS OF NATURE

131   **By what meanes:** J. Palsgrave, *Lesclarcissement 538/1*. Example in "entitle, v.," *OED Online*, http://www.oed.com/view/Entry/62903?redirectedFrom=entitle, accessed May 31, 2013.

CHAPTER 21: AND NATURE'S GOD

135   **introduced at later points in the drafting process:** Boyd.

136   **no mention of Christ:** Adams or Franklin added "Christian king" in the criticism of George III, and Congress deleted that passage. See Boyd.

137   **look into the proposition:** I take this formulation from the philosopher James Ladyman. Garry Wills also provides a very useful treatment of self-evidence; see Wills, pp. 181–83.

CHAPTER 22: KINDS OF NECESSITY

141   **"You can fool all the people":** Andrew K. McClure, *Lincoln's Own Yarns and Stories* (Philadelphia: International Publishing, 1901), p. 184. McClure knew Lincoln, but there is no other independent confirmation that Lincoln was the source of this saying. The anecdote is related this way: "Lincoln was a strong believer in the virtue of dealing honestly with the people. 'If you once forfeit the confidence of your fellow-citizens,' he said to a caller at the White House, 'you can never regain their respect and esteem. It is true that you may fool all the people some of the time; you can even fool some of the people all the time; but you can't fool all of the people all the time.'"

CHAPTER 24: SOUND BITES

147   **called maxims:** Aristotle, *Rhetoric.*

CHAPTER 25: STICKS AND STONES

154   **took as a concubine:** Annette Gordon-Reed, *The Hemingses of Monticello: An American Family* (New York: Norton, 2009).

CHAPTER 26: SELF-INTEREST?

158   **"the greatest character of the age":** Richard Brookhiser, *Founding Father: Rediscovering George Washington* (New York: Simon and Schuster, 1997), p. 103.
158   **slaves liberated themselves from plantations:** Stephanie McCurry, *Confederate Reckoning: Power and Politics in the Civil War South* (Cambridge, MA: Harvard University Press, 2010).
158   **new ideas about human equality:** John F. Witt, *Lincoln's Code: The Laws of War in American History* (New York: Free Press, 2012).

CHAPTER 27: SELF-EVIDENCE

161   **Aristotle called this method:** Aristotle, *Prior Analytics.*

CHAPTER 29: THE CREATOR

173   **when a woman was to be married:** Daniel C. Quinlan and Jean A. Shackelford, "Economy and English Families, 1500–1850," *Journal of Interdisciplinary History* 24, no. 3 (Winter 1994): 431–63; Sally Mitchell, *Daily Life in Victorian England* (Westport, CT: Greenwood, 1996).
174   **referring to a Creator:** Jefferson wrote the phrase "created equal," but either Adams or Franklin added the explicit term "Creator." See Boyd.
176   **just like any other wild creature:** For a defense of speciesism—that is, of considering human beings to have relations to one another distinct from their relations to animals—see Bernard Williams, *Philosophy as a Humanistic Discipline*, ed. A. W. Moore (Princeton: Princeton University Press, 2006), chap. 13, "The Human Prejudice," where he argues against Peter Singer.

CHAPTER 30: CREATION

178   **more than eighty years:** Darwin's *On the Origin of Species* was published on Nov. 24, 1859.
178   **earth was eternal:** Aristotle, *Physics* and *Metaphysics.*
179   **Leonardo da Vinci thought:** See, e.g., David Starr Jordan, "Extracts from Essays of Leonardo Da Vinci," *Science*, n.s., 57, no. 1479 (May 4, 1923): 520–21.
179   **validity of the Copernican revolution:** See, e.g., Rose Lockwood, "The Scientific Revolution in Seventeenth-Century New England," *New England Quarterly* 53, no. 1 (March 1980): 76–95.
179   **he should properly be called a "deist":** The Princeton scholar of religion Jeff Stout points out (personal communication with author): "What qualifies as the Christian God was itself under dispute. Many deists took themselves to be Christians in the sense of being followers of Christ. They interpreted following Christ as a matter of adhering to the teachings of Jesus, construed as especially sublime expressions of truths discoverable by the natural light of human reason."
180   **identified in 1563 by a French theologian:** Viret, Instruct. Chr. II. Ep. Ded., "J'ai entendu qu'il y en a de ceste bande, qui s'appellent Deistes, d'un mot tout nouveau, lequel ils

veulent oposer à Atheiste." Example found in "deist, n.," *OED Online*, http://www.oed.
com/view/Entry/49206?redirectedFrom=deist, accessed May 31, 2013.

181   **"a document in proof that *I* am a *real Christian*":** Thomas Jefferson to Charles Thomson, Jan. 9, 1816, quoted in Ellis, p. 257.

CHAPTER 31: BEAUTIFUL OPTIMISM

186   **recent movie hero:** The character Jonathan Banks in Steven Soderbergh's 2013 film *Side
Effects*.

CHAPTER 34: LIFE'S TURNING POINTS

199   **"Just once, later:** Sharon Olds, "Tiny Siren," in *Stag's Leap: Poems* (New York: Knopf,
2012), p. 57.

TINY SIREN

by Sharon Olds

And had it been a year since I had stood,
looking down, into the Whirlpool
in the laundry nook of our August rental, not
sure what I was seeing—it looked like a girl
brought up in a net with fish. It was
a miniature woman, in a bathing suit,
lying back after the spin cycle—
the photograph of a woman, slightly
shaped over the contours of a damp towel.
I drew it out—radiant square
from some other world—maybe the daughter
of the owners of the house. And yet it looked like
someone we knew—I said, to my husband,
This was in with the sheets and towels.
Good heavens, he said. Where?! In
with the sheets and your running shorts. Doesn't it
look like your colleague? We gazed at the smile
and the older shapely body in its gleaming
rainbow sheath—surprise trout
of wash-day. An hour later, he found me,
and told me she had given him the picture
the day that they went running together
when I was away, he must have slipped it in
his pocket, he was so shocked to see it
again, he did not know what to say.
In a novel, I said, this would be when
the wife should worry—is there even the slightest
reason to worry. He smiled at me,
and took my hand, and turned to me,
and said, it seemed not by rote,
but as if it were a physical law
of the earth, I love you. And we made love,
and I felt so close to him—I had not
known he knew how to lie, and his telling me
touched my heart. Just once, later
in the day, I felt a touch seasick, as if

a deck were tilting under me—
a run he'd taken, not mentioned in our home,
a fisher of men in the washing machine.
Just for a few minutes I had felt a little nervous.

"Tiny Siren" from *Stag's Leap: Poems* by Sharon Olds, copyright © 2012 by Sharon Olds. Used by permission of Alfred A. Knopf, an imprint of the Knopf Doubleday Publishing Group, a division of Random House LLC. All rights reserved. Any third party use of this material, outside of this publication, is prohibited. Interested parties must apply directly to Random House LLC for permission.

199   **"and I am sweating a lot by now":** Frank O'Hara, "The Day Lady Died," in *Lunch Poems* (San Francisco: City Lights, 1964). Copyright © 1964 by Frank O'Hara. Reprinted by permission of City Lights Books.

199   **"What are these words, these words?":** Sylvia Plath, "Words Heard by Accident, over the Telephone," in *Collected Poems* (New York: Harper Collins, 1960). Two lines of "Words Heard by Accident, over the Telephone" from *The Collected Poems of Sylvia Plath*, edited by Ted Hughes. Copyright © 1960, 65, 71, 81 by the Estate of Sylvia Plath. Editorial mat'l copyright © 1981 by Ted Hughes. Reprinted by permission of HarperCollins Publishers.

199   **"Over my heart, too":** Aeschylus, *Libation Bearers*, lines 184–211, trans. H. W. Smyth (1926; reprt., Cambridge, MA: Harvard University Press, 1957). *Aeschylus: Volume II*, Loeb Classical Library Volume 146, translated by Herbert Weir Smyth, p. 179, Cambridge, Mass.: Harvard University Press, Copyright 1926 by the President and Fellows of Harvard College. The Loeb Classical Library ® is a registered trademark of the President and Fellows of Harvard College.

199   **"Stop all the clocks":** W. H. Auden, "Stop all the clocks, cut off the telephone," in *Collected Poetry* (New York: Random House, 1945). Auden's first version of the poem was a satirical lament for a deceased politician, yet it has come to be read as a quintessential statement of grief, being inscribed, for instance, on a sundial sculpted by Patrick Rimoux at the Heysel Stadium (Stade Roi Baudoin) in Brussels to commemorate the deaths of 39 soccer fans in 1985 in an event of fan hooliganism. "Funeral Blues," copyright © 1940 and renewed 1968 by W. H. Auden; from *W. H. Auden Collected Poems* by W. H. Auden. Used by permission of Random House, an imprint of The Random House Publishing Group, a division of Random House LLC. All rights reserved. Any third party use of this material, outside of this publication, is prohibited. Interested parties must apply directly to Random House LLC for permissions.

CHAPTER 36: FACTS?

207   **1999 indictment:** http://www.thesmokinggun.com/documents/crime/linda-tripp-wiretap-indictment-0, accessed March 12, 2013.

208   **lawyer John Lind:** Lucas.

209   **allegedly injured a particular group:** Dumbauld, pp. 93ff.

211   **whiskey should be taxed; no one who lives upstream:** The tax on whiskey imagined here is of a level that would have been recognizable in the period; the law about water rights is an example from ancient Athens, whose political system also placed great emphasis on public depositories.

211   **precise meaning of "the rule of law":** See Brian Z. Tamanaha, *On the Rule of Law: History, Politics, Theory* (Cambridge: Cambridge University Press, 2004).

CHAPTER 37: LIFE HISTORIES

213   **Imagine a small gray gable house:** Details of colonial architecture are taken from James D. Kornwolf, *Architecture and Town Planning in Colonial North America*, vol. 2 (Baltimore: Johns Hopkins University Press, 2002).

214   **"I am cumbered about":** I have used phrases from letters between John and Abigail Adams in 1774 and 1775 to imagine this fictitious dialogue.

215 **For this one, we have to imagine:** On women and whaling, see Lisa Norling, *Captain Ahab Had a Wife: New England Women & the Whalefishery, 1720–1870* (Chapel Hill: University of North Carolina Press, 2000). On Nantucket, see J. Hector St. John de Crèvecoeur's 1782 *Letters from an American Farmer.*

215 **brings her to; "strictly search":** I have taken these phrases from a tale of impressment in John Shelburne Sleeper's 1860 book, *Jack in the Forecastle, or incidents in the early life of Hawser Martingale.* This book is available through Project Gutenberg as an e-book (#8638) produced by Theresa Armao and David Widger (2009).

215 **Soldiers board and . . . brig:** Dumbauld, pp. 143–45; Paul A. Gilje, *Liberty on the Waterfront: American Maritime Culture in the Age of Revolution* (Philadelphia: University of Pennsylvania Press, 2003); Denver Brunsman, *The Evil Necessity: British Naval Impressment in the Eighteenth-Century Atlantic World* (Charlottesville: University of Virginia Press, 2013).

217 **laws of war:** John F. Witt, *Lincoln's Code: The Laws of War in American History* (New York: Free Press, 2012).

CHAPTER 38: PLAGUES

219 **touch of hyperbole:** Lucas; Dumbauld, pp. 115–17.

219 **"Posterity must hear a Story":** John Adams to Abigail Adams, Oct. 19, 1775, in *LDC* and *AFP.*

219 **Exodus relates:** Exodus 10:3–6.

221 **the Sugar, Quartering, and Stamp Acts:** Dumbauld, pp. 115–19, 131–32.

CHAPTER 39: PORTRAIT OF A TYRANT

223 **colonists also cared about prosperity:** Dumbauld, pp. 105–8.

CHAPTER 40: THE THIRTEENTH WAY OF LOOKING AT A TYRANT

225 **"others" with whom King George combined:** Dumbauld, pp. 119–24.

225 **Board of Customs Commissioners:** On the Townshend Acts of 1767, which introduced this board, see Eric Foner and J. A. Garraty, eds., *The Reader's Companion to American History* (Boston: Houghton Mifflin, 1991).

226 **Quebec Act:** Dumbauld, p. 137; William B. Munro, "The Genesis of Roman Law in America," *Harvard Law Review* 22, no. 8 (June 1909): 579–90.

CHAPTER 43: ON POTLUCKS

233 **When Jefferson sat down:** For that matter, he had recently drafted a preamble to the new Virginia constitution that itself contained a list of charges against King George very similar to the list in the Declaration.

236 **four such letters in one day:** Oct. 19, 1775, John Adams to Abigail Adams, William Cooper, Joseph Palmer, and James Warren, in *LDC.*

237 **social knowledge:** Josiah Ober, *Democracy and Knowledge: Innovation and Learning in Classical Athens* (Princeton: Princeton University Press, 2010), pp. 90–97.

237 **"The many, of whom":** Ober's adapation of Carnes Lord's translation, ibid., p. 110.

CHAPTER 44: IF ACTIONS SPEAK LOUDER THAN WORDS . . .

241 **vice-president of the CSA:** Stephanie McCurry, *Confederate Reckoning: Power and Politics in the Civil War South* (Cambridge, MA: Harvard University Press, 2010), p. 12, citing Alexander Stephens, "Cornerstone Address in Wakelyn," *Southern Pamphlets*, pp. 405–6.

241 **start abolishing slavery:** Pennsylvania's Act for the Gradual Abolition of Slavery (1780) is

available at http://www.palrb.us/statutesatlarge/17001799/1780/0/act/0881.pdf, accessed March 13, 2013.

241   **in 1790, Benjamin Franklin:** He did this as president of the Pennsylvania Abolition Society. Ron Chernow, *Washington: A Life* (New York: Penguin Press, 2010), Kindle location 12805.

241   **decade later again, George Washington:** Ibid., Kindle location 16467–16500.

242   **He had used a letter some years earlier:** A Sept. 1786 letter from Washington to John Francis Mercer, quoted ibid., Kindle locations 10136–49.

243   **In 1782 a new law in Virginia:** Ibid., Kindle location 10110.

244   **We did not learn to spend our Sunday evenings:** I owe this example to Jonny Thakkar, "Can There Be Philosopher-Kings in a Liberal Polity? A Reinterpretation and Reappropriation of the Ideal Theory in Plato's Republic" (PhD diss., University of Chicago, Committee on Social Thought, 2013).

244   **Perhaps the single most important thing:** Richard Rothstein, "Racial Segregation and Black Student Achievement," in *Education, Justice, and Democracy*, ed. Danielle Allen and Rob Reich (Chicago: University of Chicago Press, 2013), pp. 173–98; Danielle Allen, "A Connected Society," *Soundings* 53 (2013).

245   **make a clearing:** Here I draw on A. R. Ammons's poem "Salute," a lovely meditation on the Declaration, which takes as its main subject the pursuit of happiness.

CHAPTER 45: RESPONSIVENESS

247   *Noun:* **remedy or compensation:** *Oxford Dictionaries Online*, http://oxforddictionaries. com/us/definition/american_english/redress, accessed March 12, 2013.

249   **the word "only":** Notation on original rough draft of Franklin's change; Adams's copy is the first to have "injury" instead of "injuries"; Jefferson reverts back to "injuries" in his 1783 copy for Madison. See Boyd.

250   **had occurred between two friends:** For an argument about the usefulness and validity of drawing on what we know about friendship to think about politics, see Danielle Allen, *Talking to Strangers: Anxieties of Citizenship since* Brown v. Board of Education (Chicago: University of Chicago Press, 2004).

251   **used to thinking about reciprocity:** Ibid.

251   **a king, or at least a good one:** From antiquity through the early modern period, the good, benevolent, or just king was the one who acted always in the interests of his subjects.

252   **role of talk in politics:** For an argument about the usefulness and validity of drawing on what we know about friendship to think about politics, see Allen, *Talking to Strangers*.

CHAPTER 46: WE MUST, THEREFORE, ACQUIESCE . . .

257   **"As the first work of the mind":** Isaac Watts, *Logick* . . . (Philadelphia: Thomas Dobson, 1789), p. 270.

CHAPTER 47: FRIENDS, ENEMIES, AND BLOOD RELATIONS

260   **love betrayed:** Garry Wills makes this point about this passage; see Wills, pp. 313ff.

CHAPTER 48: ON OATH

264   **Jefferson hadn't intended:** Boyd.
265   **practical syllogisms:** Aristotle, *Nicomachean Ethics*.

CHAPTER 49: REAL EQUALITY

268   **it also required any member:** For instance, Robert Alexander, a delegate from Maryland, sailed for England soon after July 4. On the general point, see Dumas Malone, *The Story of*

the Declaration of Independence (1954; repr., New York: Oxford University Press, 1975), pp. 90–92.

CHAPTER 50: WHAT'S IN A NAME?

271   **Different cultures put them:** On native American tribal names, see Elizabeth Compton, "An Exploratory Analysis of Personal Naming Practices of Western North American Indians" (MS thesis, West Virginia University, 2004).

EPILOGUE

279   **Most major scholarly books:** Julian Boyd, Alan Dershowitz, Edward Dumbauld, Joseph Ellis, Pauline Maier, Dumas Malone, and Jon Meacham respect the Jeffersonian syntax, but Carl Becker, Stephen Lucas, and David McCullough print the period. Then there are the scholars who do not commit to any particular version: John Hazelton, David Armitage, Garry Wills.

280   **"I assume the online transcription":** Email of Jan. 28, 2013, to author from National Archives staff, on file with author.

RESOURCES

A. Texts of the Declaration

Copy of Declaration in John Adams's hand. Papers of John Adams. Vol. 4, February–August 1776. Massachusetts Historical Society. Made between June 11 and June 28, 1776. Facsimile available in Boyd.

The "original rough draft" in Thomas Jefferson's hand, including all corrections, additions, and deletions made by Adams and Franklin, by the Committee of Five, and by the Congress. July, 4, 1776. Jefferson Papers. Library of Congress. Facsimile available in Boyd.

Copy of Declaration made by Jefferson for Richard Henry Lee. Sent to Lee July 8, 1776. American Philosophical Society, Philadelphia. Facsimile available in Boyd.

Unidentified copy of the Declaration made by Jefferson [Cassius F. Lee copy]. May be one of the copies Jefferson made between July 4 and July 10, 1776, for George Wythe, John Page, Edmund Pendleton, and Philip Mazzei. New York Public Library. Facsimile available in Boyd.

Unidentified Copy of the Declaration made by Jefferson [the Washburn copy]. Corresponds approximately to Richard Henry Lee copy. Massachusetts Historical Society. Facsimile available in Boyd.

The Dunlap Broadside, first printing of the Declaration, printed during the night of July 4–5 by John Dunlap in Philadelphia. Inserted in the Rough Journal of the Continental Congress. Papers of the Continental Congress. Library of Congress. Facsimile available in Boyd.

Corrected Journal manuscript by an anonymous hand. Papers of the Continental Congress. Library of Congress. Facsimile of first page available in Dumbauld.

Parchment copy, engrossed, possibly by Timothy Matlack, between July 19 and Aug. 2, 1776, and signed by members of Congress beginning Aug. 2. National Archives.

Copy of the Declaration made by Jefferson for James Madison, Spring 1783. Madison Papers, Library of Congress. Facsimile available in Boyd.

B. Descriptions of Evolutions in the Text and Transcriptions Indicating Edits

Becker, Carl L. *The Declaration of Independence: A Study in the History of Political Ideas*. New York: Harcourt, Brace, 1922. Pp. 174–84.

Boyd, Julian P. *The Declaration of Independence: The Evolution of the Text*. Washington, DC: Library of Congress, 1943.

Maier, Pauline. *American Scripture: How America Declared Its Independence from Britain*. 1997. Reprint, London: Pimlico 1999. Kindle edition. Appendix C.

C. Digital Primary Sources

Adams Family Papers: An Electronic Archive. Masschusetts Historical Society, 2003. http://www.masshist.org/digitaladams/aea/index.html.

Adams, John, *The Works of John Adams, Second President of the United States: With a Life of the Author, Notes and Illustrations, by his Grandson Charles Francis Adams*. 10 vols. Boston: Little, Brown, 1856. Available at the Online Library of Liberty, http://oll.libertyfund.org/title/2098.

Charters of Freedom website, National Archives. http://www.archives.gov/exhibits/charters/.

Early American Imprints, Series 1, Readex: Archive of Americana. Digital archive published by the American Antiquarian Society and NewsBank, 2002.

Fitzpatrick, John C., ed. *Calendar of the Correspondence of George Washington, Commander in Chief of the Continental Army, with the Continental Congress*. Library of Congress, Manuscript Division. 1906. Available as an e-book through Google books.

Journals of the Continental Congress, 1774–1789. Edited by Worthington C. Ford. Washington, DC: Government Printing Office, 1904–37. Available at http://hdl.loc.gov/loc.law/amlaw.lwjc.

Letters of Delegates to Congress, 1774–1789. Edited by Paul H. Smith et al. Washington, DC: Library of Congress, 1976–2000. Available at http://hdl.loc.gov/loc.law/amlaw.lwdg.

The Letters of Richard Henry Lee. Vol. 1, *1762–1778*. Collected and edited by James C. Ballagh. New York: Macmillan, 1911. Available at http://archive.org/details/richhenryleelet01richrich.

MacDonald, William, ed. *Documentary Source Book of American History, 1606–1913*. New ed. New York: Macmillan, 1918. Available at http://www.archive.org/details/documentarysour03macdgoog.

The Papers of Thomas Jefferson—Digital Edition. Barbara B. Oberg and J. Jefferson Looney, editors in chief. Charlottesville: University of Virginia Press, 2009. Available at http://rotunda.upress.virginia.edu/founders/TSJN.html.

Stackhouse, A. M. Col. *Timothy Matlack, Patriot and Soldier: A Paper Read before the Gloucester County Historical Society at the Old Tavern House, Haddonfield, N.J.*, April 14, 1908 Privately printed, 1910. Available at http://archive.org/details/cu31924032738365.

D. Other Primary Sources

Allen, W. B., ed. *George Washington: A Collection*. Indianapolis: Liberty Classics, 1988.

Cappon, Lester, ed. *The Adams-Jefferson Letters: The Complete Correspondence between Thomas Jefferson and Abigail and John Adams*. 1959. Reprint, Chapel Hill: University of North Carolina Press, 1987.

Warren, Mercy Otis. *History of the Rise, Progress, and Termination of the American Revolution*. 1805. Reprint edited by Lester H. Cohen. 2 vols. Indianapolis: Liberty Fund, 1988.

E. General Bibliography

Armitage, David. *The Declaration of Independence: A Global History*. Cambridge, MA: Harvard University Press, 2008.

Becker, Carl L. *The Declaration of Independence: A Study in the History of Political Ideas*. New York: Harcourt, Brace, 1922.

De Bolla, Peter. *The Fourth of July and the Founding of America*. Woodstock, NY: Overlook Press, 2008.

Dershowitz, Alan. *America Declares Independence*. Hoboken, NJ: Wiley, 2003.

Dumbauld, Edward. *The Declaration of Independence and What It Means Today*. Norman: University of Oklahoma Press, 1950.

Ellis, Joseph. *American Sphinx: The Character of Thomas Jefferson*. New York: Vintage, 1998.

Goff, Frederick R. *The John Dunlap Broadside: The First Printing of the Declaration of Independence*. Washington, DC: Library of Congress, 1976.

Hall, D. M. *Roger Sherman and the Creation of the American Republic*. Oxford: Oxford University Press, 2013.

Hazelton, John H. *The Declaration of Independence: Its History*. New York: Dodd, Mead, 1906.

Hogeland, William. *Declaration: The Nine Tumultous Weeks When America Became Independent, May 1–July 4, 1776*. New York: Simon and Schuster, 2010.

Honig, Bonnie. "Declarations of Independence: Arendt and Derrida on the Problem of Founding a Republic." *American Political Science Review* 85, no. 1 (March 1991): 97–113.

Landis, Bertha Cochran. "Col. Timothy Matlack." *Papers Read before the Lancaster County Historical Society* 42, no. 6 (1938).

Lossing, Benson John. *The Declaration of Independence with Short Biographies of Its Signers.* Bedford, MA: Applewood Books, 1997.

Lucas, Stephen E. "Justifying America: The Declaration of Independence as a Rhetorical Document." In *American Rhetoric: Context and Criticism*, edited by Thomas W. Benson. Carbondale: Southern Illinois University Press, 1989.

———. "The Stylistic Artistry of the Declaration of Independence." *Prologue: Quarterly of the National Archives* 22 (Spring 1990): 25–43.

Maier, Pauline. *American Scripture: How America Declared Its Independence from Britain.* 1997. Reprint, London: Pimlico 1999. Kindle edition.

Malone, Dumas. *The Story of the Declaration of Independence.* 1954. Reprint, New York: Oxford University Press, 1975.

McCullough, David. *1776.* New York: Simon and Schuster, 2006.

———. *John Adams.* New York: Simon and Schuster, 2008.

Meacham, Jon. *Thomas Jefferson: The Art of Power.* New York: Random House, 2012.

Peterson, Merrill D. *Thomas Jefferson and the New Nation: A Biography.* Oxford: Oxford University Press, 1970.

Selby, John E. "Richard Henry Lee, John Adams, and the Virginia Constitution of 1776." *Virginia Magazine of History and Biography* 84, no. 4 (Oct. 1976): 387–400.

Wills, Garry. *Inventing America: Jefferson's Declaration of Independence.* 1978. Reprint, New York: Houghton Mifflin, 2002.

Wood, Gordon S. *The American Revolution: A History.* New York: Modern Library, 2002.

ACKNOWLEDGMENTS

Where to begin with the thank-you's? This project originated during my childhood in discussions about the Declaration of Independence around the dinner table of my parents, William Allen and Susan Allen, to whom I owe not only this but everything, including my beloved brother, Marc Allen. Conversations with them, and my stepmother, Carol Allen, have been indispensable throughout, including for my introduction to almanacs. My many night students in the Illinois Humanities Council's Odyssey Project, and especially Teri Watkins, made this project necessary. Earl Shorris, Kristina Valaitis, and Amy Thomas Elder made the Odyssey Project itself possible and with it an invaluable continuing education for me. My former husband, Robert von Hallberg, with whom I often co-taught in the Odyssey Project and even taught this text, was very much a partner in the early development of my reading of the Declaration; he spotted the river metaphor in "course of events." My former brother-in-law, Bob Trujillo, introduced me to Mitch Albom's *Tuesdays with Morrie* and asked me whether I could perhaps write a book like that. In the end, I haven't, and still can't, but without that question, I would never have written this one. An invitation from Don Randel to deliver the 2007 commencement address at the University of Chicago issued in the first effort at this book. Sara Bershtel awakened me to the fact that most people read the second sentence of the Declaration as ending at "pursuit of happiness." She made me aware of the experience of surprise that can come from discovering the full extent of that sentence's argument. In order of appearance on this earth, Stefan von Hallberg, Isaac von Hallberg, Anthony Kveder, Isabel Kveder, Nora Doyle, and William Doyle are young people with whom I consider it a privilege to live; I am so grateful to have them to aspire to write for. The origins of this book lie with all these people, and my gratitude to them is boundless.

Tina Bennett believed in this book, and she made a beautiful match to Bob Weil, my editor at Norton. He is the real deal—what I always hoped for when in childhood I longed one day to be an author and dreamed of famous editors. This book has given me the gift of friendship with them; that in itself is reward enough.

Then there are the other people, in addition to Tina and Bob, who have taught me how to write, again in order of appearance—Elizabeth Eger, Ruth Scurr, Laura Slatkin, Maureen MacLane, Cullen Murphy, Ann Marie Lipinski, Kathleen Carroll, Fred Hiatt, and the finalists and winners of Pulitzer Prizes 2007–2013—as well as my bibliophilic in-laws—Margaret Doyle, Clare Doyle, Helen Doyle and Robin Grimes, Ursula Doyle and Dino Pappas, John and Mary Doyle. They are many things, among them the quickest, sharpest cryptic crossword solvers and Scrabble players you've ever seen.

My capable administrative assistant, Laura McCune, has supported this project for years in matters great and small. Will Menaker, Peter Miller, Phil Marino, Cordelia Calvert, and Bill Rusin at Norton/Liveright have also been of considerable assistance. As has Svetlana Katz at William Morris. I am grateful to Julia Druskin and Albert Tang for a beautifully designed book. A long list of colleagues, friends, and students helped me refine the book's arguments, concepts, and fine points, including Elizabeth Anderson; Janine Barchas; John Bowlin; John Dobard; Mitch Duneier; Joseph Ellis; Jill Frank; Bryan Garsten; Eric Gregory; David Kennedy; Nan Keohane; Melissa Lane; Jill Locke; Steven Lukes; Dan Mandell; Karuna Mantena; Clayton Marsh; Seth Moglen; Emily Nacol; Jerome Perzigian; Andrew Pyle; Kim Scheppele; Jim Schulz; Joan Scott; Earl Shorris; Max Siegel; Marc Stears; Jeff Stout; Jonny Thakkar; Michael Walzer; Cornel West; Heather Wolfe; and the students in my autumn 2012 freshman seminar at Princeton University. I am deeply in their debt, and errors are all mine.

And then there is Jimmy, hero, father of Nora and William, whose generous love, like theirs, is life-giving.

Havre de Grace, MD
June 1, 2013

ILLUSTRATION CREDITS

164   **An anonymous political cartoon:** "Federal Superstructure," *Massachusetts Centinel* (1788). *Courtesy of American Antiquarian Society.*

165   **Watt's handbook explains:** Isaac Watts, *Logick* . . . (Philadelphia: Thomas Dobson, 1789). *Courtesy of American Antiquarian Society.*

172   **Like many almanacs, this 1728 example:** Titan Leeds, *The American Almanack for the Year of Christian Account, 1728* ([Philadelphia]: S. Keimer, 1727). *Courtesy of American Antiquarian Society.*

179   **This 1739 almanac:** Nathaniel Ames, *An Astronomical Diary; or, An Almanack for the Year of Our Lord Christ, 1739. . .* (Boston: John Draper, 1738). *Courtesy of American Antiquarian Society.*

180   **This 1675 almanac:** John Foster, *An Almanack of Coelestial Motions for the Year of the Christian Aera 1675 . . .* (Cambridge [MA]: Samuel Green, 1675). *Courtesy of American Antiquarian Society.*

181   **This 1774 almanac presents:** Ezra Gleason, *The Massachusetts Calendar; or, An Almanack for the Year of Our Lord Christ 1774 . . .* (Boston: Isaiah Thomas, 1773). *Courtesy of American Antiquarian Society.*

187   **This 1774 poster advertises a new play:** Hannah More, *The Search after Happiness, a Pastoral Drama* ([Philadelphia: James Humphreys, 1774]). *Courtesy of the Library Company of Philadelphia.*

190   **This 1774 almanac depicts the traitorous statesman:** Ezra Gleason, *The Massachusetts Calendar; or, An Almanack for the Year of Our Lord Christ 1774 . . .* (Boston: Isaiah Thomas, 1773). *Courtesy of American Antiquarian Society.*

214   **This 1799 almanac lists:** *Isaiah Thomas's Massachusetts, Connecticut, Rhode-Island, Newhampshire & Vermont Almanack, with an Ephemeris, for the Year of Our Lord 1799 . . .* (Worcester, MA: Isaiah Thomas, 1798). *Courtesy of American Antiquarian Society.*

215   **Poster of an eighteenth-century ballad:** John Gay, "Ballad" ([Boston, not before 1731 and not after 1776]). *Courtesy of Connecticut Historical Society, Hartford, Connecticut.*

220   **Instruction to customs officers:** "Instructions by the Commissioners of His Majesty's Customs in America, to [blank] who is appointed [blank] of the Customs at the port of [blank] in America" (Boston?, 1768?). *Courtesy of American Antiquarian Society.*

234   **A 1774 Georgia broadside promising punishment:** *Courtesy of the National Archives UK.*

235   **A 1763 call to the townspeople in Boston:** *Courtesy of the Massachusetts Historical Society.*

236   **The author of this 1798 almanac:** Isaac Briggs, *Briggs's Maryland, Pennsylvania & Virginia Almanac; or, Baltimore Ephemeris: for the Year of Our Lord, 1798 . . .* (Baltimore: W. Pechin, 1797). *Courtesy of American Antiquarian Society.*

253   **This 1799 almanac spells out:** *Isaiah Thomas's Massachusetts, Connecticut, Rhode-Island, Newhampshire & Vermont Almanack, with an Ephemeris, for the Year of Our Lord 1799 . . .* (Worcester, MA: Isaiah Thomas, 1798). *Courtesy of American Antiquarian Society.*

256   **This 1775 almanac cover concludes:** John Anderson, *Anderson Improved: Being an Almanack, and Ephemeris, for the Year of Our Lord 1775 . . .* (Newport, RI: Solomon Southwick, 1774). *Courtesy of American Antiquarian Society.*

272   **This 1758 almanac imagines:** Nathaniel Ames, *An Astronomical Diary: or, An Almanack for the Year of Our Lord Christ, 1758 . . .* (Boston: J. Draper, 1757). *Courtesy of American Antiquarian Society.*

276   **A screenshot of the National Archives text of the Declaration:** http://www.archives.gov/exhibits/charters/declaration_transcript.html Screenshot, captured March 12, 2013.

INDEX

ABOUT THE AUTHOR

Danielle Allen is a political theorist who has published broadly in democratic theory, political sociology, and the history of political thought. Widely known for her work on justice and citizenship in both ancient Athens and modern America, Allen is the author of *The World of Prometheus: The Politics of Punishing in Democratic Athens* (2000), *Talking to Strangers: Anxieties of Citizenship since Brown v. Board of Education* (2004), and *Why Plato Wrote* (2010). In 2002, she was awarded a MacArthur Fellowship for her ability to combine "the classicist's careful attention to texts and language with the political theorist's sophisticated and informed engagement." She is currently working on books on citizenship in the digital age and civic education. Allen is a frequent public lecturer and regular guest on public radio affiliates to discuss issues of citizenship, as well as an occasional contributor on similar subjects to the *Washington Post*, *Boston Review*, *Democracy*, *Cabinet*, and *The Nation*.